A Selected Bibliography
of
Modern Historiography

EDITED BY
ATTILA PÓK

Prepared under the auspices of
the Institute of History of the Hungarian
Academy of Sciences

Bibliographies and Indexes in World History,
Number 24

Greenwood Press
New York • Westport, Connecticut • London

Library of Congress Cataloging-in-Publication Data

A Selected bibliography of modern historiography / edited by Attila
Pók.
   p.   cm. – (Bibliographies and indexes in world history, ISSN
0742-6941 ; no. 24)
   "Prepared under the auspices of the Institute of History of the
Hungarian Academy of Sciences."
   Includes index.
   ISBN 0-313-27231-X
   1. Historiography – History – 19th century – Bibliography.
   2. Historiography – History – 20th century – Bibliography.   I. Pók,
Attila.   II. Series.
   Z6208.H5S45   1992
   [D13]
   016.9'072 – dc20   91-46699

British Library Cataloguing in Publication Data is available.

Library of Congress Catalog Card Number: 91-46699
ISBN: 0-313-27231-X
ISSN: 0742-6941

First published in 1992

Greenwood Press, 88 Post Road West, Westport, CT 06881
An imprint of Greenwood Publishing Group, Inc.

Printed in the United States of America

The paper used in this book complies with the
Permanent Paper Standard issued by the National
Information Standards Organization (Z39.48-1984).

10 9 8 7 6 5 4 3 2 1

907.2
S464p

254919

Contents

3. America   207

4. Africa and the Middle East   234

5. Asia   238

6. Australia   244

Acknowledgements

The material of this bibliography has been collected between 1984 and 1990. Besides various national and international historical bibliographies the editor has used catalogues of numerous big national and university libraries in Bloomington, Budapest, Cambridge, Erfurt, Frankfurt am Main, Leipzig, London, Moscow, New York, Oxford, Prague, Utrecht, and Vienna. The infinite number of titles could not have been arranged into the present form without the most valuable help of colleagues. It was Professor Georg G. Iggers who read the first draft, encouraged the editor to continue his work and recommended it to Greenwood Press for publication. Colleagues from a number of the countries dealt with in this bibliography have been asked to revise the respective chapters. I am most grateful also to Professors Robert Bonnaud (France), A. Djakov (Soviet Union), Dinu Giorescu (Roumania), Andrzej Felix Grabski (Poland), Ivan Ilchev (Bulgaria), Ivan Kamenec (Czechoslovakia), John Kenyon (Great Britain), Walter Schmidt (Germany), Vojislav Stanovcic (Yugoslavia), and Al Zub (Roumania) for their corrections and suggestions.

The Institute of History of the Hungarian Academy of Sciences offered indispensable moral and practical help during the long period of the preparation of this book.

Cynthia Harris of Greenwood Press has devoted much time, energy and lots of patience to this project; without her support it could not have been completed.

All mistakes are, of course, the editor's sole responsibility.

Introduction

Historiography is a frequently used concept whose content, however, is far from being unequivocal. In the strict sense of the word, naturally, it means history writing; when hearing this word, however, most historians have in mind not the whole of history writing but an independent discipline investigating the history of history *writing* and historical *science*. History writing and historical science are not synonymous concepts at all: many authors draw a very strict line between the two.

We classify all the works beginning from ancient times which give an account in one way or another of the events of the past or, perhaps, of the present, with the conscious purpose of informing the future as creations of history *writing*. These writings are generally not based upon a methodical revealing of some kind of material. Instead, the sources arrive at the author more or less by accident, and the author's purpose is not so much to reconstruct the past in the most complete form possible but rather to ennoble, teach, educate the present by conjuring up the past, and, last but not least, to entertain the reader.

In accordance with the general characteristics of scientific research, historical *science* (without giving up its aim to mould the future) investigates historical reality in a methodological manner: with the help of its conceptual, theoretical apparatus it uses the investigated sources, selected with versatile, internal and external criticism, to arrive at historical facts. An important moment in the development of scientific accuracy is the process of specialization. As a consequence of time-consuming data collecting, necessary for a versatile reconstruction, historical literature is dominated more and more by the elaboration of topics with a more limited range, although the outstanding representatives of the first generations of history writing rarely gave up the idea of writing a comprehensive history of the whole of their nation, of a great era or, on occasion, of a universal historical period.

Another important moment is the formation of the system of institutions of historical science: historical departments are created in universities; archives are founded; historical periodicals are started; and academies, institutions, and societies are established for organizing and directing research. This process developed as European societies became increasingly more conscious of the idea of historicity at the turn of the 18th and 19th centuries. For the formation of historical science the transition from feudalism to capitalism — with the spreading of enlightenment and of the idea of progress — was a decisive ideological moment, and there were two decisive moments of social-political history: the French Revolution and the American War of Independence. Existing institutions and political systems broke down, and values that had been considered eternal became relative.

These events required an explanation, more exactly a new explanation, and that explanation was provided by the gaining ground of historicity, as well as the deduction of economic, political and social events resulting from these. Scholars, representing several approaches and belonging to different schools, were not sparing of their explanations. These explanations are of two types: they are either of a philosophical character (concerning the sense, laws, and cognizability of the whole of history) or works of historical science which, relying upon critically selected sources, introduce historical facts. These facts may be within a longer or shorter stretch of time.

The above is related here in order to throw light upon the viewpoints manifested in the selection of the material for the present bibliography. For historiography is frequently considered to be a science introducing the history of works of both a philosophical nature and of historical sience. Thus, for example, according to J.G.A. Pocock, a historian of ideas of high renown, historiography embraces the history of the relationship of mankind towards its own past as well as the study of all the instruments and methods necessary for getting acquainted with this past.

The idea to compile this work came from L. D. Stephens' bibliography (1975) which interprets historiography in a manner narrower than that, but still very widely. In his view, historiography studies the processes of historical cognition; thus it includes the history of the philosophy of history, history writing, historical science, the analysis of the careers of certain historians as well as the studying of the methods and techniques of historical research. The present work, less for theoretical than for practical reasons, uses a more stringent interpretation of historiography aiming to bring fuller coverage and lucidity to that interpretation. By *modern historiography* figuring in the title it means the *history of historical science* established at the beginning of the 19th century, as a result of the process outlined above in a sketchy manner, the first outstanding representatives of which were Niebuhr and Ranke. The book aims to list works that discuss the development of historical science beginning at that time up to 1990 in general or in a given age and field.

Historiography in this sense is one of the special fields of historical science, interested in the internal and external factors which form the individuals and institutions of historical science. This interpretation not only excludes a great part of the works on the philosophy of history and methodology but it also neglects the history of research of a given historical problem, mostly discussed in the introduction of monographs but frequently in independent works as well. The works belonging to the latter type have only been included in the bibliography if the author introduces the research of the given topic as of decisive importance from the point of view of the formation of the whole of the historical science of an age and a region.

At the same time this interpretation considers works, which may be looked upon on the basis of their title as belonging to the philosophy of history or historical theory, as historiographical ones, for which the source material frequently referred to is the history of historical science. In a similar manner, the sources dealing with the general situation of historical thought have been included if they allow an indirect insight into the history of the profession in some way.

Naturally, as is the case of every selected bibliography, it was the subjective judgment of the editor which decided the inclusion or omission of a given work. The main point in making the judgement was that the bibliography should serve as a *stable starting point* with significant works that may be properly surveyed for those interested in any moment in the historical science of the period from Ranke up to our days. (In a few cases I also included works dealing with preceding periods if they contained statements or evaluations of a general character as well.)

*

The present work expands on Stephens' earlier work, *Historiography: A Bibliography*. Stephens divided that work into three chapters in accordance with his definition of historiography: Theories of History, Historiography, and Historical Methods. The works included in the second chapter, bearing the same title as that of the book, essentially constitute the interpretation of historiography presented in this bibliography. The present work differs in other ways from Stephens' 1975 book which focused on English-language works. It arranges the material according to geographical regions and includes more regions and languages. At the same time, it provides fuller coverage of works within its interpretation of historiography and, of course, it has collected material from the fifteen years since the appearance of Stephens' work.

Susan Kinnel's recent historiographical manual (1987) provides a comprehensive survey of publications from 1970 to 1985. The present selected bibliography covers a longer time period. Its aim is to provide access to the most important works on nineteenth- and twentieth-century historiography.

*

The books and the studies have not been separated from each other. I have only adopted as an independent title collections of studies on historiography including writings on different topics (mainly from the Soviet Union where a great many works of this type are published) if they discuss the same topic (no matter how wide it may be). In other cases, the individual studies of such volumes figure in the place appointed for their topic. It was not theoretical consideration but lucidity which was the main viewpoint when forming the structure of the bibliography. In addition to the individual countries and nations, the works of comprehensive topics have been included in a special unit. In the case of this bulk of materials, it seemed to be superfluous to make a further classification for the great number of overlappings would have made usability more difficult rather than easier.

I have not succeeded in making the description of the titles fully uniform, since the materials have been collected from quite a few bibliographies, library catalogues, footnotes utilizing methods of describing titles of a great diversity. In transcribing the Cyrillic letters, I followed the standard of the former Council of Mutual Economic Aid (CMEA 1362—78, Table 1) using accents and diacritical signs. In certain cases when the title does not elucidate unequivocally the contents of the work, a brief remark refers to the topic of the book or the study and sometimes to the most important reviews and debates dealing with the work. Naturally, the titles of the works are given in the original language, and the most frequently occuring placenames and titles of periodicals are abbreviated.

Abbreviations

1

General

1. 1. *Abelove, Henry—Blackmar, Betsy—Dimock, Peter — Schner, Jonathan (eds.)* Visions of History. Interviews with E.P. Thompson, Eric Hobsbawm, Sheila Rowbotham, Linda Gordon, Natalie Zemon Davis, William Apleman Williams, Staughton Lynd, David Montgomery, Herbert Gutman, Vincent Harding, John Womaek, D. L. R. James, Moshe Lewin. By MARHO, the Radical Historians Organization. Manchester University Press, 1984.324p.

1. 2. *Alföldy, Géza et al. (eds.)* Probleme der Geschichtwissenschaft. Düsseldorf, 1973.

1. 3. *Anderle, Othmar F.* "Theoretische Geschichte. Betrachtungen zur Grundlagenkrise der Geschichtswissenschaft". HZ 85 (1958) 1–54 p. On the state of historical studies.

1. 4. *Anderle, Othmar F.* "Die Geschichtswissenschaft in der Krise". *In:* Festschrift J. Lortz 2. Glaube und Geschichte. Baden-Baden, 1958. 491—550 p.

1. 5. *Andrea, Alfred J.—Schmokel, Wolfe W. (eds.)* The living past. Western historiographical traditions. N. Y., 1975. 298 p.

1. 6. *Andreano, R. L. (ed.)* The new economic history. Recent papers on methodology. N. Y., 1965.

1. 7. Angehrn, Emil Geschichte und Identität. Berlin (West), 1985.397p.

1. 8. Aron, Raymond (ed.) L'histoire et ses interpretations. Entretiens autour de Arnold Toynbee. Paris, 1961.

1. 9. Aron, Raymond La Philosophie critique de l'histoire. Paris,1969.

1. 10. Aron, Raymond Politics and history. Collected, translated and edited by *Conant, Miriam Bernheim.* L.,1978.

1. 11. Asendorf, Manfred Geschichte und Parteilichkeit. Berlin (West), 1984.

1. 12. Bailyn, Bernard "The challenge of modern historiography". AHR 87 (1982) 1/1—24 p.

1. 13. Ballard, M. (ed.) New movements in the study and the teaching of history. L., 1970.

1. 14. Barg, Mikhail Abramovic Problemy socialnoj istorii. V osveščentii sovremennoj zapadnoj medievistiki. M., 1973. 228 p.

1. 15. Barnes, Harry Elmer A history of historical writing. Norman, Oklahoma, 1937. N. Y. 450 p. An important review of the book: Becker, Carl "What is historiography?" AHR 44 (1938) 4/20—28p.

1. 16. Barnes, Harry Elmer Learned crusader. The New History in action. Edited by *Goddard Arthur.* Colorado Springs, 1968. 884p.

1. 17. Barraclough, Geoffrey History in a changing world. L., 1955.

1. 18. Barraclough, Geoffrey History and the common man:

presidential address. Diamond Jubilee Conference, London, 12-16 April, 1966. L., 1967.

1.19.Barraclough,Geoffrey Main trends in history. N. Y., 1979. Available also in French: Tendences actuelles de l'histoire. Paris, 1980. 342 p.

1.20.Barzun,Jacques—F.Graff,Henry The modern researcher. N. Y.–Chicago–San Francisco–Atlanta, 1957. Second, revised edition, 1970.

1. 21. Barzun, Jacques Clio and the doctors: psycho-history, quanto-history. Chicago—L., 1974. 173 p.

1. 22. Bataillon, M.—Bremont, C. (eds.) Histoire et historiens depuis cinquante ans. Paris, 1927.

1. 23. Bauer, W. Einführung in das Studium der Geschichte. Tübingen, 1921. Reprinted Frankfurt, 1961.

1. 24. Bauer, C.—Boem, J.—Müller, M. (eds.) Speculum Historiale: Geschichte im Spiegel von Geschichtsschreibung und Geschichtsdeutung. München, 1965.

1. 25. Bauer, Gerhard Geschichtlichkeit. Wege und Irrwege eines Begriffs. Berlin, 1963.

1. 26. Baumgartner, H. M. and *Rüsen, A. (eds.)* Seminar: Geschichte und Theorie. Frankfurt, 1976.

1.27.Baur,Karl Zeitgeist und Geschichte: Versuch einer Deutung. München, 1978. 484 p.

1. 28. Beck, R. N.—Lee, D. S. "The meaning of »historicism«". AHR 59 (1953—54) 568—577 p.

1.29.Below,Georg von "Die neue historische Methode". HZ 81 (1898) 193—273 p.

1. 30. Below, Georg von Naturwissenschaft und Geschichte. Beilage zur Allgemeinen Zeitung, 279, 1899.

1. 31. Below, Georg von "Das gute Recht der politischen Historiker". Preußische Jahrbücher 193 (1923) 288—308 p.

1. 32. Benson, L. Toward the scientific study of history. N. Y., 1972.

1. 33. Benz, Wolfgang—Müller, Martin Geschichtswissenschaft. Darmstadt, 1973. 272 p. (Das Wissen der Gegenwart. Geisteswissenschaften)

1. 34. Berdahl, Robert et al. Klassen und Kultur. Sozialanthropologische Perspektiven in der Geschichtsschreibung. Berlin (West), 1982 *Kocka, Jürgen's* review: Merkur 36 (1982). 955–965 p. On the ensuing debate cf.: *Wehler, Hans-Ulrich* "Geschichte – von unten gesehen. Wie bei der Suche nach dem authentischen Engagement mit Methodik verwechselt wird". Die Zeit 10. Mai, 1985.20.p.

1.35. Berding, Helmut Bibliograpie zur Geschichtstheorie. (Arbeitsbücher zur modernen Geschichte, 4, Vandenhoeck and Ruprecht). Göttingen, 1977. (With a chapter on historiography.)

1. 36. Berend T., Iván "History as a discipline-scholarly and scholastic". Etudes Historiques Hongroises 1980. Budapest, 1980. I.515—551 p.

1. 37. Beringer, R. E. Historical analysis: contemporary approaches to Clio's craft. N. Y., 1978. 317 p.

1. 38. Berlinguer, Luigi Considerazioni su storiografia e dritto. Bologna, 1974.

1. 39. Bernheim, Eduard Lehrbuch der historischen Methode und der Geschichtswissenschaften. Leipzig, 1889.

1. 40. Bernheim, Eduard Einleitung in die Geschichtswissenschaft. Berlin, 1926.

1. 41. Berr, Henri La synthese en histoire. Son rapport avec la synthèse générale. Paris, 1901. Nouvelle edition revue et nise à jour, Paris, 1952.

1. 42. Berr, Henri—Febvre, Lucien "History". *In:* Encyclopedia of Social Sciences. vol. 7. N. Y., 1959.

1. 43. Bertels, Cornelis Patrus Geschiedenis tussen struktur en evenement. Amsterdam, 1973. With an English summary. 381 p.

1. 44. Berthold, Werner (Autorenkollektiv unter Leitung von) Zur Geschichte der marxistischen Geschichtswissenschaft 1-2. Lehrmaterial. Manuskriptdruck, Berlin, 1986.

1. 45. Besson, Waldemar "Historismus". *In: Besson, Waldemar (ed.)*Das Fischer Lexikon. Geschichte. Frankfurt, 1961. 102–116 p.

1. 46. Best, Geoffrey Francis Andrew History, politics und universities: inaugural lecture. Edinburgh, 1969. 19 p.

1. 47. Bianco, Franco Storicismo ed ermeneutica. Roma, 1974. 274p.

1. 48. Birkes, Alexander S.—Tambs, Lewis A. Historiography, method, history teaching: a bibliography of books and articles in English 1965—1973. Hamden (Connecticut), 1975. 130 p.

1. 49. Blanchard, Lydia Burman The narrator in history. A study of Thomas Babington Macaulay's History of England and Jacob Burckhardt's Civilization of the Renaissance. Ann Arbor (Michigan), 1973.

1. 50. Blank, A. S. Istoriografiâ novoj i noveǰej istorii. Vologda, 1975. A university coursebook.

1. 51. Blanke, Horst Walter—Rüsen, Jörn (eds.) Von der Auf-klärung zum Historismus: zum Strukturwandel des historischen Denkens. München—Wien—Zürich, 1984. 324 p.

1. 52. Bloch, Marc Apologie pour l'histoire ou le métier d'historien. Paris, 1949, 112 p.

1. 53. Bober, M. Karl Marx's interpretation of history. Cambridge, 1948.

1. 54. Bobinska, Celina Historiker und historische Wahrheit. Zu erkenntnistheoretischen Problemen der Geschichtswissenschaft. Berlin, 1967.

1.55. Bogue, Allan G. Emerging theoretical models in social and political history. Beverly Hills—L., 1973. 151 p.

1. 56. Böhning, P. (ed.) Geschichte und Sozialwissenschaften. Göttingen, 1972. Including: *Kocka, Jürgen* Zu einigen sozialen Funktionen der Geschichtswissenschaft.

1. 57. Bonanno, Carmela L'evoluzione dell'Europa nella critica storica. Dal Congresso di Vienna alla fine della seconda guerra mondiale. Padova, 1963.

1. 58. Borowsky, Peter et al. Einführung in die Geschichtswissenschaft. 1-2. Opladen, 1975—1980.

1. 59. Bosl, K. "Der soziologische Aspekt der Geschichte. Wertfreie Geschichtswissenschaft und Idealtypus". HZ 20 (1965) 613—630p.

1.60. Bourdé, Guy—Martin, Hervé Les écoles historiques. Paris, 1983. 341 p.

1. 61. Bourdeau, L. Histoire et les historiens. Essai sur l'histoire considérée comme science positive. Paris, 1888.

1. 62. Bowman, F. A handbook of historians and history writing. Dubuque (Iowa), 1951.

1.63. Bradley, Francis Herbert The presuppositions of critical history. Edited with introduction and commentary by Lionel Rubinoff. Chicago, 1968. 147 p. First published Oxford, 1874, reprinted in his Collected essays, Oxford, 1935.

1. 64. Brandi, Karl Einführung in die Geschichtswissenschaft und ihre Probleme. Berlin, 1922. Geschichte der Geschichtswissenschaft, Bonn, 1947. 147 p. (New, revised edition of the 1922 work.)

1. 65. Braudel, Fernand Écrits sur l'histoire. Paris, 1969. 315 p. An important review by *Salmon, J.H.M.* HT 10 (1971).

1. 66. Breisach, Ernst Historiography. Ancient, medieval and modern. The University of Chicago Press, 1983. 487 p. Bibliography, 429—464 p.

1. 67. Breysig, Kurt Aufgaben und Maßstäbe einer allgemeinen Geschichtsschreibung. Berlin, 1900.

1. 68. Breysig, Kurt Vom Sein und Erkennen geschichtlicher Dinge.
I. Psychologie der Geschichte. Berlin, 1935.
II. Die Meister der entwickelnden Geschichtsforschung. Berlin, 1936.
III. Gestaltungen des Entwicklungsgedankens. Berlin, 1940.
IV. Das neue Geschichtsbild im Sinn der entwickelnden Geschichtsforschung. Berlin, 1943.

1. 69. Bridbury, A. R. Historians and the open society. L., 1972. 163p.

i. 70. Brinton, Crane "The New History: twenty-five years after". Journal of Social Philosophy 1 (January 1936). 137—147 p. (A review of Barnes's The history of western civilization). The author's reply: "The New History and common-sense" ibid., 148—153p.

1.71. Brunner, Otto Neue Wege der Verfassungs- und Sozialgeschichte. 2. vermehrte Auflage. Göttingen, 1968. 344 p.

1.72. Bullock, Alan Is history becoming a social science?: The case of contemporary history. Cambridge, 1977. 23 p. (The Leslie Stephen lecture).

1.73. Burksnek, V. Some historians of modern Europe. L., 1942.

1.74. Butterfield, Herbert The study of modern history. L., 1944.

1.75. Butterfield, Herbert Man on his past. Cambridge, 1955. 237p.

1.76. Butterfield, Herbert The history of the writing of history. Rapports du XIe Congrès International des Sciences Historiques. Stockholm, 21—28 Août 1960. I. 25—40 p.

1.77. Butterfield, Herbert History and Man's attitude to the past: their role in the story of civilization. L., 1961.

1.78. Butterfield, Herbert The present state of historical scholarship. Cambridge, 1964.

1.79. Butterfield, Herbert "Delays and paradoxes in the development of historiography". *In:* Studies in international history. Essays presented to W. N. Medlicott, ed. K. Bourne and A. C. Watt. L., 1967.

1.80. Butterfield, Herbert Some trends in scholarship, 1868—1968, in the field of modern history. Transactions of the Royal Historical Society. 5th series, 19 (1969).

1.81. Butterfield, Herbert The origins of history. L., 1981.

1. 82. Canary, Robert H. —Kozicki, Henry (eds.) The writing of history. Literary form and historical understanding. The University of Wisconsin Press, 1978.

1. 83. Cantimori, Delio Storici e storia. (Metodo, caratteristiche e significato del lavoro storiografico). Torino, 1971. 693 p.

1. 84. Cappelletti, Vincenzo La scienza tra storia e societa. Roma, 1978. 537 p. (La cultura 16.)

1. 85. Carbonell, Charles-Olivier L'historiographie. Paris, 1981. 127 p. (Que sais-je? 1966)

1. 86. Carbonell, Charles-Olivier "Pour une histoire de l'historiographie". Storia della storiografia 1982, 1/7—25 p.

1. 87. Cardoso, Ciro—Perez Brignoli, Hector Los metodos de la Historia. Barcelona, 1976.

1. 88. Carr, David–Dray, William–Geraeto, Theodore F.–Quellet, Fernand–Watelet, Hubert (eds.) La Philosophie de l'histoire et la pratique historienne d'aujourd'hui–Philosophy of history and contemporary historiography. Colloque international sur la philosophie de l'histoire. Ottawa, 18 au 20 avril 1980. Ottawa, 1982. 396 p.

1. 89. Carr, Edward Hallett What is history? L., 1961.

1. 90. Carvalho, Joaquim Burradas de Da istoria cronica a historia-ciencia. Lisboa, 1979. 118 p.

1. 91. Cebik, L. B. "Colligation in the writing of history". The Marxist, 1969/40—57p.

1. 92. Cebik, L. B. Concepts, events and history. Washington, 1978.

1. 93. de Certau, Michel L'écriture de l'histoire. Paris, 1975. 358 p.

1. 94. Chadwick, Owen The secularisation of the European mind in the nineteenth century. Cambridge, 1975.

1.95. Chadwick, Owen Catholicism and history: the opening of the Vatican archives. Cambridge, 1978. 174 p.

1. 96. Chartier, Roger—Le Goff, Jacques—Ravel, Jacques (eds.) La nouvelle histoire. Paris, 1978.

1. 97. Chaunu, Pierre Histoire, science sociale: le durée, l'espace et l'homme a l'époque moderne. Paris, 1983.

1.98. Chesneaux, Jean Du passe faisons table rase? Paris, 1976. English version: Pasts and futures or what is history for? L., 1978. 150p.

1.99. Childe, V. Gordon What is history? N. Y., 1953.

1. 100. Christ, Karl Von Gibbon zu Rostovtzeff. Leben und Werk führender Althistoriker der Neuzeit. Darmstadt, 1972. 384 p. On outstanding specialists of ancient history: Gibbon, Niebuhr, Droysen, Curtius, Mommsen, Burckhardt, Delbrück, Pöhlmann, Beloch, Eduard Meyer, Rostovtzeff.

1. 101. Ciardo, Maulio Le quattro epoche dello storicismo. Vico, Kant, Hegel, Croce. Bari, 1947.

1. 102. Clark, Sir George Norman Historical scholarship and historical thought. L.—Cambridge, 1944.

1. 103. Cochran, T. C. The uses of history. Wilmington, 1974.

1. 104. Cohen, Lester H. The revolutionary histories. L., 1980.

1. 105. Collingwood, R. G. The idea of history. Oxford, 1946.

1. 106. Commager, Henry Steele The nature and the study of history. (Columbus Ohio), 1965.

1.107. Conkin, Paul K.—Stromberg N. Roland The heritage and challenge of history. N. Y.—Toronto, 1971. Bibliography 260—271 p. Part 1. is a short survey of the history of historical writing. New edition: Heritage and challenge. The history and theory of history. Arlington Heights (Illinois), 1988.

1. 108. Cornell-Smith, Gordon The future of history. Hull, 1975. 22 p. (University of Hull. Inaugural lectures).

1.109. Cristian, Vasile Istoriografia generala. Bucureşti, 1979. 311 p. A university coursebook.

1. 110. Crubellier, Maurice Sens de l'histoire et religion: August Comte, Northrup, Sorokin, Arnold Toynbee. Paris, 1957.

1. 111. Croce, Benedetto Zur Theorie und Geschichte der Historiographie.Tübingen, 1915. 269 p.;Teoria e storia della storiografia. Roma, 1916.; History: its theory and practice. N. Y., 1960.

1. 112. Croce, Benedetto "La monotonia e la vacuita della storiografia communistica". Quaderni della 'Critica' V (1949) 34—45p.

1.113. Cuneo, Ernest Science and history. N. Y., 1963.

1.114. Cernak, E. Istoriografiâ protiv istorii. (Kritika reakcionnoj istoriografii epohi krušeniâ kapitalizma) M., 1962.

1. 115. Dahlmann-Waitz Quellenkunde der deutschen Geschichte. Band 1. Abschnitt 1-8. 35—43 p. Stuttgart, 1969. A good selection of standard works on the history of modern historiography.

1. 116. Dance, E. H. History, the betrayer: a study in bias. L., 1960. On slanted treatment of certain topics in textbooks.

1. 117. Danilov, A. I.—Cernâk, E. B. et al. "Istoriografiâ". *In:* Sovetskaâ Enciklopediâ 6. M., 1965. 455—514 p.

1. 118. Dardel, E. L'histoire, science du concret. Paris, 1946.

1. 119. Dehne, Harold Aller Tage Leben. Zu neuen Forschungsanalysen im Beziehungsfeld von der Alltagsgeschichte, Lebensweise und Kultur der Arbeiterklasse. Jahrbuch für Volkskunde und Kulturgeschichte 28 (1985) 1—35 p.

1. 120. Delanglez, Jean—Garraghan, Gilbert J. (eds.) A guide to historical method. N. Y., 1946.

1. 121. Delzell, Charles F. (ed.) The future of history. Nashville, 1977.

1. 122. Demandt, Alexander Geschichte als Argument. Drei Formen politischen Zukunftsdenkens im Altertum. Konstanz, 1972. Deals also with some general problems of the political uses of history.

1. 123. Demandt, Alexander "Natur- und Geschichtswissenschaft im 19. Jahrhundert". HZ (1983) 3/37—66 p.

1. 124. Deutsch, Robert—Joyeux, Frank—Sznapka, Marion "Die Entwicklung der Kooperation durch die Internationale Kongresse für Historische Wissenschaften". Revue roumaine historique 15 (1976) 93—117 p.

1. 125. Dietrich, Richard (ed.) Historische Theorie und Geschichtsforschung der Gegenwart. Berlin, 1964.

1. 126. Di Maio, Alfonso Storicismo e non storicismo, discussione e prospettive. Napoli, 1966. 293 p.

1. 127. Diwald, Hellmut Das historische Erkennen. Untersuchungen zum Geschichtsrealismus im 19. Jahrhundert. Leyden, 1955. 109 p.

1. 128. *D'âkov, V. A.* Metodologiâ istorii v prošlom i nastoâš-
čem. M., 1974. 189 p.

1. 129. *Djordejvic, Miroslav* Savremeni problemi istoriske
nauke. Beograd, 1959. 103 p.

1. 130. *Domarch, Jean* Marx et l'histoire. Paris, 1972. 271 p.

1. 131. *Dovring, F.* History as a social science. An essay on the
nature and purpose of historical studies. Den Haag, 1960.

1. 132. *Dray, William H.* Perspectives on history. L.—Boston,
1980. 142 p.

1. 133. *Dray, William H. et al. (eds.)* Philosophy of history and
contemporary historiography. Ottawa, 1982.

1. 134. *Drobizev, V. Z. (ed.)* Velikij Oktâbr, rabocij klass i
sovremennaâ burzuaznaâ istoriografiâ. M., 1977.

1. 135. *Droysen, Johann Gustav* Historik [1858]. *Hübner, R.
(ed.)*München, 1977.

1. 136. *Droysen, Johann Gustav* Texte zur Geschichtstheorie.
Birtsch, Günter—Rüsen, Jörn (eds.), Göttingen, 1972.

1. 137. *Droz, Jacques (ed.)* Les historiens des pays successeurs
sur l'Autriche-Hongrie. Austriaca (Université de Haute-Norman-
die, Centre d'Etudes et de Recherches Autrichiennes). No. 18.
(Mai 1984) 9—126 p. On the works of Austrian, Hungarian, Czech
and Transylvanian Romanian historians.

1. 138. *Dyson, Anthony Oakley* The immortality of the past. L.,
1974. 116 p.

1. 139. *Eckermann, W.* Neue Geschichtswissenschaft. Rudolf-
stadt, 1949.

1. 140. Eckermann, E.—Mohr, H. (ed.) Einführung in das Studium der Geschichte. Berlin, 1966.

1.141. Economic History in the Nineteen Seventies. A Contemporary Reckoning and New Departures (Papers Presented at the Thirty-Seventh Annual Meeting of the Economic History Association). The Journal of Economic History XXXVIII (1978) 1. Includes three studies on the development of economic history: *McCloskey, Donald N.* "The Achievements of the Cliometric School". 13—26; *Cohen, Jon S.* "The Achievements of Economic History: The Marxist School". 29—57; *Forster, Robert* "Achievements of the Annales School". 57—76 p.

1. 142. Ehrard, J.—Palmade, G. P. Histoire de l'histoire. Paris, 1964. Revised edition Paris, 1965.

1. 143. Elekes, Lajos Korszerű műveltség, történelmi gondolkodás. Budapest, 1969.

1. 144. Elekes, Lajos "Connaissance historique — consience sociale. Quelques tendences de l'historiographie et de la philosophie de l'histoire, leur influence sur la pensée contemporaine". Études Historiques Hongroises 1970. Budapest, 1970. I/89—147 p.

1. 145. Elekes, Lajos A történelem felfogása korunk polgári tudományában. Budapest, 1975. 341 p.

1. 146. Elekes, Lajos "Historisme, ahistorisme, antihistorisme dans la science bourgeoise de notre temps". Études Historiques Hongroises 1975. Budapest, 1975. I/59—88 p.

1. 147. Elton, Geoffrey Rudolph The practice of history. Sidney, 1957.

1. 148. Elton, Geoffrey Rudolph Political history: principles and practice. N.Y., 1969. 184 p.

1. 149. Elton, Geoffrey Rudolph "The historian's social function". Transactions of the Royal Historical Society. 5th Series, 27 (1977)197—211p.

1. 150. Enderwitz, Ulrich Kritik der Geschichtswissenschaft: der historische Relativismus, die Kategorie der Quelle und das Problem der Zukunft in der Geschichte. Berlin (West)—Wien, 1983.300p.

1. 151. Engelberg, Ernst (ed.) Probleme der Geschichtsmethodologie. Berlin, 1972.

1. 152. Engelberg, Ernst—Küttler, Wolfgang (eds.) Formationstheorie und Geschichte. Berlin, 1978.

1. 153. Engelberg, Ernst Theorie, Empirie und Methode in der Geschichtswisenschaft. Berlin, 1980.

1. 154. Engel-Jánosi, Friedrich Die Wahrheit der Geschichte. Versuche zur Geschichtsschreibung in der Neuzeit. Wien, 1973. 280p.

1. 155. Engel-Jánosi, Friedrich—Klingenstein, G.—Lutz, Heinrich(eds.) Denken über Geschichte. Aufsätze zur heutigen Situation des geschichtlichen Bewußtseins und der Geschichtswissenschaft. München, 1974. 257 p.

1. 156. Erdmann, Karl Dietrich "Die Zukunft als Kategorie der Geschichte". HZ 198 (1964) 44—61 p.

1. 157. Erdmann, Karl Dietrich "A History of the International Historical Congresses. Work in Progress". Storia de la Storiografia. 8 (1985) 1—20 p.

1. 158. Erdmann, Karl Dietrich "Stuttgart und der Neohistorismus". GWU 37 (1986) 2/75—80 p.

1. 159. Erich, Hermann Die misshandelte Geschichte: historische Schuld- und Freisprüche. Düsseldorf, 1983. 230 p.

1. 160. Evans, Howard V. "Current Trends in American and European Historiography". Michigan Academician 4 (Fall, 1971), 143—160p.

1. 161. Faber, Karl Georg Theorie der Geschichtswissenschaft. München, 1971.

1. 162. Faber, Karl-Georg "Ausprägungen der Historismus". HZ 228 (1979) 1—22 p.

1. 163. Fain, H. "History as science". HT 9 (1970) 104—173 p.

1. 164. Fatta, Corrado L'esperienza della storia. Palermo, 1970. 342 p.

1. 165. Fatta, Corrado Il mito della potenza. L'esperienza della storia II. Palermo, 1974. 326 p.

1. 166. Febvre, Lucien Combats pour l'Histoire. Paris, 1953. 458 p.

1. 167. Febvre, Lucien Pour une histoire à part entière. Paris, 1962. 859 p.

1. 168. Febvre, Lucien A new kind of history, and other essays. *Edited by Burke, Peter.* N.Y., 1973. 275 p.

1. 169. Fehl, Noah Eduard Personality and pattern in history. Hong-Kong, 1975. 171 p.

1. 170. Ferguson, W. K. The Renaissance in historical thought: five centuries of interpretation. Boston, 1948.

1. 171. Fernandez Alvarez, Manuel Evolucion del pensamiento historico en los tiempos modernos. Madrid, 1974. 149 p.

1. 172. Ferrater Mora, José Cuatro visiones de la historia universal. Madrid, 1982. 107 p.

1. 173. Ferro, Marc L'histoire sous surveillance. Science et conscience de l'histoire. Paris, 1987. 256 p

1. 174. Finberg, H. P. R. (ed.) Approaches to history. L., 1962. A series of essays on historical disciplines:
    Eindoff, T. Political history.
    Court, W. H. B. Economic history.
    Perkin, H. J. Social history.
    Barraclough, G. Universal history.
    Finberg, H. P. R. Local history.
    Darby, H. C. Historical geography.
    Rice, Talbot A. The history of art.
    Rupert Hall, A. The history of science.
    Wainwright, F. E. Archeology and place names.

1. 175. Finley, Moses L. The use and abuse of history. L., 1975. 254p.

1. 176. Fischer, D. H. Historians' fallacies: towards a logic of historical thought. L., 1971. An important review: *Mink, Louis O.* HT X (1971) 107 ff.

1. 177. Fischer, H. A. L. Studies in history and politics. Freeport, N. Y., 1920. reprinted in 1967. Essays, among others, on Lord Acton and modern German historians.

1. 178. Fitzsimons, M. A.—Pundt, A. G.—Nowell, Charles E. (eds.) The development of historiography. Harrisburg, Pa., 1954. 471 p. Rich bibliography.

1. 179. Fitzsimons, Matthew Anthony The past recaptured. Great historians and the history of history. Notre Dame (Ind.), 1983. 230 p. Studies among others on Acton, Burckhardt and Ranke.

1.180. Geschichte, Objektivität und Parteinahme in der Geschichtsschreibung. Von *Fontana, Jose Maria* und *Carr, Edward
Hallett* als Interviewpartner. Reinbek bei Hamburg, Rowohlt,
1979.125p.

1. 181. Fontana, Jose Maria Historia. Análisis del pasado y
proyecto social. Barcelona, 1942. 339 p.

*1. 182. Francais, Michel—Milne, A. Taylor—Mommsen, Wolf-
gang—Shafer, Boyd* Historical study in the West. N. Y., 1968.
USA, France, FRG, Great-Britain.

1. 183. Frèdericq, Paul The study of history in Germany and
France, Belgium and Holland. Baltimore, 1890.

1. 184. Freyer, Hans "Soziologie und Geschichtswissenschaft".
GWU 1 (1952) 3/14—20 p.

1.185.Friesen,Abraham Reformation and utopia. The Marxist
interpretation of the Reformation and its antecedents. Wiesbaden,1974.271 p.

1.186.Fueter,Eduard Geschichte der neueren Historiographie.
München, 1911. 626 p. Reprinted in 1968, a new German edition
with a preface by *Peyer, Hans* Ovell Füssli, 1985. The French
version: Histoire de l'historiographie moderne. Paris, 1914. An
important review by *Below, Georg von* in Vierteljahrschrift für
Sozial-und Wirtschaftsgeschichte 1912, p. 457 ff.

1. 187. Furet, François L'atelier de l'histoire. Paris, 1982. 312
p. Especially the study "La naissance de l'histoire".

1. 188. Galbraith, V. H. An introduction to the study of history.
L.,1964.

1. 189. Galkin, I. S.—Kolpakov, A. D. "Osnovnye problemy
istoriografii novogo vremeni". VI (1965) 10/67—88 p.

1. *190. Galkin, I. S. et alii* Istoriografiâ novogo vremeni stran Evropy i Ameriki. M., 1967. 670 p.

1. *191. Galkin, I. S. et al. (eds.)* Istoriografiâ novoj i novejšej istorii stran Evropy i Ameriki. M., 1968. 597 p. New edition 1977. 576p.

1. *192. Galkin, I. S.* V. I. Lenin i razvitie istoriografii novoj i novejšej istorii stran Evropy i Ameriki. M., 1977. 364 p.

1. *193. Gandy, D. Ross* Marx and history. L., 1976.

1. *194. Gardiner, Juliet (ed.)* What is history today? Houndsmills, Basingstoke (England), 1988. 167 p.

1. *195. Gardiner, Patrick* The nature of historical explanation. Oxford, 1952.; L., 1962.; Oxford, 1978.

1. *196. Gargallo di Castel Lentini, Gioacchino* Storiografia e sociologia. Roma, 1971. 111 p.

1. *197. Gargallo di Castel Lentini, Gioacchino* Lettere di storici –scritti di storia della storiografia. Roma, 1982. 219 p.

1. *198. Gay, Peter Jack* Style in history. N. Y., 1974.; L., 1975. 242p.

1. *199. Gefter, M.A. (ed.)* Istoričeskaâ nauka i nekotorye problemy sovremennosti. M., 1969. 428 p.

1. *200. Geiss, Imanuel* Studien über Geschichte und Geschichtswissenschaft. Frankfurt, 1972.

1. *201. Geiss, Imanuel* "Zwischen Marx und Stalin. Kritische Anmerkungen zur marxistischen Periodisierung der Weltgeschichte". Aus Politik und Zeitgeschichte 24 (1974) 41/3—22 p.

1. 202. Geiss, Imanuel—Tamchina, Rainer (eds.) Ansichten einer künftigen Geschichtswissenschaft. 1-2. München, 1974. 191, 226p.

1. 203. Génicot, Leopold Simples observations sur la façon d'écrire l'histoire. Louvain-la-Neuve, 1980. 120 p.

1. 204. Gervinus, G. G. Grundzüge der Historik, Leipzig,1937.

1. 205. "Gesellschaftliche Aufgaben der Geschichtswissenschaft in der Gegenwart". GWU 24 (1973) 354—56 p. A statement of "Verband der Historiker Deutschlands" of 10 February, 1973.

1. 206. Geyl, Pieter Napoleon: for and against. Yale University Press,1949.

1. 207. Geyl, Pieter From Ranke to Toynbee. 5 lectures on historians and historiographical problems. Northampton (Mass), 1952.80p.

1. 208. Geyl, Pieter Use and abuse of history. New Haven, 1955.

1. 209. Geyl, Pieter Debates with historians. L., 1955. 286 p. Revised German version: Die Diskussion ohne Ende. Darmstadt, 1958. 256 p. Ranke, Macaulay, Carlyle, Michelet, Toynbee, Sorokin, Dutch historiography and the national state, the French historians and Talleyrand, Isaiah Berlin.

1. 210. Geyl, Pieter Encounters in history. Cleveland, 1961.

1. 211. Geyl, Pieter—Sorokin, P.—Toynbee, Arnold J. The pattern of the past: can we determine it? Boston, 1944.

1. 212. Gilbert, A. N. (ed.) In search of a meaningful past. Boston, 1971.

1. 213. Gilbert, Felix History: choice and commitment. Cambridge (Mass.), 1977.

1. 214. Gilbert, Felix—Graubard, Stephen R. (eds.) Historical studies today. N. Y., 1972.

1. 215. Glatz, Ferenc "A történettudomány és a közgondolkodás történeti elemei". Társadalmi Szemle 35 (1980) 1/47—58 p.

1. 216. Glatz, Ferenc "Marxi elmélet és történeti szaktudomány". Történelmi Szemle 26 (1983) 3-4/353—366 p.

1. 217. Goetz, Walter Intuition in der Geschichtswissenschaft. München, 1935.

1. 218. Goetz, Walter "Die Entstehung des Historismus". *In: Goetz, Walter* Historiker in meiner Zeit. München—Graz, 1957.

1. 219. Gooch, George P. History and historians in the nineteenth century. L., 1913, revised edition 1952, with a new preface 1959. 604 p. The German version: Geschichte und Geschichtsschreiber im 19. Jahrhundert. Frankfurt, 1964. 680 p.

1. 220. Gooch, George P. Historical surveys and portraits. N. Y. 1966. (General problems and English historians).

1. 221. Goodfriend, June—Toulmin, Stephen The discovery of time. N. Y., 1965.

1. 222. Gorman, J. L. The expression of historical knowledge. Edinburgh, 1982. 123 p.

1. 223. Gorodeckij, E. N. "Istoriografiâ kak special'naâ otrasl istoričeskoj nauki". Istoriâ SSSR (1974) 4/19—116 p.

1. 224. Gottschalk, Louis Understanding history. A primer of historical method. N. Y., 1950.

1.225. Gottschalk, Louis (ed.) Generalization in the writing of history. Chicago, 1963. A review by *Mink, Louis O.* Journal of Philosophy 61 (1964).

1. 226. Görlitz, W. Idee und Geschichte. Die Entwicklung des historischen Denkens. Freiburg, 1949.

1. 227. Görög József Történetírás és történetszemlélet fejlődése. Budapest, 1963. Manuscript, used as a textbook of teacher training colleges in Hungary.

1. 228. Graham, Gordon Historical explanation reconsidered. Aberdeen, 1983. 82 p.

1. 229. Grekov, B. D. "Istoriâ". *In:* Bol'šaâ sovetskaâ enciklopediâ. Vol. 19. M., 1953. 28—33 p.

1. 230. Groh, D. Kritische Geschichtswissenschaft in emanzipatorischer Absicht. Stuttgart, 1973.

1. 231. Groningen, B. A. In the grip of the past. Leiden, 1953.

1. 232. Gründer, Karlfried Reflexion der Kontinuitäten: zum Geschichtsdenken der letzten Jahrzehnte. Göttingen, 1982. 177.

1. 233. Gubernatis, Angelo de Storia universale della letteratura. Vol. 11. Storia della storia. Milano—Napoli—Pisa, 1884. 329 p.

1. 234. Guggenberger, Bernd Die Neubestimmung des subjektiven Faktors im Neomarxismus. Eine Analyse des voluntaristischen Geschichtsverständnisses der Neuen Linken. Freiburg—München, 1973. 444 p.

1. 235. Guilday, Peter (ed.) Church historians. N. Y., 1926.

1. 236. Guinsburg, T. N. (ed.) The dimensions of history. Readings on the nature of history and the problems of historical interpretation. Chicago, 1971.

1. 237. Gulyga, Arsenij V. Estetika istorii. M., 1974. 126 p. A general analysis.

1.238. Gulyga, Arsenij V. Iskusstvo istorii. M., 1980. 287 p.

1. 239. Gusev, K. V.—Naumov, V. P. (eds.) Velikij Oktâbr v rabotah sovetskih i zarubeznyh istorikov. M., 1971.

1.240. Gustavson, Carl A. A preface to history. N. Y., 1955.

1. 241. Gutnova, E. V. "Mesto i značenie buržuaznoj positivistskoj istoriografii vtoroj poloviny XIX veka v razvitii istoričeskoj nauki". Srednie veka. Vypusk 25. M., 1964.

1.242. Gutnova, E. V. Istoriografiâ istorii srednih vekov. (Seredina XIX. v. — 1917 g.) M., 398 p. A university coursebook.

1. 243. Haddock, B. A. An introduction to historical thought. L.,1980.

1. 244. Hahn, Manfred Historiker und Klassen. Zur Grundlegung einer Geschichte der bürgerlichen Gesellschaft. Frankfurt am Main—N. Y., 1976.

1. 245. Halevy, Daniel Essai sur l'accélération de l'histoire. Paris,1948.

1.246. Halperin, Samuel William (ed.) Some twentieth century historians. Chicago, 1961. [Pirenne, Trevelyan, Lefebvre, Butterfield, Renouvin, Febvre].

1. 247. Halperin, Samuel William (ed.) Essays in modern European historiography. Chicago—L., 1970. 378 p.

1. 248. Halphen, L. Introduction a l'histoire. Paris, 1946.

1. 249. Hampl, Franz—Weiler, Ingoma (eds.) Vergleichende Geschichtswissenschaft: Methode, Ertrag und ihr Beitrag zur Universalgeschichte. Darmstadt, 1978. 294 p.

1. 250. Handelsman, Marceli Historyka. Zamosc, 1921. Second revised and enlarged edition: Historyka. Zasady metodologii i teorii poznania historycznego. Warszawa, 1928.

1. 251. Handlin, Oscar Truth in history. Cambridge (Mass.) — L., 1981. 437 p.

1. 252. Harrison, Frederic The history schools: an Oxford dialogue, *In:* The meaning of history, and other historical pieces. N. Y., 1984.

1. 253 . Harte, N. B. (edited and introduction by) The study of economic history: collected inaugural lectures 1893—1970. L., 1971. 390p.

1. 254. Hauser, Oswald (ed.) Geschichte und Geschichtsbewusstsein. 19 Vorträge für die Ranke-Gesellschaft, Vereinigung für Geschichte im öffentlichen Leben. Göttingen, 1981.

1. 255. Hayek, Friedrich (ed.) Capitalism and historians. L., 1954. 188 p. Essays by Ashton, T. S., Hacker, L. M., Hutt, W. H., de Jouvenel, B.

1. 256. Hearder, Harry Ideological commitment and historical interpretation. An inaugural lecture. Cardiff, 1969. 23 p.

1. 257. Hedinger, Hans-Walter Subjektivität und Geschichtswissenschaft. Grundzüge einer Historik. Berlin, 1969. 691 p.

1. 258. Hedinger, Hans-Walter "Theorienpluralismus in der Geschichtswissenschaft". *In: Diener A. (ed.)* Der Methoden — und Theorienpluralismus in den Wissenschaften. Meisenheim, 1971.

1. 259. Hedinger, Hans-Walter "Über Zielsetzungen der Geschichtswissenschaft". GWU 23 (1972) 21—26 p.

1. 260. Heffer, J. La nouvelle histoire économique. Paris, 1977.

1. 261. Heimpel, Hermann "Über Organisationsformen historischer Forschung". HZ 189 (1959) 139—222 p.

1. 262. Heitzer, Hans—Küttler, Wolfgang Marx, Lenin und die Geschichtswissenschaft. Berlin, 1983. 269 p.

1. 263. Heller, Ágnes A theory of history. N. Y., 1982.

1. 264. Helton, Tinsley (ed.) The Renaissance: a reconsideration of the theories and interpretations of the age. Madison, University of Wisconsin Press, 1961.

1. 265. Heussi, K. Die Krise des Historismus. Tübingen, 1932.

1. 266. Hexter, Jack H. Reappraisals in history. New views on history and society in early modern Europe. Foreword by Lasslett, Peter N. Y., 1963. Including essays on "The historian and his day" and "A new framework for social history". A new edition: Chicago—London, 1979. 278 p.

1. 267. Hexter, Jack H. The history primer. N. Y., 1971.

1. 268. Hexter, Jack H. Doing history. L., 1971.

1. 269. Hexter, Jack H. On historians. Reappraisals of some of the makers of modern history. Harvard University Press, Cambridge (Mass.), 1979. 310 p. [Carl Becker, Wallace K. Ferguson, Hiram Hayden, Fernand Braudel, Lawrence Stone, Christopher Hill, J. G. A. Pocock]

1. 270. Himmelfarb, Gertrude The new history and the old. Cambridge (Mass.), 1987. 209 p.

1. 271. Hintze, Otto "Über individualistische und kollektivistische Geschichtsauffassung". HZ 78 (1897)

1. 272. Hintze, Otto Soziologie und Geschichte. Göttingen, 1964.

1. 273. Hirst, Paul Q. Marxism and historical writing. L., 1985. 184p.

1.274. Histoire et historiens depuis cinquante ans. Méthodes, organisation et résultats du travail historique de 1876 à 1926. Paris, 1927.

1.275. "The historian and the world of the twentieth century". Daedalus 100/1971/2.

1.276. "Historians on the twentieth century". Journal of Contemporary History 2 (January, 1967) A whole issue devoted to the subject.

1. 277. Hobsbawm, Eric J. "Karl Marx's contribution to historiography". Diogenes 64 (Winter, 1968) 37—56 p.

1. 278. Hobsbawm, E. J. "From social history to the history of society". *In: Flinn, M. W.—Smaut, T. C.* (eds.) Essays in social history. Oxford, 1974.

1. 279. Hockett, Homer C. The critical method in historical research and writing. N. Y., 1955.

1. 280. Hofer, Walther Geschichte zwischen Philosophie und Politik. Basel, 1956.

1. 281. Hofstadter, Richard—Lipset, Seymour M. (eds.) Sociology and history. N. Y.—L., Basic Books, 1968.

1. 282. Holborn, H. History and the humanities. Garden City (N. Y.), 1972.

1. 283. Holborn, H. "Greek and modern conceptions of History". Journal of the History of Ideas 10 (1949) 3—13 p.

1. 284. Holldack, H. "Historismus heute". Deutsche Beiträge 1974/5.

1. 285. Hook, S. (ed.) Philosophy and history. N. Y., 1963.

1. 286. Horák, P. Studie z dejin historického pozitivismu. Praha, 1971.

1. 287. Hours, J. Valeur de l'histoire. (Coll. »Initiation philosophiques«) Paris, 1963. 90 p.

1. 288. Hughes, H. Stuart Consciousness and society: the reorientation of European social thought, 1890—1930. N. Y., 1958.

1. 289. Hughes, H. S. History as art and science: twin vistas on the past. N. Y., 1964. 107 p.

1. 290. Huizinga, Johan Mein Weg zur Geschichte. Basel, 1947. (General, autobiographical and on Carlyle, Burckhardt).

1. 291. Hulme, Edward Maslin History and its neighbours. Oxford University Press, 1942.

1. 292. Humboldt, Alexander von "Über die Aufgabe des Geschichtsschreibers". [1822]. *In:* Gesammelte Schriften, Berlin, 1903—1936. IV. 35—63 p. English translation HT 6 (1967) 57—71 p. Some important comments: *Erhardt, L.* HZ 55 (1886), *Spranger, E.* HZ 100 (1908), *Kessel, E.* Studium Generale 2 (1949).

1. 293. Hübner, K. (ed.) Natur und Geschichte. Hamburg, 1974.

1. 294. Hünermann, P. Der Durchbruch des geschichtlichen Denkens im 19. Jahrhundert. Freiburg, 1967.

1. 295. Hunt, Lynn (ed.) The New cultural history: essays. Berkeley (Cal.), 1989. 244 p.

1. 296. Hyslop, Beatrice F. "Trends in historical writing about modern Europe in the last five years". The Annals (American Academy of Political and Social Science) January, 1970.

1. 297. Iggers, Georg G. New directions in European historiography. Middletown, 1975. 229 p. Revised, extended edition Middletown, 1984. In German: Neue Geschichtswissenschaft. Vom Historismus zur historischen Sozialwissenschaft. München, 1978. An important review by *Ward, Paul L.* HT XV (1976) 2, 202—212p.

1. 298. Iggers, Georg G. "The »Methodenstreit« — in international perspective. The reorientation of historical studies at the turn from the nineteenth to the twentieth century". Storia della Storiografia 6 (1984) 21—32 p.

1. 299. Iggers, Georg G.—Schulz, W. "Geschichtswissenschaft". *In:* Sachwörterbuch der Geschichte. Vol. 2. Freiburg, 1968. 914—959p.

1. 300. Iggers, Georg G.—Parker, H.T. (eds.) International handbook of historical studies. Contemporary research and theory. Westport (Conn.), 1979. 452 p.

1. 301. Iribadzakov, Nikolaj Klio pred sda na buržoaznata filozofiâ. Sofiâ, 1970. 814 p. With Russian and English summaries.

1. 302. Irmschler, Konrad—Lozek, Gerhard "Historismus und Sozialgeschichte in der gegenwärtigen bürgerlichen Geschichtsschreibung". ZfG 27 (1979) 3/195—208 p.

1. 303. Iser, Wolfgang—Schalk, Fritz (eds.) Dargestellte Geschichte in der europäischen Literatur des 19. Jahrhunderts. Frankfurt am Main, 1970.

1. 304. Iskenderov, A.A. (ed.) Kritika sovremennoj buržoaznoj i reformistskoj istoriografii. M., 1974. 221 p.

1. 305. Jäckel, E.—Wegnar, E. (eds.) Die Funktion der Geschichte in unserer Zeit. Stuttgart, 1975.

1. 306. Janosi, Janina Optimism si pessimism istoric. Bucureşti, 1972.

1. 307. Jaspers, Karl Vom Ursprung und Ziel der Geschichte. Zürich, 1949. English version: The origin and goal of history. L., 1953.

1. 308. Jaures, Jean Idéalism et matérialisme dans la conception de l'histoire. Paris, 1895.

1. 309. Jeismann, Karl-Ernst Geschichte als Horizont der Gegenwart: über den Zusamenhang von Vergangenheitsdeutung, Gegenwartsverständnis und Zukunftsperspektive. Padeborn, 1985.348p.

1. 310. Jodl, Friedrich Die Culturgeschichtsschreibung, ihre Entwicklung und ihr Problem. Halle, 1878. 125 p.

1. 311. Johnson, Richard—McLennan, George—Schwarz, Bill—Sutton, David Making histories. Birmingham, 1982. Marxist theory and historical analysis, problems of modern social history.

1. 312. Jones, Gareth S. Klassen, Politik und Sprache. Für eine theorieorientierte Sozialgeschichte. Münster, 1988. 320 p.

1. 313. Jordáky, Lajos Szocializmus és történettudomány. Bukarest, 1974. 417 p. A collection of studies.

1. 314. Joyce, Davis D. History and historians. Some essays. Washington D. C., 1983. General and American.

1. 315. Kaegi, Werner Chronica Mundi. Grundformen der Geschichtsschreibung seit dem Mittelalter. Einsiedeln, 1954. 89 p.

1. 316. Kaltenbrunner, G. K. (ed.) Die Zukunft der Vergangenheit. München, 1975.

1. 317. Kann, A. Betrachtungen zum Relevanzproblem in der Geschichtsschreibung der Neuzeit. Anzeiger der Philosophisch-Historischen Klasse der Österreichischen Akademie der Wissenschaften 116 (1979) 129—44 p.

1. 318. Kaplan, Steven L.—La Capra, Dominick (eds.) Modern European intellectual history. Reappraisals and new perspectives, Ithaca,1982.

1. 319. Kelle, Vladislav Zanovic—Koval'zon, Matvej Âkovlevic Teoriâ i istoriâ. Problemy istoriceskogo processa. M., 1981. 287 p.

1. 320. Kelley, D. R. Foundations of modern historical scholarship. N. Y., 1970.

1. 321. Kesting, Hanno Geschichtsphilosophie und Weltbürgerkrieg. Deutungen der Geschichte von der französischen Revolution bis zum Ost-West Konflikt. Heidelberg, 1959.

1. 322. Key, Kerim Kami Some observations on modern historiography. Washington, 1966. 23 p. (A lecture on general problems of modern historiography.)

1. 323. Keyser, E. Die Geschichtswissenschaft. Aufbau und Aufgaben. München, 1931. 243 p.

1. 324. Kinnel, Susan (ed.) Historiography. An Annotated Bibliography of Journal Articles, Books, and Dissertations. ABC-Clio, Santa Barbara, California—Oxford, England, 1987. I-II. 376, 482p.

1.325. Kirn, P.—Leuschner, J. Einführung in die Geschichtswissenschaft. Berlin, 1947., 5 more editions until 1972.

1. 326. Kirn, P. Das Bild des Menschen in der Geschichtsschreibung von Polybios bis Ranke. Göttingen, 1955.

1. 327. Klempt, A. Die Säkularisierung der universalhistorischen Auffassung. Göttingen, 1960.

1. 328. Knowles, David The historian and character. N. Y., 1955. Also published in: The historian and character and other essays. Collected and presented to him by his friends, pupils and colleagues on the occasion of his retirement as Regius Professor of Modern History in the University of Cambridge. Cambridge, 1963. 387 p.

1. 329. Knowles, David Great historical enterprises. Problems in Monastic history. L., 1963. On mediaeval scholarship.

1. 330. Knowles, David Some trends in scholarship 1868—1968, in the field of mediaeval history. Transactions of the Royal Historical Society, 5th series, 19 (1969).

1. 331. Koch, Gertrud H. Zum Verhältnis von Dichtung und Geschichtsschreibung.Theorie und Analyse. Frankfurt am Main–N. Y., 1983.

1. 332. Kocka, Jürgen Geschichte. München, 1976.

1. 333. Kocka, Jürgen (ed.) Theorien in der Praxis des Historikers. Göttingen, 1977.

1. 334. Kocka, Jürgen Sozialgeschichte: Begriff, Entwicklung, Probleme. Göttingen, 1977. 173 p.

1. 335. Kocka, Jürgen—Nipperdey, Thomas (eds.) Theorie und Erzählung in der Geschichte. München, 1979.

1. 336. Kon, I. S. Die Geschichtsphilosophie des 20. Jahrhunderts. Berlin, 1964.

1. 337. Kosáry, Domokos "Strukturalizmus és történettudomány". Valóság 20 (1977) 9/39—48 p.

1. 338. Kosáry, Domokos "Modellalkotás és történettudomány". Történelmi Szemle 21 (1978) 2/117—157 p.

1. 339. Kosminskij, E. A. Istoriografiâ srednih vekov, V.v. — seredina XIX. v. Lekcii. M., 1963. 429 p. The last lectures deal with French and German historiography in the first half of the 19th century.

1. 340. Kosseleck, Reinhart "Wozu noch Historie?" HZ 212 (1971) 1—18 p.

1. 341. Kosseleck, Reinhart—Stempel, W. D. (eds.) Geschichte-Ereignis und Erzählung. Poetik und Hermeneutik. Vol. 5. München, 1973. 600 p.

1. 342. Kosseleck, R. et al. "Geschichte, Historie". *In: Brunner, Otto—Conze, Werner—Kosseleck, Reinhart (eds.)* Geschichtliche Grundbegriffe. Vol. 2. Stuttgart, 1975. 593—713 p.

1. 343. Kovács, Endre A mai polgári történetírás. Budapest, 1962. 209 p.

1. 344. Kovács, Endre "Ismeretelméleti problémák a mai polgári történetírásban". Történelmi Szemle 11 (1968) 4/349—372 p.

1. 345. Král, Václav Historiografie — její retrospektivy a perspektivy. Praha, 1973. 200 p.

1. 346. Krey, August History and the social web. A collection of essays. Minneapolis, 1955.

1. 347. Krieger, Leonard "Marx and Engels as historians". Journal of the History of Ideas XIV (1953) 381—403 p.

1. 348. Krieger, Leonard "The horizons of history". AHR 63 (1957) 62—74 p.

1. 349. Krieger, Leonard "The uses of Marx for history". Political Sciences Quarterly LXXV (1960) 255—78 p.

1.350. Kritik der bürgerlichen Geschichtswissenschaft (I.). Das Argument. Zeitschrift für Philosophie und Sozialwissenschaften Nr. 70 (Sonderband). Berlin, 1972.

1. 351. Krzystof, Pornian "L'histoire de la science et l'histoire de l'histoire". Annales 30 (1975)

1. 352. Kudrna, Jaroslav "Die politisch-ideologische Rolle des Individualitätbegriffs in der Geschichtsschreibung der Neuzeit". Sbornik Praci Filosofické Fakulty Brnenské University. 15 (1968) 93—110p.

1. 353. Kudrna, Jaroslav Kapitoly z dejin marxisticke historiografie. 1. vyd. Brno, Univ. J. E. Purkyne. 1981. 66 p.

1. 354. Kudrna, Jaroslav Ke kritice pozitivismu v soucasné burzoazní nemecké francousské a italiské historiografii 19. a 20. století. Univrsita J. E. Purkyne v Brne, 1983. 151 p. With a German summary.

1. 355. Kuczynski, Jürgen Die Muse und der Historiker. Studien über Jacob Burckhardt, Hypolite Taine, Henry Adams. Berlin, 1974. 247 p. (Jahrbuch für Wirtschaftsgeschichte. Sonderband)

1. 356. Küttler, Wolfgang (ed.) Marxistische Typisierung und idealtypische Methode in der Geschichtswissenschaft. Berlin, 1986. 315p.

1. 357. La Capra, Dominick History and criticism. Ithaca—L., 1985. 145p.

1.358. Lacombe, P. De l'histoire considerée comme une science. Paris, 1894.

1. 359. Lamprecht, Karl Alte und neue Richtungen in der Geschichtswissenschaft. Berlin, 1896.

1. 360. Lamprecht, Karl Moderne Geschichtswissenschaft. Fünf Vorträge. Freiburg i. Br., 1905. 130 p.

1. 361. Langlois, Ch. V.—Seignobos, Ch. Introduction aux Etudes Historiques. Paris, 1898. English version: Introduction to the study of history. L., 1898 — reprinted N. Y., 1966.

1. 362. Langlois, Ch.V. Manuel de bibliographie historique 1-2. Paris, 1901—1904.

1. 363. Lapeyre, Henri Ensayos de historiografia. Valladolid, 1978. 247 p.

1. 364. Laqueur, Walter—Mosse, George (eds.) The new history. Trends in historical research and writing since world war II. N. Y., 1967. Originally an issue of the Journal of Contemporary History: 3 (1968) No. 4. Another edition of the same work: *Watt, Donald Cameron (ed.)* Contemporary history in Europe. L. 1969.

1. 365. Laqueur, W.—Mosse, G. L. (eds.) Historians in politics. L.—Beverly Hills, 1974.

1. 366. Lecky, W. E. H. The political value of history. L., 1892.

1. 367. Léderer, Emma A történelem tudományossága. Budapest, 1968.

1. 368. Lefebvre, G. La naissance de l'historiographie moderne. Paris, 1971. 348 p. Lectures delivered at the Sorbonne in 1946.

1. 369. Leff, Gordon History and social theory. L., 1969.

1. 370. Le Goff, Jacques (ed.) La nouvelle histoire. Paris, 1978. 575 p. (Les encyclopédies du savoir moderne)

1. 371. Le Goff, J.—Nora, Pierre (eds.) Faire de l'histoire. 1-3. Paris,1974.
1. Nouveaux problèmes. 230 p.
2. Nouvelles approches. 250 p.
3. Nouveaux objets. 281 p.

1. 372. Le Roy Ladurie, Emmanuel Le territoire de l'historien. Paris, 1974. 542 p. English version: The territory of the historian. Chicago, 1979. The mind and method of the historian. Chicago,1981.

*1. 373. Leskiewicz, Janina—Kowalska—Glikman, Stefania (eds.)*Historia i nowoczesnosc. Problemy unowoczesnienia metodologii i warsztatu badawczego historyka. Wroclaw, 1974. 354 p.

1. 374. Levy-Leboyer, H. "La New economic history". Annales 1969/1035—1065p.

1. 375. Lewis, I. M. (ed.) History and social anthropology. L., 1968.

1.376. L'Histoire. Textes et documents sur l'histoire. Paris, 1980. 1-3. 192+160+160 p.
1. *Julliot, André—Quillet, Pierre (eds.)* Les Philosophies de l'histoire.
2. *Fremeaux, Jacques—Valette, Bernard (eds.)* L'Ecriture de l'histoire.
3. *Hanrion, Régis (ed.)* L'Histoire au présent.

1.377. L'historiographie moderne. N° special. Revue international des sciences sociales 1981/4.

1. 378. L'histoire sociale. Sources et méthodes. Colloque d' l'Ecole Normale Supérieure de Saint-Cloud. 15—16 mai 1965. Paris,1967.

1. 379. Linehan, P. A. "The making of the Cambridge Medieval History". Saeculum 57 (1982) 3/463—494 p.

1.380. Litt, Theodor Wege und Irrwege geschichtlichen Denkens. München, 1948. 155 p.

1.381. Litt, Theodor Die Wiederweckung des geschichtlichen Bewußtseins. Heidelberg, 1956.

1.382. Lord, Clifford L. (ed.) Keepers of the past. Chapel Hill, 1965.

1.383. Lorenz, Ottokar "Die »bürgerliche« Geschichte und die naturwissenschaftliche Geschichte". HZ 39 (1878) 458—485 p.

1.384. Lorenz, Ottokar Die Geschichtswissenschaft in Hauptrichtungen und Aufgaben. 1-2. Berlin, 1886, 1891.

1.385. Lovejoy, Arthur O. "The historiography of ideas" in his Essays in the history of ideas. Baltimore, 1948.

1.386. Lowenthal, David The past is a foreign country. Cambridge, 1985. The development of historical consciousness and historiography in Britain, France and the USA.

1.387. Lozek, Gerhard "Zur Theoriediskussion in der nicht-marxistischen Geschichtswissenschaft Ende des 19., Anfang des 20. Jahrhunderts". ZfG 32 (1984) 5/395—404 p.

1.388. Lübbe, Hermann Geschichtsbegriff und Geschichtsinteresse. Analytik und Pragmatik der Historie. Basel—Stuttgart, 1977.

1.389. Ludz, Peter Christian Soziologie und Sozialgeschichte. Aspekte und Probleme. Opladen, 1974.

1.390. Lüthy, H. Wozu Geschichte? Zürich, 1969.

1.391. Macurek, Josef Dejepisectví evropského vychodu. V Praze, 1946. 349 p.

1. 392. *Mâgkov, G. P.—Carev, V. B.* "K metodologičeskim voprosam istoriografičeskih issledovanij". *In: Sofman, A. S. (ed.)* Kritika buržuaznych koncepcij vseobsčej istorii. Kazan', 1973. Vypusk. 1.

1. 393. *Malin, J. C.* Essays on historiography. Lawrence (Kan.), 1946.

1. 394. *Mandelbaum, Maurice* "Lovejoy and the theory of historiography". Journal of the History of Ideas IX (1948) 412—23 p.

1. 395. *Mandelbaum, Maurice* History, man and reason. A study in nineteenth-century thought. Baltimore, 1971.

1. 396. *Mandelbaum, Maurice* The anatomy of historical knowledge. Baltimore—L., 1977. 232 p.

1. 397. *Mann, Golo* "Die alte und die neue Historie". *In: Padevils, C. (ed.)*Tendenzwende. Stuttgart, 1975. 40—58 p.

1. 398. *Mann, Golo* "Geschichte und Geschichtswissenschaft heute". Universitas 32 (1977) 6/587—588 p.

1. 399. *Mann, Golo* Geschichte und Geschichten. Frankfurt am Main, 1961. 532 p.

1. 400. *Maravall, José Antonio* Teoria del 'aber histórico. Madrid, 1967. 310 p.

1. 401. *Marcus, John T.* "Time and the sense of history: East and West". Comparative Studies in Society and History III (1961) 123—139p.

1. 402. *Marrou, Henri—Irénée* "La méthodologie historique: orientations actuelles à propos d'ouvrages récents". Revue Historique CCIX (1953) 256—70 p.

1. 403. Marrou, Henri—Irénée "L'histoire et les historiens. Seconde chronique de l'méthodologie historique". Revue Historique CCXVII (1957) 270—89 p.

1. 404. Marrou, Henri—Irénée De la connaissance historique. Paris,1954.

1. 405. Marwick, A. The nature of history. L., 1970. 316 p.

1. 406. Marxismus. A comprehensive Literaturbericht. GWU 26/1979/6-7.

1. 407. Masur, Gerhard "Distinctive traits of Western civilization through the eyes of Western historians". AHR LXVII (1962) 591—608p.

1. 408. Masur, Gerhard Prophets of yesterday. Studies in European culture, 1890—1914. N. Y., 1961.

1. 409. Masur, Gerhard Geschehen und Geschichte. Berlin, 1971.189p.

1. 410. McClelland, Peter Dean Causal explanation and model building in history, economics and the new economic history. Ithaca—L.—Cornell University Press, 1975. 290 p.

1. 411. McCullagh, C. Behan Justifying historical descriptions. Cambridge University Press, 1984. Numerous analyses of modern British and American historical works.

1. 412. McLennan, George Marxism and the methodologies of history. L., 1981.

1. 413. Meduševskaâ, O. M. Sovremennaâ buržoaznaâ istoriografiâ i voprosy istočnikovedeniâ. M., 1979. 72 p. A university coursebook.

1. 414. Meinhold, P. Geschichte der kirchlichen Historiographie. Freiburg—München, 1967. 1-2. 533, 628 p. Bibliography: 1. 495—515, 2. 600—616p.

1. 415. Meister, A. Grundzüge der historischen Methode. Leipzig, 1913.

1. 416. Mercalov, A. N. (ed.) Kritika sovremennyh buržuaznyh istoričeskih koncepcij. Gor'kij, 1976.

1. 417. Meron, Josef Theorien in der Geschichtswissenschaft: die Diskussion über die Wissenschaftlichkeit der Geschichte. Göttingen, 1985. 227 p.

1. 418. Meyer, E. Zur Theorie und Methodik der Geschichte. Halle, 1902.

1. 419. Mezlish, Bruce (ed.) Psychoanalysis and history. Englewood Cliffs (N. J.), 1963.

1. 420. Mirsky, D. S. "Bourgeois history and historical materialism". Labour Monthly 13 (1931) 453—459 p.

1. 421. Mises, Ludwig von Theory and history: an interpretation of social and economic evolution. New Haven, 1957.; N. Y., 1969..

1. 422. Miskiewicz, Benon Wstep do badan historucznych. Warszawa—Poznan, 1973. 283 p.

1. 423. Mogil'nickij, B. G. "Marksistskij i buržuaznyj istorizm". V. I. (1982) 7/71—85 p.

1. 424. Momigliano, Arnoldo "A hundred years after Ranke". Diogenes 7 (1954) 52—58 p.

1. 425. Momigliano, Arnoldo "Sullo stato presente degli studi di storia antica". *In:* X. Congreso Internazionale di Scienze Storiche. Roma 4-11 Settembre 1955. Relazioni VI. 1—40 p.

1. 426. Momigliano, Arnoldo Studies in historiography. N. Y., 1966. 263 p.

1. 427. Momigliano, Arnoldo "Linee per una valutazione della storiografia nel quindicennio 1961—1976". Rivista storica italiana 89 (1977) 596—608 p.

1. 428. Momigliano, Arnoldo Essays in ancient and modern historiography. Oxford, 1977. 387 p.

1. 429. Momigliano, Arnoldo Problème d'historiographie ancienne et moderne. Paris, 1983. 432 p.

1. 430. Momigliano, Arnoldo Tra Storia e Storicismo. Pisa, 1985. 264 p.

1. 431. Moreno Fraginals, Manuel La Historia como arma. Barcelona, 1983. 178 p.

1. 432. Morris, W. Towards a new historicism. Princeton, 1972.

1. 433. Mortet, Ch. et V. La science de l'histoire. Paris, 1894.

1. 434. Muhlack, Ulrich "Probleme einer erneuerten Historik". HZ 228 (1979) 335—364 p.

1. 435. Muller, Herbert, J. The uses of the past. Profiles of former societies. N. Y., — Oxford University Press, 1957.

1. 436. Munby, L.—Wangermann, E. Marxism and history. A bibliography of English language works. L., 1967.

1. 437. Murphey, Murray G. Our knowledge of the historical past. Indianapolis—N. Y., 1973. 209 p.

1. 438. Murray, Michael Edward Modern philosophy of history: its origin and destination. The Hague, 1970. 137 p.

1. 439. *Nagl-Docekal, Herta* Die Objektivität der Geschichtswissenschaft. Wien—München, 1982. 268 p.

1. 440. *Nagl-Docekal, Herta—Wimmer, Franz (eds.)* Neue Ansätze in der Geschichtswissenschaft. Wien, 1984. 167 p.

1. 441. *Namier, L. B.* Avenues of history. L., 1952.

1. 442. *Neale, R. S. (ed.)* History and class. Essential reading in theory and interpretation. L., 1983.

1. 443. *Neff, Emery* The poetry of history. The contribution of literature and literary scholarship to the writing of history since Voltaire. N. Y.—London, 1947. 258 p.

1. 444. *Neron, Josef* Theorien in der Geschichtswissenschaft. Göttingen, 1985.

1. 445. *Niebuhr, Reinhold* Faith and history: a comparison of Christian and modern views of history. N. Y., 1949.

1. 446. *Nietzsche, Friedrich* "Vom Nutzen und Nachteil der Historie für das Leben". *In:* Unzeitgemäße Betrachtungen, Nietzsche Werke in Einzelausgaben, herausgegeben von Georg Matthäi, Leipzig 1883. Auch in Nietzsches Werke, Vol. 2. Leipzig, 1906.

1. 447. *Nipperdey, Thomas* "Historismus und Historismuskritik heute". *In: Nipperdey, Thomas* Gesellschaft, Kultur, Theorie. Göttingen, 1976. 59—73 p.

1. 448. *Nisbet, Robert A.* Social change and history. Aspects of the Western theory of development. N. Y. — Oxford University Press, 1969.

1.449. Nordisk fagkonferense for historisk metodelaere 10th, Rovos 1974. Periferi og sentrum i historien. Oslo (1975). 195 p. (Studier i historisk metode; 10)

1. 450. Nolte, E. "Über das Verhältnis von bürgerlicher und marxistischer Geschichtswissenschaft". Aus Politik und Zeitgeschichte 3 (1973).

1. 451. Norling, Bernard Timeless problems in history. L., 1970. 301 p.

1. 452. North, Douglas "The state of economic history". American Economic Review LV /1965/2.

1. 453. North, Douglas "The new economic history after twenty years". American Behavioral Scientist N°21 (November-December 1971)

1. 454. Novack, George Understanding history. Marxist essays. N. Y., 1972.

1. 455. Nowell, Charles E. "Has the past a place in history?" Journal of Modern History XXIV (December, 1952) 331—340 p.

1. 456. Oakeshott, Michael "The activity of being an historian". *In:* Historical Studies: Papers read before the Second Irish Conference of Historians. Edited by T. Bermand Williams, L., 1958. Reprinted in his Rationalism in Politics. N. Y., 1962. 137—167 p.

1. 457. Oakeshott, Michael On history and other essays. Oxford, 1983. 198 p.

1. 458. Obenga, Theophile Pour une nouvelle histoire. Paris, 1980. 170 p.

1. 459. Oelmüller, W. (ed.) Wozu noch Geschichte? München, 1976.

1. 460. Oexle, Otto G. "Die Geschichtswissenschaft im Zeichen des Historismus". HZ 238 (1984) 17—56 p.

1. 461. Oman, Sir Charles On the writing of history. L., 1939.

1. 462. Pamlényi, Ervin "A historiográfia tárgyáról". Történelmi Szemle 17 (1974) 4/552—560 p.

1. 463. Pane, Luigi dal La storia come storica del lavoro. Discorsi di concezione et di metodo. Bologna, 1971. 279 p.

1. 464. Papaioannou, Kostas "The consecration of history. An essay on the genealogy of the historical consciousness". Diogenes 31 (1960) 29—55 p.

1. 465. Pares, Richard The historian's business and other essays. *Edited by R. A.* and *Elizabeth Humphreys.* N. Y.—Oxford, 1961.

1. 466. Pašuto, V. T. Revanšisti — psevdoistoriki Rossii. M., 1971.157p.

1. 467. Pašuto, V. T.—Cerepnin, L. V.—Štrankl, M. M. (eds.) Kritika buržoaznych koncepcij istorii Rossii v periode feodalizma. M., 1962. 429 p.

1. 468. Patrides, C. A. The grand design of God: the literary form of the Christian view of history. Toronto, 1972.

1. 469. Peachey, Paul "Marxist historiography of the radical reformation: causality or covariation?" Sixteenth Century Essays and Studies 1 (1970) 1—16 p.

1. 470. Pearce, R. H. Historicism once more. Princeton, 1969.

1. 471. Petran, Josef Problémy dejin historiografie. Praha, 1983.

1. 472. Petsche, Ernst Geschichte und Geschichtsschreibung unserer Zeit. Leipzig, 1865. 218 p.

1. 473. Plumb, J. H. (ed.) Crisis in the humanities. Baltimore, 1964. A chapter on history by Plumb, J. H.

1. 474. Plumb, J. H. The death of the past. London, 1969. Second edition 1973. An important review of the book: *Himmelfarb, Wilton* "Is history dead?" Commentary 50 (August, 1970) 45—48p.

1. 475. Plumb, J. H. Die Zukunft der Geschichte. München, 1971.

1. 476. Pocock, J. G. A. "The origins of the study of the past: a comparative approach". Comparative Studies in Society and History 4 (1962) 209—46 p.

1. 477. Pomian, K. "L'histoire de la science et l'histoire de l'histoire". Annales 1975/5.

1. 478. Ponceau, Amédée Le temps dépassé. L'art d'l'histoire. Paris, 1973. 122 p.

1. 479. Porter, Dale M. The mergence of the past: a theory of historical explanation. Chicago—London, 1981. 205 p.

1. 480. Porter, D. M. "The historian's use of nationalism and vice versa". AHR 67 (1962) 924—950 p.

1. 481. Powicke, F. M. Modern historians and the study of history. Essays and papers. L., 1955. 256 p.

1. 482. Pundeff, Martin Communist history: its theory and practice. Northridge (Calif.), 1962. A selection of articles with comments.

1. 483. Quandt, Siegfried—Süssmuth, Hans (eds.) Historisches Erzählen. Formen und Funktionen. Göttingen, 1982.

1. 484. Quazza, Guido "Storia dela storiografia. Storia del potere, storia sociale". Rivista storica contemporanea 1979/8/ 210—230p.

1. 485. Rabb, Theodore K.—Rotberg, Robert J. (eds.) The New History: the 1980s and beyond, studies in interdisciplinary history. Princeton, 1982. 334 p.

1. 486. Radkau, J. und O. Praxis der Geschichtswissenschaft. Düsseldorf, 1972.

1. 487. Radkau, J. und O. "Geschichtswissenschaft heute — Ende der Selbstmystifikation?" NPL 17 (1972) 1—14, 141—67 p.

1. 488. Randa, Alexander (ed.) Mensch und Weltgeschichte. Zur Geschichte der Universalgeschichtsschreibung. Salzburg—München, 1969. 313 p.

1. 489. Randall, J. G. "Historianship". AHR LVIII (1953) 249—264 p. Historian and society: their relationship.

1. 490. Ránki, György Közgazdaság és történelem, a gazdaságtörténet válaszútjai. Budapest, 1977. 95 p. English version: Economics and history. Alternatives of economic history. Acta Historica Academiae Scientiarum Hungaricae 23 (1977) 3-4/343—396 p.

1. 491. Reinisch, Leonhard Die Europäer und ihre Geschichte. München, 1961. With a bibliography.

1. 492. Renouvin, Pierre "L'orientation actuelle des travaux d'histoire contemporaine". *In:* X. Congresso Internazionale di Scienze Storiche. Roma 4—11 Settembre 1955. Relazioni, VI. 331—388p.

1. 493. Revanonkov, V. G. Marksism i problema âkobinskoj diktatury. (Istoriografičeskij očerk) Leningrad, 1966.

1. 494. Riasanovsky, A. V.—Riznick, B. (eds.) Generalization in historical writing. Philadelphia, 1963.

1. 495. Rigby, S. H. Marxism and history: a critical introduction. Manchester, 1987. 314 p.

1. 496. Ritter, Gerhard "Leistungen, Probleme und Aufgaben der internationalen Geschichtsschreibung zur neueren Geschichte (16—18. Jahrhundert)" *In:* X. Congresso Internazionale di Scienze Storiche. Roma 4—11 Settembre 1955. Relazioni VI. 167—330p.

1. 497. Ritter, J. "Die Aufgabe der Geisteswissenschaften in der modernen Gesellschaft." *In:* Ders.: Subjektivität. Frankfurt, 1974..

1. 498. Ritter, Moritz Die Entwicklung der Geschichtswissenschaft an den führenden Werken betrachtet. München—Berlin, 1919.461 p.

1. 499. Rocha, Filipe Teorias sobre a historia. Braga, 1982. 381 p.

1. 500. Rota, Ettore (ed.) Questioni di storia contemporanea. 1-3. Milano, 1952—1955. The third volume is devoted to the history of historical writing.

1. 501. Rotenstreich, N. Between past and present. An essay on history. New Haven, 1958.

1. 502. Rothacker, E. "Die dogmatische Denkform in den Geisteswissenschaften und das Problem des Historismus." *In:* Akademie der Wissenschaften und der Literatur. Abhandlungen der Geistes- und Sozialwissenschaften. Mainz. 6 (1954) 243—298 p.

1. 503. Rothacker, E. Das Wort "Historismus". Zeitschrift für deutsche Wortforschung 16 (1960) 3-6 p.

1. 504. Rowse, A. L. The use of history. L., 1946.; N. Y., 1947.

1. 505. Ruffili, Roberto Crisi dello stato e storiografia contemporanea. Roma, 1979.

1. 506. Ruloff, Dieter Geschichtsforschung und Sozialwissen-schaft. München, 1981.

1. 507. Russell, Bertrand "History as art." *In:* Portraits from memory and other essays. N. Y., 1956.

1. 508. Rutenburg, V. I. "Reakcionnaâ suščnost' sovremennoj klerikal'noj istoriografii". *In: Vajnštejn, O. L. et al. (eds.)* Kritika novejšej buržuaznoj istoriografii. M.-Leningrad, 1961. 150-194 p.

1. 509. Rüdinger, Karl Unser Geschichtsbild. Der Sinn in der Geschichte. München, 1950.

1. 510. Rüsen, Jörn (ed.) Historische Objektivität. Göttingen, 1973.

1. 511. Rüsen, Jörn Ästhetik und Geschichte. Stuttgart, 1976.

1. 512. Rüsen, Jörn Für eine erneuerte Historik. Stuttgart, 1976.

1. 513. Rüsen, Jörn New directions in historical studies. *In:* Proceeding of the Symposium on the History of Chinese and Western Historiography 2. Taichung, 1987. 445—485 p.

1. 514. Rüsen, Jörn—Süssmuth, H. (eds.) Theorien in der Geschichtswissenschaft. Düsseldorf, 1980.

1. 515. Ryszka, Franciszek Politische Wissenschaft und Geschichtswissenschaft. Einige methodologische Bemerkungen. Acta Poloniae Historica 1973 (27) 139—157 p.

1. 516. Saharov, A. M. "O nekotorych voprosach istoriografičeskich issledovanij." Vestnik Moskovskogo Universiteta, seriâ istorii, 1973/6.

1. 517. Saharov, A. M. "O predmete istoriografičeskich issledovanij". Istoriâ SSSR 1974/4.

1. 518. Saitta, Armando Avviamento allo studio della storia. Firenze, 1974. 644 p.

1. 519. Saitta, Armando Guida critica alla storia e alla storiografia. Roma, 1980.

1. 520. Salmon, Pierre Histoire et critique. Bruxelles, 1976. 198 p.

1. 521. Salov, V. I. "Rol' istoriografii v sovremennych usloviach". Vestnik AN SSSR 1974/6/58—65 p.

1. 522. Salov, V. I. Istorism i sovremennaâ burzoaznaâ istoriografiâ. M., 1977. 253 p.

1. 523. Samaran, Ch. (ed.) L'histoire et ses methodes. (Encyclopedie de la Pléiade) Paris, 1961.

1. 524. Sanchez Albornoz, Claudio Historia y libertad. Ensayos sobre historiologia. Madrid, 1978. 158 p.

1. 525. Saskar, Susobban A Marxian glimpse of history. New Delhi, 1975. 153 p.

1. 526. Schachenmayer, Helmut Arthur Rosenberg als Vertreter des historischen Materialismus. Wiesbaden, 1964.

1. 527. Scheschkewitz, Jürgen (ed.) Geschichtsschreibung. Epochen, Methoden, Gestalten. Düsseldorf, 1968. 168 p.

1. 528. Schewill, Ferdinand Six historians. Chicago, 1956. (On Thucydides, St. Augustine, Machiavelli, Voltaire, Ranke, Henry Adams)

1. 529. Schieder, Theodor "Strukturen und Persönlichkeiten in der Geschichte". HZ 195 (1962) 265—296 p.

1. 530. Schieder, Theodor "Karl Marx und seine Stellung in der europäischen Geschichte." GWU 15 (1964) 16—32 p.

1. 531. Schieder, Theodor Geschichte als Wissenschaft. Wien— München, 1965.

1. 532. Schieder, Theodor (ed.) Methodenprobleme der Geschichtswissenschaft. München, 1974.

1. 533. Schleier, Hans "Narrative Geschichte und strukturgeschichtliche Analyse im traditionellen Historismus". ZfG 34 (1986) 2/99—112 p. In this issue further GDR contributions to the discussion on the "Narrative and structural history: past, present, perspectives" at the XVIth Congress (session organized by the Commission Internationale d'Historiographie) of Historical Sciences in Stuttgart, 1985 are also published: — *Lozek, Gerhard* "Narration und Sozialgeschichte" (113—116 p.), *Küttler, Wolfgang* "Marxistische Geschichtswissenschaft und »narrative Geschichte«" (116—119 p.), *Schmidt, Walter* "Narrative und Strukturgeschichte im Marxismus. Eine Fallstudie zu Friedrich Engels' »Zur Geschichte des Bundes der Kommunisten«" (120—125 p.).

1. 534. Schmidt, Alfred "Über Geschichte und Geschichtsschreibung in der materialistischen Dialektik". *In:* Folgen einer Theorie. Essays über »das Kapital« von Karl Marx. Frankfurt, 1967.

1. 535. Schmidt, Alfred Geschichte und Struktur. Fragen einer marxistischen Historik. München, 1971.

1. 536. Schmitt, Bernadotte E. (ed.) Some historians of modern Europe. Essays in historiography by former students of the Department of History in the University of Chicago. Chicago, 1942. Discusses historians not mentioned in the standard works of Fueter and Gooch.

1. 537. Schmitt, Eberhard (ed.) Die Französische Revolution. Anlässe und langfristige Ursachen. Wege der Forschung. Vol. 193.

Darmstadt, o. J. 533 p. Excerpts from the works of Henri Sée, Louis R. Gottschalk, E. Rudé, Alfred Cobban, Georges Lefebvre, Denis Richet, Albert Soboul, Régine Robine and Eberhard Schmitt on the French Revolution with a short preface.

1. 538. Schmitt, Hans A. (ed.) Historians of modern Europe. Essays. Baton Rouge (La.) 1971. 338 p. A »Festschrift« for S. William Halperin.

> *Edward Whiting Fox:* Arnold J. Toynbee: The paradox of Prophecy
> *CarterJefferson*Carlton J. H. Hayes
> *Kenneth F. Lewolski* Oscar Halecki
> *Louis L. Snyder* Hans Kohn: Historian of Nationalism
> *H. Russell Wiliams* A. J. P. Taylor
> *Henry R. Winkler:* J. L. Hammond
> *Charles F. Delzell* Adolfo Omodeo: Historian of the "Religion of Freedom"
> *William Harvey Maehl* Gerhard Ritter
> *George T. Peck* Gaetano Salvemini: Meridionalista
> *Pierre Renouvin* Ernest Labrousse
> *A. William Salomone* Federico Chabod: Portrait of a Master Historian
> *William Savage* The France of M. Chastenet
> *Edward R. Tannenbaum* Giocchino Volpe

1. 539. Schoeps, Hans Joachim Was ist und was will die Geistesgeschichte: über Theorie und Praxis der Zeitgeistforschung. Göttingen, 1959.

1. 540. Scholte, G. Geschichte, Historie. Historisches Wörterbuch der Philosophie. Vol. 3. 1974. 344—398 p.

1. 541. Schröder, Hans-Christoph (ed.) Kontroversen über Historiographie. Göttingen, 1981. 624 p. Geschichte und Gesellschaft. Jg. 7. H.2.

1. 542. Schulin, Ernst Weltgeschichte und europäische Geschichte in der Auffassung des 20. Jahrhunderts. Qulu (Finland), 1969.33 p.

1. 543. Schulin, Ernst Traditionskritik und Rekonstruktionsversuch: Studien zur Entwicklung von Geschichtswissenschaft und historischem Denken. Göttingen, 1979.

1. 544. Schulin, Ernst Geschichtswissenschaft in unserem Jahrhundert. Probleme und Umrisse einer Geschichte der Historie. HZ 245 (1987) 1/1—30 p.

1. 545. Schulz, G. (ed.) Geschichte heute. Göttingen, 1973.

1. 546. Schulz, Winfried Soziologie und Geschichtswissenschaft. München, 1974.

1. 547. Schütz, A. Das Problem der Relevanz. Frankfurt, 1971.

1. 548. Scott, E. Men and thought in modern history. L., 1920.

1. 549. Sechi, Salvatore Movimento operaio e storiografia marxista: rassegne e note critiche. Bari, 1974. 325 p.

1. 550. See, H. The economic interpretation of history. N. Y., 1929.

1. 551. Seignobos, Ch. La methode historique appliquée aux sciences sociales. Paris, 1901.

1. 552. Seligman, Edwin R. A. The economic interpretation of history. N. Y., 1907.

1. 553. Shafer, Boyd et al. Historical study in the West. N. Y., 1968. On the academic study of history in France, Great Britain, FRG, USA.

1. 554. Shaw, W. H. Marx's theory of history. L., 1978.

1. 555. Shotwell, James Thomson The history of history. I. Revised edition of "An introduction to the history of history". N. Y., 1950. 393 p.

1. 556. Sieburg, Heinz-Otto Deutschland und Frankreich in derGeschichtsschreibung des 19. Jahrhunderts. 1-2. Wiesbaden, 1954—1958. 340, 394 p. On the period 1815—1871.

1. 557. Siles Salinas, Jorge Ante la historia. Conciencia histórica y revolución. Madrid, 1969.

1. 558. Simon, W. M. European positivism in the nineteenth century. Ithaca, 1963.

1. 559. Skotheim, R. A. (ed.) The historian and the climate of opinion. Reading (Mass.), 1969.

1. 560. Small, Melvin Public opinion and historians. Interdisciplinary perspectives. Detroit, 1970. 199 p.

1. 561. Smith, Page The historian and history. N. Y., 1964. With a rich bibliography.

1. 562. Southern, R. W. The shape and substance of academic history. Oxford, 1961.

1. 563. Stearns, Peter Nathaniel (ed.) A century for debate, 1789—1914: problems in the interpretation of European history. N. Y.—Toronto, 1969. 511 p.

1. 564. Steinberg, Siegfrid (ed.) Die Geschichtswissenschaft der Gegenwart in Selbstdarstellungen. 1-2. Leipzig, 1925—1926.
  1. Georg von Below, Alfons Dopsch, Heinrich Finke, Walter Goetz, A. F. Kaindl, Max Lehmann, Georg Steinhausen.
  2. Karl Julius Beloch, Harry Bresslau, Victor Gordthausen, George Peabody Gooch, Nicolaus Japiske, Ludwig Frh. von Pastor, Felix Rachfohl.

1. 565. Stephens, L. D. Historiography: a bibliography. Metuchen, N. Y., 1975.

1. 566. Stern, F. (ed.) The varieties of history. Cleveland—N. Y.1956. 421 p. German version: Geschichte und Geschichtsschreibung. München, 1966. Extracts from works of great historians. From Voltaire and Niebuhr to Hofstadter and Namier, with most informative comments. The best selection of its kind.

1. 567. Stern, Leo Zur geistigen Situation der bürgerlichen Geschichtswissenschaft der Gegenwart. (Rektoratsrede) Halle—Wittenberg, 1953. 30 p.

1. 568. Stiehler, Gottfried Geschichte und Verantwortung. Zur Frage der Alternativen in der gesellschaftlichen Entwicklung. Berlin, 1972. 100 p.

1. 569. Stone, L. The past and the present. L., 1982.

1. 570. Stone, Lawrence The revival of narrative. Commented by *Hobsbawm, E.* The revival of narrative — some comments. Past and Present 85—86 (1979—80).

1. 571. Strayer, Joseph R. (ed.) The interpretation of history. Princeton, N. Y., 1943. Reprinted, N. Y., 1950.

1. 572. Strong, E. W. "How is practice of history tied to theory?" Journal of Philosophy XLVI (1949) 637—44 p.

1. 573. Süssmuth, Hans (ed.) Historische Anthropologie. Der Mensch in der Geschichte. Göttingen, 1984.

1.574. Sywottek, Arnold Geschichtswissenschaft in der Legitimationskrise. Bonn, 1974. Archiv für Sozialgeschichte. Beiheft 1.

1. 575. Teng, Ssu-yu "The predispositions of Westerners in treating Chinese history and civilization". Historian 19 (May 1957) 307—327p.

1. 576. Tessitore, Fulvio Dimensioni dello storicismo. Napoli, 1971.310p.

1. 577. Tessitore, Fulvio Storicismo e pensiero politico. Milano, 1974.

1. 578. Tessitore, Fulvio Comprensione storica e cultura. Revisioni storicistiche. Napoli, 1979. 461 p.

1. 579. Tessitore, Fulvio Profilo dello storicismo politico. Torino, 1981. 179 p.

1. 580. Tessitore, Fulvio "La storiografia come scienza". Storia de la Storiografia 1/1982/ 48—88 p.

1. 581. Theorie der Geschichte. Beiträge zur Historik. 1-4. München, 1977—1982.

Band 1.: Objektivität und Parteilichkeit in der Geschichtswissenschaft. Herausgegeben von *Reinhart Kosseleck, Wolfgang J. Mommsen* und *Jörn Rüsen.*

Band 2.: Historische Prozesse. Herausgegeben von *Karl-Georg Faber* und *Christian Meier.*

Band 3.: Theorie und Erzählung in der Geschichte. Herausgegeben von *Jürgen Kocka* und *Thomas Nipperdey.*

Band 4.: Formen der Geschichtsschreibung. Herausgegeben von Reinhart Kosseleck, Heinrich Lutz und Jörn Rüsen.

1.582. Theory and Practice in Historical Study. A report of the [USA] Committee on Historiography. Social Science Research Bulletin 54. N. Y., 1946. Bulletin 64. N. Y., 1954.

Commentaries:

Holt, W. Stull "An Evaluation of the Report on Theory and Practice in Historical Study". Pacific Historical Review XVIII (May 1949) 23—42 p.

Tonham, George K. "A Discussion of Historiography". Historian 10 (Spring 1948) 152—156 p.

1. 583. Thompson, Paul The voice of the past. Oral history. Oxford University Press, 1978.

1. 584. Thompson, J. W.—Holm, B. J. A history of historical writing. 1-2. N. Y., 1942., 676, 674 p. A remarkable review by *Vajnštein, O. L.*VI1946/11—12/153—155p.

1. 585. Tihvinskij, S. L.—Tiškov, V. A. "XVI Meždunarodnyj Kongress istoričeskich nauk". VI 1986/1/3—25 p.

1.586. Tillinghoyt, Pardon E. The spacious past: historians and others. Reading (Mass.)—L., 1972. 198 p.

1. 587. Tilly, Charles As sociology meets history. N.Y.—L.— Toronto, 1981. 237 p.

1. 588. Times Literary Supplement, Special supplements of April 7, July 28, September 8 1966 on "New Ways in History".

1.589. Topolski, Jerzy Metodologia historii. Warszawa, 1973. English version: Methodology of History. Dordrecht—Boston, 1976. 690p.

1. 590. Topolski, Jerzy Nowe idee w spolczesnej historiografii o roli teorii w badaniach historycznych. Warszawa, 1980.

1. 591. Topolski, Jerzy Prawda i model w historiografii. Warszawa, 1982.

1. 592. Torodeckij, E. I. "Istoriografiâ kak special'naâ otrasl' istoričeskoj nauki". Istoriâ SSSR 1974/4.

1. 593. Tosh, John The pursuit of history: aims, methods and new directions in the study of modern history. L.—N. Y., 1984. 205 p.

1. 594. Trevelyan, George Clio, a muse and other essays. Freeport, N. Y., 1913. Reprint 1968. (Books for Libraries Press)

1. 595. Trevor-Roper, H. R. Men and events: historical essays. N. Y., 1957. Includes chapters on Jacob Burckhardt, G. Lytton Strachey, Karl Marx and Arnold Toynbee.

1. 596. Troeltsch, E. Der Historismus und seine Probleme. Tübingen, 1922.; Aalen, 1961.

1. 597. Troeltsch, E. Der Historismus und seine Überwindung, Berlin, 1924.; Aalen, 1965.

1. 598. Trompf, G. W. The idea of historical recurrence in western thought. L., 1979.

1. 599. Tûmenev, A. "Marksizm i burŽuaznaâ istoričeskaâ nauka". *In:* Akademiâ Nauk SSSR. Pamati K. Marxa. Sbornik statej k patigesâtiletiû s dnâ smerti. 1883—1933. Leningrad, 1933.

1. 600. Uhlig, Ralph Historische Grundlagenforschung als Problem der Geschichtswissenschaft. Zur Analyse der historischen Aussage. Berlin /West/, 1980. 435 p.

1. 601. Architects and craftsmen in history. Festschrift für *Abbott Payson Usher.* Tübingen, 1956.
> I. The German Design for Social History. Some Heirs of Gustav von Schmoller by *Frederic C. Lange* /USA/ /Werner Sombart, Arthur Spiethoff, Joseph A. Schumpeter, Walter Eucken/ Sombart and the German Approach by *Edgar Salin* /Switzerland/
> II. Social Historians: Ancient and Medieval.
> Michael I. Rostovtzeff by *C. Bradford Welles* /USA/
> Marc Bloch by *Lucien Febvre* /France/
> Henri Pirenne by *Charles Verlinden* /Belgium/
> III. Toward an Economic History of Modern Times.
> Henri See by *Melvil M. Knight* /USA/
> Eli F. Heckscher by *Arthur Montgomery* /Sweden/
> John F. Clapham by *W.H.B. Court* /England/
> Abbot Payson Usher by *Wiliam N. Parker* /USA/

1. 602. Vajnštejn, O. L'. Istoriografiâ srednih vekov v svâzi s razvitiem istoričeskoj mysli ot načala srednih vekov do našich dnej. M.—Leningrad, 1940.

1. 603. Vajnštejn, O. L'. "Die neueste bürgerliche Literatur über die Geschichte der Geschichtswissenschaft". ZfG 4 (1956)

1.604. Vajnštejn, O.L'. (ed.) Kritika novejšej buržuaznoj istoriografii. Leningrad, 1961. 444 p.

1.605. Vajnštejn, O.L'.(ed.) Kritika novejšej buržuaznoj istoriografii. Leningrad, 1967. 380 p.

1.606. Vajnštejn, O.L'.(ed.) Kritika novejšej buržuaznoj istoriografii. Leningrad, 1967. 267 p.

1. 607. Vajnštejn, O. L'. Očerki razvitiâ buržuaznoj filozofii i metodologii istorii v XIX—XX vv. Leningrad, 1979. 270 p. Useful also for the history of historical scholarship.

1. 608. Valsecchi, Franco Lineamenti di storia della storiografia moderna. Dal rinascimento al romanticismo. Milano, 1956. 263 p.

1. 609. Valsecchi, Franco La storiografia del positivismo. Milano, 1958. 96 p.

1. 610. Vangalovskaa, M. G. "K izučeniu recenzii kak istoriografičeskogo istočnika". *In: Salimova, E. (ed.)* Voprosy istoriografii i istočnikovedeniâ. Kazan', 1974.

1. 611. Vasquez de Prada, Valentin et al. (eds.) Conversaciones internacionale de Historia. La historiografia en Occidente desde 1945. Pamplona /Spain/, 1985. 502 p.

1.612. Vazquez, Josefina Zoraida Historia de la historiografia. Peru /Pormaca/, 1965. 178 p. Mexico, 1978. 174 p.

1.613.Venturi, Franco Historiens du XXe siècle. Jaures, Salvemini, Namier, Maturi, Tarle. Genéve, 1966. 269 p.

1.614. Vercauteren, F. "Rapport Général sur les travaux d'histoire du moyen age de 1945 a 1954". *In:* X. Congresso Internazionale di Scienze Storiche. Roma 4—11 Settembre 1955. Relazioni VI.41—166p.

1. 615. Veyne, Paul Comment on ecrit l'histoire. Paris, 1978. 384p.

1. 616. Vilar, P. Une histoire en construction. Approches marxistes et problématiques conjoncturelles. Paris, 1982. 428 p.

1.617. Vogt, Joseph Wege zum historischen Universum. Von Ranke bis Toynbee. Stuttgart, 1961.

1.618. Wagar, Warren W. Good tidings. The belief in progress from Darwin to Marcuse. Indiana University Press, Bloomington—L.,1972.

1. 619. Wagner, Fritz Der Historiker und die Weltgeschichte. Freiburg,1965.

1.620.Wagner, Fritz Moderne Geschichtsschreibung. Ausblick auf eine Philosophie der Geschichtswissenschaft. Berlin, 1960, 127 p.

1.621. Ware, C. F. The cultural approach to history. N. Y., 1940.

1.622.Wehler, Hans-Ulrich "Zum Verhältnis von Geschichtswissenschaft und Psychoanalyse". HZ 208 (1968).

1.623. Wehler, Hans-Ulrich (ed.) Geschichte und Soziologie. Köln,1972.

1.624. Wehler, Hans-Ulrich (ed.) Geschichte und Ökonomie. Köln,1973.

1.625. Wehler, Hans-Ulrich Geschichte als historische Sozial-wissenschaft. Frankfurt, 1973.

1.626. Wehler, Hans-Ulrich "Geschichtswissenschaft heute". *In: Habermas, Jürgen (ed.)* "Stichworte zur geistigen Situation der Zeit". Frankfurt, 1979. 709—753 p.

1.627. Wehler, Hans-Ulrich Die moderne deutsche Geschichte in der internationalen Forschung. Geschichte und Gesellschaft 4 (1978) 286 p.

1.628. Wehler, Hans-Ulrich Historische Sozialwissenschaft und Geschichtsschreibung. Göttingen, 1980.

1. 629. Weil, Erik Wert und Würde der erzählenden Ge-schichtsschreibung. Göttingen, 1976. 14 p. A lecture.

1.630. Weintraub, Karl J. Visions of culture. Voltaire, Guizot, Burckhardt, Lamprecht, Huizinga. University of Chicago Press. Chicago—L., 1966.

1.631. Weiss, A. von. Neomarxismus. Freiburg, 1970.

1. 632. Wetzel, Paul (ed.) Von Wesen und Sinn der Geschichte, eine Auswahl aus den Geschichtstheorien des 19. und 20. Jahr-hunderts 1-3. Frankfurt am Main, 1951—1953.

1. 633. White, Andrew D. European schools of history and politics. Baltimore, 1887.

1. 634. White, Hayden Metahistory: the historical imagination in nineteenth-century Europe. Baltimore (Md.)—L., 1973. 448 p. Some reviews: A provocative argument against the conception of history as a science. A review by *Nelson, J. S.* HT XIV /1975/ 74—91. *Iggers, Georg G.* Style in history? History as art and as science. Review in European history 2 /1976/. Six critiques HT Beiheft 19 (1980).

1.635. White, Hayden The content of the form: narrative discourse and historical representation. Baltimore (Md.), 1987. 244 p.

1.636. Widgery, A. G. Interpretations of history. Confucius to Toynbee. L., 1961. 260 p.

1.637. Wiegelmann, Günter Geschichte als Alltagskultur. Aufgaben und neue Ansätze. Münster, 1980.

1. 638. Williams, C. H. The modern historian. L., 1938. A thorough methodological survey + excerpts from the works of master historians.

1.639. Wilson, Edmund To the Finland station. A study in the writing and acting of history. Garden City (N. Y.) 1953. 502 p.

1.640. Wimmer, Franz Martin Verstehen, Beschreiben, Erklären: zur Problematik geschichtlicher Ereignisse. München, 1978. 231 p.

1.641. Winkler, H.A. Revolution, Staat, Faschismus. Zur Revision des historischen Materialismus. Kleine Vandernhoeck Reihe 1440 /Göttingen und Zürich/, 1978.

1.642. Wolf, G. Einführung in das Studium der neueren Geschichte. Berlin, 1910.

1.643. Wolman, Benjamin B. et al. (ed.) The psychoanalytic view of history. N. Y.—L., 1971. 240 p.

1. 644. Xenopol, A. D. La théorie de l'histoire. Paris, 1908. VIII+483 p.

1.645. Zaprâkova, Todorova Antoanet "Istorik na istoričeskata nauka—prdmet i zadači". Istoričeski Pregled 38 (1983) 5/98—105 p.

1. 646. Zimmermann, Monika Die Synopse als Mittel universalhistorischer Orientierung. Eine kritische Untersuchung der Geschichtschreibung. Göttingen—Frankfurt—Zürich (Musterschmidt), 1977. 228 p.

1. 647. Zinn, H. The politics of history. Boston, 1970.

1. 648. Zitomersky, Joseph On making use of history. L., 1982.

1. 649. Zub, Alexandra A scrie si a face istoria. Iasi, 1981. 368 p.

1. 650. Zunz, Oliver (ed.) Reliving the past: the worlds of social history. Chapel Hill (N.C.), University of North Carolina Press, 1985. 334 p. Bibliography 297—323 p.

2
Europe

2.1. East and Central Europe in general

2.1.1. Baráth, Tibor Kelet-Európa fogalma a modern történet-írásban. In: Emlékkönyv Domanovszky Sándor születése hatvana-dik fordulójának ünnepére. Budapest, 1937.

2.1.2. Belâvskaja, I. M. (ed.) Slavânkaâ istoriografia. Sbornik statej. M., 1966. 281 p. The most important study of the volume: *Belâvskaja, I. M.* "Osnovnye certy razvitiâ istoričeskoj nauki v zarubežnyh slavjanskih stranah v poslevoennoj periode." 69—84 p.

2.1.3. Birke, Ernst—Lemberg, Eugen (eds.) Geschichtsbewußt-sein in Ostmitteleuropa. Marburg/Lahn, 1961. 149 p.

2.1.4. Deletant, Dennis — Hanak, Harry (eds.) Historians as nation-builders: Central and South-East Europe. Basingstoke (Hampshire), 1988. 245 p.

2.1.5. Mohov, N. A. — Sytnik, M. K. (eds.) Voprosy istorii i istoriografii Ugo-Vostočnoj Evropy. Kišinev, 1977. 169 p.

2.1.6. Niederhauser, Emil "Geschichtsschreiber und Politiker. Lelewel und Palacky." Annales Universitatis Scientiarum Buda-pestinensis de Rolando Eötvös nominatae. Sectio Historica XXI (1981)205—219p.

2.1.7. Niederhauser, Emil "A kelet-európai történetírás útja a mitosztól a tudományig". Világosság 24 (1983) 8—9/512—519 p.

2.1.8. Niederhauser, Emil "A marxista történetírás kezdetei Kelet-Európában". Történelmi Szemle 27 (1984) 1—2/172—181 p.

2.1.9. Niederhauser, Emil "A dicső múlt — mitosz és realitás". Világtörténet, 1984/1/ 74—83 p. The same study in French: "Le passé glorieux — mythe et realité". Hungaro-Slavica, 1983. Budapest, 1983. 211—222 p.

2.1.10. Niederhauser, Emil "Polgári történeti iskolák és politika Kelet-Európában". Kortárs 29 (1985) 7/81—83 p.

2.1.11. Pech, S. Z. "New Avenues in East European history". Canadian Slavonic Papers 10 (1968) 3—18 p.

2.1.12. Pfitzner, J. "Die Geschichte Osteuropas und die Geschichte des Slaventums als Forschungsprobleme". HZ 150 (1934)

2.1.13. Philippi, Paul (ed.) Studien zur Geschichtsschreibung im 19. und 20. Jahrhundert. Köln-Graz (Böhlau), 1967. Including: *Möckel, Andreas* Geschichtsschreibung und Geschichtsbewußtsein bei den Siebenbürger Sachsen.; *Berger, Hans* Geschichtsbewußtsein und Nationalprogramm der Siebenbürger Saschen.

2.1.14. Seton Watson, R. W. The historian as a political force in Central Europe. A lecture. L., 1922. 36 p.

2.1.15. Stoekl, Guenther Die Interdependenz von Geschichte und Politik in Osteuropa seit 1945. Köln, 1977.

2. 2. Albania

2.2.1. Bozhori, Kogo – Koka, Viron "L'historiographie albanaise dans ces 25 ans". Studia Albanica, Tirana 6/1969/2/21—34 p.

2.2.2. Buda, A. Mbi disa te historiografise sonë. Buletin per shkencot natyrose. Tiranë. 2/1952/21—30 p.

2.2.3. Ducellier, Alain "Les études historiques en République Populairee d'Albanie 1945—1966." Revue Historique/Paris/ 91/1967/481,125—144p.

2.3. Austria

2.3.1. Dachs, Herbert Österreichische Geschichtswissenschaft und Anschluss, 1918-1930. Wien-Salzburg, 1974. 265 p.

2.3.2. Grass, Nikolaus (ed.) Österreichische Geschichtswissenschaft der Gegenwart in Selbstdarstellungen. 1-2. Innsbruck, 1950-1951.201,279p.

2.3.3. Grass, Nikolaus Österreichische Historiker-Biographien. Beiträge zur Geschichte der historischen Forschung in Österreich. Folge 1. (No more published) Innsbruck₁1957. 156 p.

2.3.4. Höflechner, Walter Das Fach Geschichte an der Universität Graz 1729-1848. Graz, 1975. 155 p.

2.3.5. Lhotsky, Alphons Geschichte des Instituts für Österreichische Geschichtsforschung, 1854-1954. Graz-Köln, 1954.

2.3.6.Lhotsky,Alphons Österreichische Historiographie. Wien-München, 1962. 235 p.

2.3.7. Lhotsky, Alphons Aufsätze und Vorträge. Ausgewählt, herausgegeben von Hans Wagner, Heinrich Koller, Bd.3. Historiographie, Quellenkunde, Wissenschaftsgeschichte. Wien, 1972. 296p.

2.3.8. Oberkofler, Gerhard Die geschichtlichen Fächer an der Philosophischen Fakultät der Universität Innsbruck 1850-1945. Innsbruck, 1975. 239 p.

2.3.9. Ottenthal, E. v. Das K.-K. Institut für österreichische Geschichtsforschung 1854-1904. Festschrift. Wien, 1904. 96 p.

2.3.10. Ramhardter, Günther Geschichtswissenschaft und Patriotismus. Österreichische Historiker im Weltkrieg 1914-1918. München-Wien, 1973. 230 p. (Bibliography 196-218 p.)

2.3.11. Santifaller, Leo Das Institut für Österreichische Geschichtsforschung. Festgabe zur Feier des zweihundertjährigen Bestandes des Wiener Haus-, Hof- und Staatsarchivs. Wien, 1950. 164 p.

2.4. Belgium

2.4.1. Académie royale de Belgique. La commission royale d'histoire, 1834—1934. Livre jubilaire, composé a l'occasion du centième anniversaire de sa fondation par les membres de la commission. Bruxelles, 1934. 372 p.

2.4.2. Harighurst, Alfred F. (ed.). The Pirenne thesis: analysis, criticism and revision. Boston, 1958.

2.4.3. van Houttte, J. A. et al. (eds.) Un quart de siècle de recherche historique en Belgique, 1944—1968. Louvain, 1970. 586 p.

2.4.4. Kracauev, Sigfried History: the last things before the last. N. Y. — Oxford University Press, 1919. Shows how Pirenne used time-worn rhetorical tricks to bring together relatively discontinuous persons and events in a single, continuous and unified narrative.

2.4.5. Lyon, Bryce Dale The origins of the Middle Ages. Pirenne's challenge to Gibbon. N. Y., 1972. 96 p. (Historical controversies.)

2.4.6. Lyon, Bryce Dale Henri Pirenne. A biographical and

intellectual study. Ghent, 1974. 477 p. The standard book on Pirenne.

2.4.7. Pirenne, Henri "Sciences historiques". In: L'Académia royale de Belgique depuis sa fondation. 1772—1922. Histoire de la classe des lettres. Bruxelles, 1922. 171—196 p.

2.4.8. Sadretdinov, G. K. "K karakteristike stanovleniâ i evolûcii obšeistoriceskih vzglâdov Henri Pirenne-a." In: Metodologičeskie i istoriografičeskie voprosy istoričeskoj nauki. Vypusk 4. Tomsk,1966.

2.4.9. Vercauteren, Fernand Cent ans d'histoire nationale en Belgique. Bruxelles, 1959.

2.4.10. Wils, Lode De groot-nederlandse geschiedschriyuing. Revue Belge Philologique—Historique 61 (1983) 322—366 p.

2.5. Bulgaria

2.5.1. Andreeva, M. A. "V. N. Zlatarski" Slavia XV/1937/38/

2.5.2. Angelov, Dimitâr "Imenit balgarski istorik. (100 godini ot rozdenieto na prof Petar Mutafciev) Vekove, 12.1 (1983) 5—11 p.

2.5.3. Angelov, Dimitâr — Nikolov, J. "Naucnoto delo na akad. Snegarov."III 1964/14—65p.

2.5.4. Bejlis, Alexandr S. Stanovlenie marksistkoj istoriograffii v Bolgarii (s konca XIX. v. do socialističeskoj revoljuci 1944 g.) Lvov,1970.240p.

2.5.5. Bidlo, J. V. N. Zlatarski. Praha, 1937.

2.5.6. Birman, M. A. "Osnovnye napravleniâ v issledovanii novoj i novejsej istorii Bolgarii v bolgarskoj istoriografii (1918—1944 gg.)"Sovetskoe slavjanovedenie 1967/2/69—75 p.

2.5.7. Burmov, Alexsandâr K. Marin Drinov Kato istorik na Bâlgariâ. Studia in honorem M. Drinov. Sofiâ, 1960. 105—118. p. With a German summary.

2.5.8. Canev, Petr Marksistskata istoričeska nauka v Bulgaria, 1885—1944. Istoriko-bibliografičeski ocerk. Sofiâ, 1972. 178 p.

2.5.9. Chadzinikolov, Veselin "Rusofily i rusofoby v bolgarskoj istoričeskoj literature do Oktjabr'skoj revoljucii". Études historiques. Sofiâ. 4 (1968) 55—81 p.

2.5.10. Clarka, James F. "Zlatarski and Bulgarian historiography". The Slavonic Review XV (1937)

2.5.11. Dujcev, Ivan "Übersicht über die bulgarische Geschichtsscreibung." *In:* Antike und Mittelalter in Bulgarien. Berlin, 1960. 51—69 p.

2.5.12. Gorina, Ludmila V. "Političeskite vazgledi na Marin Drinov do osbovozdenieto." Istoričeski Pregled 41 (1985) 7/56—65 p.

2.5.13. Gorinov, N. Marin Drinov. Sofiâ, 1936.

2.5.14. Hristov, Hristo "Dimitâr Blagoev — osnovatelna bâlgarskata naučna istoriografiâ". Izvestiâ na Instuta za bâlgarska istoriâ (Sofiâ) 1951/1—2/8—38 p.

2.5.15. Hristov, Hristo "G. S. Rakovski kato istoriograf." *In:* G. S. Rakovski, Vazgledi, dejnost, zivot. I. Sofiâ, 1964.

2.5.16. Hristov, Hristo "Krupen isledovatell na bâlgarskoto nacionalnorevolûcionno dvizenie (Mihail Dimitrov)" Vekove 1981/ (10.6.) 5—17 p.

2.5.17. Kosev, Dimitar "Razvitieto na istoričeskata nauka v Bâlgariâ sled pobedata na Velikata Oktovurijska Socialističeska Revolucija." Istoričeski Pregled 13 (1957) 6/3—16 p.

2.5.18. Kosev, Dimitar "Razvitieto na bâlgarskata istoričeska nauka sled pobedata na. IX. 1944. g." Istoričeski Pregled 15/1959/ 4/26—41.p.

2.5.19. Kosev, Dimitar "Die Geschichtswissenschaft in der Volksrepublik Bulgarien." Jahrbuch für Geschichte der UdSSR und der volksdemokratischen Länder Europas. Berlin 6 (1962) 313—336p.

2.5.20. Kosev, Dimitar et al. Problemi na bâlgarskata istoriografiâ sled Vtorata svetovna vojna (Materiali ot naučnata Konferenciâ po slucaj 70. godishninata ot osnovovaneto na Bâlgarskoto istoričesko druzestvo.) Sofiâ, 1973. 701 p.

2.5.21. Mosely, Philip E. "The post-war historiography of modern Bulgaria". Journal of Modern History 9/September, 1937/ 348—366p.

2.5.22. Natan, Zak "Akad. T. Pavlov i bâlgarska istoričeska nauka." Istoričeski Pregled 16/1960/2.

2.5.23. Natan, Zak "Mestoto na G. Bakalov v razvitieto na marks-leninskata istoriografiâ." Istoričeski Pregled 20/1964/6.

2.5.24. Niederhauser, Emil "A bolgár történettudomány fejlődése."Századok88/1955/270—286p.

2.5.25. Pundeff, Martin "Bulgarian Historiography, 1942—1958".AHR66(April, 1961)682—693 p.

2.5.26. Veleva, Mariâ Nikolova Dimitâr Strasimirov. Istoriografičeski očerk. Sofiâ, 1972. 203 p.

2.5.27. Veleva, Mariâ Nikolova "Zahari Stoânov—istorik /120 godini ot rozidenito Emu/". Vekove (1972) 1. 1. 30—41 p.

2.5.28. Veleva, Mariâ Nikolova "Viden istorik i patriot (100 godini ot smârta na Spiridon Palauzov". Vekove (1972) 1. 6. 89—94p.

2.5.29. *Veleva, Mariâ Nikolova* "Marin Drinov". Vekove (1982)1.1—2.139—146p.

2.5.30. *Vlachov, Tuse* Sastojanie i zadači na Balgarskata istori- česka nauka. Sofiâ, Darzvana pec. 1948. 42 p.

2.6. Czechoslovakia, Bohemia, Slovakia

2.6.1. Bartošek, Karel "Czechoslovakia: the state of histori- ography". Journal of Contemporary History 2 (January, 1967) 143—155p.

2.6.2. Butvin, Jozef "K historickým koncepciam Jozefa Škul- tétyho so zretel'om na novodobé dejiny Slovákov". HČ 29 (1981) 1/51—63p.

2.6.3. Česká a slovenská historiografie od vystoupení školy Gellovy do vítězství marxistické metodologie. Materiály. Autor- Kol. pod. ved. Lumíra *Dokoupila* 1. vyd. Ostrava, 1980. 340 p.

2.6.4. Filip, Jan et al. 25 ans d'historiographie tchécoslovaque 1935—1960.Praha,1960.493p.

2.6.5. Glassl, Horst Die slovakische Geschichtswissenschaft nach 1945. Wiesbaden, 1971. 166p.

2.6.6. Glejdura, Stefan "Súcasná slovenská historiografia". Literárny almanach Slováka v Amerike. Chicago, 1968. 46—55 p.

2.6.7. Goll, Jaroslav "Dejiny a dejepis". In: Goll, Jaros- lav,Vybrané spisy drobné. I. Praha, 1928. 1—27 p.

2.6.8. Holotík, Ľudovít "Rozvoj slovenskej historickej vedy a československá historiografia". HČ 10 (1962) 489—503 p.

2.6.9. Holotík, Ľudovít "Súčasny stav a problémy slovenskej historiografie". HČ 14 (1966) 1/1—9. p.

2.6.10. Horváth, Pavel "Slovenská regionálna historiografia v 19. storocí". HC 29 (1981) 2/217—243. p.

2.6.11. Jetmarová, Milena František Palacký. /Studie s ukázkami z díla/ Praha, 1961. 263 p.

2.6.12. Kamenec, Ivan Začiatky marxistického historického myslenia na Slovensku. (Historizmus a jehoúloha v slovenskom revolučnom robotnickom hnutí.) Bratislava, 1984. 142 p.

2.6.13. Kirschbaum, J. M. Pavel Josef Šafařík and his contribution to Slavic studies. Cleveland-Winnipeg, 1962.

2.6.14. Kopcan, Vojtech "Michaľ Matunák a jelo dielo". HČ (1981) 1/75—83. p.

2.6.15. Král, Václav Myšlenkový svět historie. Praha: Univ. Karlova 1974. 206 p. On Czechoslovak historiography before and after 1968.

2.6.16. Kutnar, František Přohledné dejiny českého a slovenského dejepisectví 1. Od počatko národní kultury až po vyznění obrodného úkolu dějepisectví v druhé polovině 19. století Brno, 1973. 274 p. 2. Od počatkii pozitivistického dějepisectví na práh historiografie marxistické. Brno, 1978. 501 p.

2.6.17. Kutnar, František — Králík, Oldrich — Belic, Jaromír Tri studie o Paláckém. /Palacký, F./ Olomouc, 1949. 242 p.

2.6.18. Lütsow, F. Lectures on historians of Bohemia. L., 1905.

2.6.19. Macek, Josef "Cechoslovaskaâ istoričeskaâ nauka v period zaverseniâ stroitel'stva socialisma". VI, 3 (1960) 102—119 p.

2.6.20. Magdolenova, Anna "Peter Kellner Hostinský ako historik". HČ 29 (1981) 1/103—115 p.

2.6.21. Myl'nikov A. S. Pavel Šafařik, vydausi jsa učennyj — svist. M.-Leningrad, 1963.

2.6.22. Myška, M. Památník Palackého 1798—1968. Ostrava, 1968.

2.6.23. Novotny, Jan Pavel Josef Šafařík. Praha, 1971.

2.6.24. Odlozilik, Ottokar "Modern Czechoslovak Historiography". The Slavonic and East European Review 30 (June, 1952)376—392p.

2.6.25. Paul, Karel Pavel Josef Šafarík. Život a dílo. Praha, 1961.

2.6.26. Pech, Stanley Z. "Ferment in Czechoslovak Marxist historiography". Canadian Slavonic Papers 10 (1968) 502—522. p.

2.6.27. Plaschka, Richard Georg Von Palacký bis Pekář. Geschichtswissenschaft und Nationalbewußtsein bei Tschechen. Mit einem Nachwort von Heinrich Felix Schmid. Graz-Köln, 1955. 119 p. (Bibliography 111—119. p.)

2.6.28. Potemra, M. (ed.) Slovenská historiografia v rokoch 1901—1918. Košice, 1980.650p.

2.6.29. Precan, Vilém (ed.) Acta Creationis. Unabhängige Geschichtsschreibung in der Tschechoslovakei, 1969—1980. Hanover, 1980.252 p.

2.6.30. Prinz, Fiedrich "František Palacký und das deutsch-tschechische Verhältnis aus der Sicht der tschechischen Geschichtswissenschaft unseres Jahrhunderts". *Bohemia* 18 (1977) 129—143.p.

2.6.31. Rosenbaum, Karol Pavel Josef Šafárik. Bratislava, 1961.

2.6.32. Tibensky, Ján "Slovenská historiografia v období slovenského národného obrodenia (1780—1830)". HČ 28 (1980) 4/531—553.p.

2.6.33.Tomic, J. Kniževni i naučni rad P. J. Safaříka. Novi Sad, 1900.

2.6.34. Válka, Josef La theorie de l'histoire chez F. Palacký. Sborník Prací Filosofické Fakulty Brnenské University 1967. c. 14. 79-100.p.

2.6.35. Vojtech, Tomáš "České buržoazní dějepisectví o svém vyvoji: Pokus o kritickou rekonstrukci". Československy časopis historický30/1982/383—861.p.

2.6.36.Vojtech,Tomáš "Die tschechische bürgerliche Historiographie und der Positivismus bis zum Jahre 1918". Historica 21 (1982)5—61.p.

2.6.37. Vojtech, Tomáš Česká buržoasní historiografie a studium kapitalizmu. *In:* Historiografie celem k budocnosti. Sbornik k sedesatinam akademika Jaroslava Purše. Praha, 1982. 77—102. p.

2.6.38.Vojtech,Tomáš Česka historiografie a positivismus. Praha,1984.164p.

2.6.39.Werstadt,Jaroslav "The philosophy of Czech history". Slavonic Review 3 (March, 1925) 533—546. p.

2.6.40. Zácek, Joseph Frederick Palacky. The historian as scholar and nationalist. The Hague-Paris, 1970. 137 p.

2.7.Denmark

2.7.1. Bach, Erik Danske historieskrivere. Kobenhavn, 1942. 115p.

2.7.2. Danske historiske forening. Linier i dansk historieskrivning i nyere ticl (ca. 1890—1950) udgivet a anledining of Historik sanfunds 75 ors jubilaem of Den danske historiske Forening 1976.Copenhagen, 1976. 136 p.

2.7.3. Holm, Soren Peter Soren Kierkegaards Historiefilosofii. Kobenhavn, 1952. 119 p.

2.7.4. Manniche, Jens Chr. Den radikale historikertradition: Studier i Dansk Historievidenskab s Forudsaetninger og Normer. Aarhus, 1981.

2.7.5.Mitchell, Philipp Marshall Vilhelm Gronbech. En indforing. Copenhagen, 1970. 255 p.

2.7.6.Westergaard, Waldemar "Danish history and Danish historians". Journal of Modern History XXIV (1952) 167—180 pp.

2.8.Finland

2.8.1. Mustelin, Olof Studier i finländsk historie forskning, 1809—1865.Helsingfors,1957.630p.

2.9.France

2.9.1. Afanasev, J. Istorizm protiv ékléktiki. Francuskaâ istoričeskaâ skola Annales v sovremennoj buržuaznoj istoriografii. M., 1980. 277 p. A review by *Ingerflom, S.* in Annales 1982/1.

2.9.2. Allegra, Luciano — Torre, Angela La nascita della storia sociale in Francia della commune alle "Annales". Torino, 1977.

2.9.3. Alpatov, M. A. Političeskie idei francuskoj buržuaznoj istoriografii XIX veka. M-Leningrad, 1949. 405 p.

2.9.4. Aries, Philippe Le temps de l'histoire. Monaco, 1954.

2.9.5. Atkinson, J. L. Boone "Taine on the French Revolution: A study in historiographic controversy". Historian 15 (Spring, 1953) 188—216. (The Taine-Aulard controversy)

2.9.6. Aymard, M. The Annales and French historiography (1929—1971)". Journal of European Economic History 1 (1972) 491—511.

2.9.7. Bandyopadhyay, Pradeep "The many faces of French Marxism" Science and Society 36 (1972) 129—157. On the institutional and ideological background of Marxist studies in social sciences and history in France.

2.9.8. Bann, Stephen The clothing of Clio. A study of the representation of history in 19th century Britain and France. Cambridge, 1984. 196p.

2.9.9. Becher, Ursula A. J. Geschichtsinteresse und historischer Diskurs: Ein Beitrag zur Geschichte der französischen Geschichtswissenschaft im 19. Jahrhundert. Wiesbaden, 1986. 222 p.

2.9.10. Becher, Ursula A.J. Methodenkonzeption und politische Funktionalisierung der Geschichtsschreibung Frankreichs im 19.Jahrhundert. In: Historische Methode-Beiträge zur Historik 5. München, 1988. 181—199p.

2.9.11. Bendrikova, Ljubov Arksentievna Luis Blanc kak istorik. Istoriograficesky ocerk. M., 1959. 99 p.

2.9.12. Bendrikova, Ljubov Arksentievna Francuskaâ istoriografiâ revolûcii 1848—1849 gg. vo Francii, 1848—1968. M., 1969. 396p.

2.9.13. Berding, Helmut Rationalismus und Mythos. Geschichtsaufassung und politische Theorie bei Georges Sorel. München-Wien,1969.

2.9.14. Bloch, Marc Actes du colloque de Paris 1986 à l'occasion de son Centenaire. Paris, 1988.

2.9.15. Boia, Lucian "Historiens des Annales". Acta Univ. Bucuresti 30 (1981) 42—72. p. 31 (1982) 47—77 p.

2.9.16. Born, K. E. "Neue Wege in der Wirtschafts- und Sozialgeschichte. Die Gruppe der Annales". Saeculum 15 (1964)

2.9.17. Bourde, Guy. — Martin, Hervé Les écoles historiques. Paris, 1983. 341 p. A short survey of the development of French historiography with some perspective on the general evolution of historical scholarschip.

2.9.18. Bourguière, André "Histoire d'une histoire: la naissance des Annales (1929)". Annales 1979 (6) 1346—1359. p.

2.9.19. Braudel, Fernand "Personal Testimony". Journal of Modern History 44/1979/ The whole issue devoted to study of the "monde braudellien".

2.9.20. Brogan, Hugh Tocqueville. L., 1973. 95 p.

2.9.21. Burguiere, André "The fate of history of *mentalites* in the Annales". Comparative Studies in Society and History 24/1982/424—437p.

2.9.22. Cantin, Eiken Mounier : a personalist view of history. N.Y., 1973. 176 p.

2.9.23. Carbonell, Charles-Olivier Histoire et historiens. Une mutation ideologique des historiens francais 1865—1885. Toulouse, 1976. 605 p.

2.9.24.Carbonell,Charles-Olivier "La naissance de la Revue Historique" La Revue Historique No. 516 (Avril-Juin, 1976) 331—351p.

2.9.25.Carbonell,Charles-Olivier "L'histoire dite positiviste en France". Romantisme 1978/21—22 p.

2.9.26.Carbonell,Charles-Olivier—Livet,G.(eds.) Au berceau des Annales. Le milieu strasbourgeois. L'histoire en France au début du XXe siècle. Toulouse, 1983.

2.9.27.Cedronio, M.—Diaz, F. Storiografia francese di ieri e di oggi.Napoli, 1977.

2.9.28.Clark, TerryNichols Prophets and patrons: The French university and the emergence of social sciences. Cambridge (Mass.), 1973.

2.9.29.Cobban,Alfred Historians and the causes of the French Revolution. L., 1958. 40 p.

2.9.30.Cobban,Alfred The social interpretation of the French Revolution. Cambridge, 1964.

2.9.31. Cobban, Alfred "Hippolyte Taine, historian of the French Revolution". History LIII (1968) October

2.9.32. Comité Français des Sciences Historiques La recherche historique en France de 1940—1965. Paris, 1965. 518 p. With an introduction by *Glénisson, Jean* "L'historiographie francaise contemporaine: tendances et réalisations". IX—LXIV p.

2.9.33. Comité Français des Sciences Historiques La recherche historique en France depuis 1965. Paris, 1980.

2.9.34. Coornaert, Emile Destins de Clio en France depuis 1800.Paris, 1977.190p.

2.9.35. Coutau-Begarie, Hervé Le phenoméne "Nouvelle Histoire". Stratégie et ideologie des nouveaux historiens. Paris, 1983.354p.

2.9.36.Dalin, V. M. Istoriki Francii XIX—XX vekov. M., 1981. 324 p. An important review by *Ado, A. V.* in Novaâ i noveĵaâ istoriâ1982/5/180—183.

2.9.37. Davies, R. R. "Marc Bloch". History LII (1967) October.

2.9.38. Diligenskij, J. "Les Annales vues de Moscov". Annales 1963/107—128.

2.9.39. Dosse, François L'Histoire en miettes: des Annales a la Nouvelle histoire. Paris, 1987. 272 p.

2.9.40. Eeles, G. N. Guizot as historian of England. B. Litt. thesis Oxford, 1926. (Manuscript)

2.9.41. Ehrard, Jean — Palmade, Guy P. (Textes choisis et présentés par) L'histoire. Paris, 1964, 1971 3. An anthology of French historiography.

*2.9.42.Engel–Janosi,Friedrich*Four studies in French Romantic historical writing. Baltimore, 1955. (Chateaubriand, de Barante, Thierry, Tocqueville)

2.9.43. Erbe, Michael Zur neueren französichen Sozialge-schichtsforschung. Die Gruppe um die Annales. Darmstadt, 1979. 159p.

2.9.44. Evans, Colin Taine. Essai de biographie intérieure. Paris, 1975.615p.

2.9.45.Farmer, Paul France reviews its revolutionary origins. N.Y.,1944.147p.

2.9.46. Fonville, Robert Desire Mounier. Paris, 1974. 338 p.

2.9.47. Friguglietti, James Albert Mathiez, historien révolution-naire, 1874—1932. Paris, 1974.

2.9.48. Gembicki, Dieter Histoire et politique à la fin de l'Ancien regime. J. N. Moreau (1717—1801) Paris, 1979.

2.9.49. Geoffroy, M.A. —Zeller, J.S.—Thienot J. Rapports sur les études historiques. Paris, 1867. 356 p.

2.9.50. Gérard, Alice La Révolution Française, mythes et inter-prétations. 1789—1870. Paris, 1970. 142 p.

2.9.51. Gérard, A. "La Revue Historique face à l'histoire con-temporaine" La Revue Historique No. 518 (avril-juin 1976) 352—405 p.

2.9.52. Gerstenberger, Peter Der deutsche Imperialismus im Spiegel französischer bürgerlicher Geschichtsschreibung. Berlin, 1975. 273 p.

2.9.53. Goedde-Baumanns, Beate Deutsche Geschichte in fran-zösischer Sicht. Die französische Historiographie von 1871 bis 1918 über die Geschichte Deutschlands und der deutsch-französi-schen Beziehungen in der Neuzeit. Wiesbaden, 1971. 461 p.

2.9.54. Gore, Keith L'idée de progrès dans la pensée de Renan. Paris, 1970. 314 p.

2.9.55. Gorgon, Edward T. De Tocqueville. N. Y., 1965.

2.9.56. Gossmann, Lionel Augustin Thierry and liberal histori-ography. With introductory comments by Hayden White. HT Beiheft 15 (1976) 83 p.

2.9.57. Guirol, Pierre — Temime, Emile (eds.) "L'historiographie du Second empire"· *In:* Revue d'histoire moderne et contemporaine 21 (1974) 1—185 p.

2.9.58. Gutnova, E. "Sintez v oblasti istorii prava i gosudarstva v francuskoj medievistike vtoroj polovini XIX v.". *In:* Evropa v srednie veka. M., 1972.

2.9.59. Haac, Oscar Les principes inspirateurs de Michelet: Sensibilité et philosophie de l'histoire. New Haven, 1951.

2.9.60. Haac, Oscar Jules Michelet. Boston, 1982. [Twayne's World Authors Series] 199 p.

2.9.61. Halévy, Daniel Jules Michelet. Paris, 1928.

2.9.62. Halphen, Louis L'histoire en France depuis cent ans. Paris, 1914.

2.9.63. Halphen Louis "Les historiens français et la science historique allemande" Sciencia Mai 1923/333—340 p.

2.9.64. Heising, Harald Die Deutung der französischen Revolution in der französischen Historiographie 1815 — 1852 Köln (Phil. Diss.) 1971. 258 p.

2.9.65. Herr, Richard Tocqueville and the Old Regime. Princeton, 1962.

2.9.66. Herrick, Jane The historical thought of Fustel de Coulanges. Washington, 1954.

2.9.67. Herter, J. H. "Ferdinand Braudel and the Monde Braudellien" Journal of Modern History 44 (1972)

2.9.68. Hoeges, Dirk François Guizot und die Französische Revolution. Bonn, 1973. 199 p.

2.9.69. Hughes, H. S. The obstructed path. French social thought in the years of desperation. New York, 1966. (Chapter II on the Annales School)

2.9.70. Jaeck, Hans-Peter "Das Geheimnis der europäischen Revolutionen. Marx rezensiert Guizot (1850)". Storia della Storiografia 4(1983)84—98.

2.9.71. Johnson, Douglas Guizot. L., 1963.

2.9.72. Jullian, Camille Extraits des historiens français du XIXe siècle. Paris, 1951. 684 p. An anthology.

2.9.73. Kaplam, Edward K. Michelet's poetic vision. A romantic philosophy of nature, man and woman. University of Massachusettes Press. Amherst, 1977. 211 p.

2.9.74. Kellley, Donald R. Historians and the law in postrevolutionary France. Princeton, 1984. 184 p.

2.9.75. Keylor, William R. A. Academy and community. The foundation of the French historical profession. Cambridge (Mass.), 1975. 286 p. Bibliography: 266—278 p.

2.9.76. Kinser, S. "Annaliste paradigm: the geohistorical structure of Ferdinand Braudel" AHR 86 (1981) 61—105 p.

2.9.77. Kippur, A. Stephen Jules Michelet. A study of mind and sensibility. N. Y., 1981. 269 p. The first Michelet-biography in English.

2.9.78. Kniebiehler, Yvonne Naissance des sciences humaines: Mignet et l'histoire philosophique au XIXe siècle. Paris, 1973. 506 p.

2.9.79. Krieser, Hannes Die Abschaffung des "Feudalismus" in der Französischen Revolution: Revolutionärer Begriff und begriffene Realität in der Geschichtsschreibung Frankreichs (1815—1914). Frankfurt am Main-Bern-N.Y., 1984. 390 p.

2.9.80. Kudrna, Jaroslav "Ideologische Aspekte und methodologische Grundlagen der französischen Annales Schule". ZfG 29(1981)3.

2.9.81. Kudrna, Jaroslav "Zu einigen Fragen des Methodenstreits in der französischen Historiographie um 1900". Storia della Storiografia 1983/3/62—78p.

2.9.82. Kudrna, Jaroslav "Sur la differentiation intèrieure de l'historiographie bourgeoise française avant l'École des Annales (1890—1945)". Ceskoslovensky casopis historicky 33/ 1985/5/739—755p.

2.9.83. Larat, P. Expliquez moi les Historiens du XIXe siècle. Tome 1. Thierry, Guizot, Michelet, Tocqueville, Tome 2. Fustel de Coulanges, Taine, Renan. Paris, 1946—47. 71, 64 p.

2.9.84. Lamberti, Jean Claude La notion d'individualisme chez Tocqueville. Paris, 1970. 86 p.

2.9.85. Locatelli, R. La Franche-Comte a la recherche de son histoire (1800—1914) Besancon, 1982. 488 p.

2.9.86. LeGoff, Jacques "Le Moyen Age de Michelet". *In:* Pour un autre Moyen Age. Paris, 1977. 19—45 p.

2.9.87. Lutz, Heinrich "Braudels La Méditerranée." *In: Kosseleck, R. — Lutz, H. — Rüsen, J. (eds.)* Formen der Geschichtssreibung. (Theorie der Geschichte, Beiträge zur Historik, Bd. 4.) München, 1982.

2.9.88. Mann, Hans Dieter Lucien Febvre. La pensée vivante d'un historien... Paris, 1971. 189 p.

2.9.89. Markova, U.D. "Nekotorye problemy istorii Parizskoj

Kommuny v sovremennoj francuzskoj istoriografii". *In: Kurginan, E. A. (ed.)*Voprosy istoriografii novoj i novejšej istorii. M., 1973.

2.9.90. Massicotte, Guy L'histoire probléme: la méthode de Lucien Febvre. Saint-Hyacinthe (Canada) et Paris, 1981. 121 p.

2.9.91. Mastrogregori, Massimo Il genio dello storico, le considerazioni sulla storia di Marc Bloch e Lucien Febvre. Napoli, 1987. 274p.

2.9.92. Melon, Stanky The political uses of History: A study of historians in the French Revolution. Stanford, 1958. 226 p.

2.9.93. Michelet. (By various authors) *In:* Europe année 51. (1973)No.535/536.p.1—234.

2.9.94. Mitchell, A, "German History in France after 1870". Journal of Contemporary History 3 (1967).

2.9.95.Monod,Gabriel La vie et la pensée de Jules Michelet. Edited by Charles Bénart et Henri Hauser. 1—2. Paris, 1923. 388+262 p. A standard biography.

2.9.96. Moreau, P. L'histoire en France au XIXe siècle. Etat présent de travaux et esquisse d'un plan d'études. Paris, 1937.

2.9.97. Moreau, Thérése Le sang de l'histoire. Michelet, l'histoire et l'idée de la femme au XIXe siècle. Paris, 1982. 526 p.

2.9.98. Moretti, Mauro Parlando di eventi un aspetto del dibattito storiografia attorne alle Annales dal secondo dopoguerra ad oggi. Societa e Historia (Milan) 7/1985/28/373—442 p.

2.9.99. Nantet, Jacques Tocqueville. Paris, 1970. 188 p.

2.9.100. Nora, Pierre "E. Lavisse, son role dans la formation du sentiment national". La Revue Historique Juillet 1962, 73–106 p.

2.9.101. Nora, Pierre (sous la direction de) Les Lieux de Mémoire 1—3. Paris, 1984—1987.

2.9.102. O'Connor, Sister Mary Consolata The historical thought of François Guizot. Washington, 1955.

2.9.103. Orr, Linda Jules Michelet. Nature, history and language. L., 1976.

2.9.104. Orr, Linda Headless history: nineteenth century French historiography of the revolution. Ithaca (N. Y.), 1990. 185 p.

2.9.105. Picon, Gaätan L'étudiant. Précédé de Michelet et la parole historienne. Paris, 1970. 182 p.

2.9.106. Pillarget, R. "From a classical to a serial and quantitative study of history". Durham University Journal 1978. On the "Annales School".

2.9.107. Reizov, B. G. Francuskaâ romanticeskaâ istoriografiâ (1815—1830) Leningrad, 1956. 533 p. Available also in French: L'Historiographie romantique française (1815—1830) M., without date. 808 p.

2.9.108. Renouvin, Pierre "Research in modern and contemporary history: Present trends in France". Journal of Modern History 28/1966/1/1—12.p.

2.9.109. Revel, J. "Histoire et sciences sociales, les paradigmes des Annales". Annales 1979/6/1360—1376 p.

2.9.110. Ricoeur, Paul The contribution of French historiography to the theory of history. Cambridge, 1980. (The Zaharoff lecture)

2.9.111. Rioux, J. P. "Les métamorphoses d'E. Lavisse". Politique aujourd'hui, 1975. (nov—déc) 3—12 p.

2.9.112. Roubichou-Stretz, Antoinette La vision de l'histoire dans l'eouvre de la Pléiade. Themes et structures. Paris, 1973. 254 p.

2.9.113. Schmidt, Jörg Der historiographische Ansatz Fernand Braudels und die gegenwärtige Krise der Geschichtswissenschaft. München, 1971. 238 p. (Phil. Diss.)

2.9.114. Schuin, Aniz Le pessimisme historique au XIXe siecle: Hippolyte Taine. Genéve, 1982. 87 p.

2.9.115. Siegel, Martin Science and the historical imagination in French historiographical thought, 1866—1914. A Columbia University (N. Y.) Ph. D. Dissertation, 1965.

2.9.116. Smithson, Aulon Nephi Augustin Thierry: social and political consciousness in the evolution of a historical method. Genéve, 1972. 316 p.

2.9.117. Social historians in contemporary France. Essays from the Annales. Edited and translated by the staff of the Annales. Paris — N. Y., 1972.

2.9.118. Sokolova, M. N. Sovremennaâ francuzskaâ istoriografiâ. Osnovnye tendencii v objasnenii istoričeskogo processa. M., 1979. 364 p. With a French summary.

2.9.119. Stadler, Peter Geschichtsschreibung und historisches Denken in Frankreich. 1789—1871. Zürich, 1958. 350 p.

2.9.120. Starke, D. England and the English: as presented in Michelet's History of France. M. A. thesis, L., 1922. (Manuscript)

2.9.121. Stengers, J. "Marc Bloch et l'histoire". Annales VIII (1953) 329—338 p.

2.9.122. Stoianovich, Trainan French historical method: The "Annales" paradigm. With a foreword by Fernand Braudel. Ithaca — L. Cornell University Press, 1976. 260 p.

2.9.123. Stowski, Fortunat Les historiens français au XIXe siècle d'Augustin Thierry à Michelet. Paris, 1935. 68 p. (Manuscript)

2.9.124. Struve, Paul Taine. Bruxelles, 1947. 57 p. A lecture given at the Palais de Justice in Bruxelles on 8 June, 1944.

2.9.125. Walch, Jean Les maîtres de l'histoire, 1815-1850: Augustin Thierrry, Mignet, Guizot, Thiers, Edgard Quinet. Geneve, 1986. 307p.

2.9.126. Viallaneix, Paul La Voie royale. Essai sur l'idée de peuple dans l'ouvre de Michelet. Paris, 1959. 511 p.

2.9.127. Vossler, Otto Alexis de Tocqueville. Freiheit und Gleichheit. Frankfurt am Main, 1973. 279 p.

2.9.128. Weintraub, Viktor Profjeca i profesura. Mickiewicz, Michelet i Quinet. Warszawa, 1975.

2.9.129. Weiss, G. The emergence of modern universities in France 1863—1914. L., 1983.

2.10. Germany, GDR, FRG

2.10.1. Acton, J. Lord "German schools of history". English Historical Review 1 (January 1886) 7—42 p. Published also in German: Die neuere deutsche Geschichtswissenschaft. Berlin, 1887. Reprinted in *Acton, J. Lord* Historical essays and studies. L., 1929.

2.10.2. Aly, Friedrich "Der Einbruch des Materialismus in die historischen Wissenschaften". Preußische Jahrbücher 81(1895) On Lamprecht.

2.10.3. Antoni, Carlo Dallo storicismo alla sociologia. Firenze, 1948. In German: Vom Historismus zur Soziologie. Stuttgart, 1949. In English: From history to sociology. The transition in German historical thinking. Detroit, 1959.; London, 1962. (Dilthey, Meinecke, Troeltsch, Max Weber, Huizinga, Wölfflin)

2.10.4. Antoni, Carlo La storicismo. Roma, 1957.

2.10.5. Arnscheidt, Margit Wandlungen in der Auffassung des deutschen Bauernkrieges zwischen 1790 und 1848. Ein Beitrag zum Verhältnis von Geschichtsschreibung und Gegenwartsinteresse. Heidelberg, 1976. 324 p.

2.10.6. Aron, Raymond La philosophie critique de l'histoire, essai sur une theorie allemande de l'histoire. Paris, 1970. 318 p.

2.10.7. Asendorf, Manfred Aus der Aufklärung in die permanente Restauration. Geschichtswissenschaft in Deutschland. Hamburg, 1974. 438 p. (Introduction + excerpts.)

2.10.8. Asendorf, Manfred Geschichte und Parteilichkeit: historisches Bewußtsein in Deutschland. Berlin, 1984. 326 p.

2.10.9. Astholz, H. Das Problem "Geschichte" untersucht bei J. G. Droysen. Berlin, 1933.

2.10.10. Aycoberry, P. "Histoire de l'Allemagne au XIXe siècle". Annales XXI (1966) 1402—1409 p. (Deals with post-World War II GDR and FRG historiography.)

2.10.11. Bach, Wolfgang Geschichte als politisches Argument. Eine Untersuchung an ausgewählten Debatten des Deutschen Bundestages. (Diss.) Münster, 1976.

2.10.12. Backs, Silvia Dialektisches Denken in Rankes Geschichtsschreibung bis 1854. Köln—Wien, 1985. 360 p.

2.10.13. Baldwin, Peter (ed.) Reworking the past: Hitler, the Holocaust, and the historians' Debate. Boston, 1990.

2.10.14. Barker, F. Nietzsche and Treitschke. Oxford, 1914.

2.10.15. Bauer, C. "Die Freiburger Lehrstühle der Geschichtswissenschaft im letzten Jahrzehnt des 19. bis zum ersten Viertel des 20. Jahrhunderts". *In:* C. Bauer, E. W. Zeeden, H. G. Zmarclik Beiträge zur Geschichte der Freiburger Philosophischen Fakultät. Freiburg/Br. 1957.

2.10.16. Bauer, Wilhelm "Treitschke und die Juden". Weltkampf (Mai—August/1944) 68—77 p.

2.10.17. Baumgart, Franzjörg Die verdrängte Revolution. Düsseldorf, 1976. (On pre-1918 interpretations of the 1848 German revolution.)

2.10.18. Baumgarten, H. Treitschke's "Deutsche Geschichte". Straßburg, 1883.

2.10.19. Beard, Charles A.–Vagts, Alfred "Currents of thought in historiography". AHR 42 (April 1937), 460–483 p. (Mainly on German philosophy of history)

2.10.20. Beck, Reinhart Die Geschichtsschreibung in der Sowjetzone. Ideologische Grundlagen und politische Zielsetzungen. Bonn—Berlin, 1965.

2.10.21. Beck, Reinhart Die Geschichte der Weimarer Republik im Spiegel der sowjetzonalen Geschichtsschreibung. Bonn, 1966. 367 p.

2.10.22. Becker, Berta J. G. Droysens Geschichtsauffassung. Hamburg, 1928. (Diss.)

2.10.23. Becker, Gerhold Neuzeitliche Subjektivität und Religiosität: die religions-philosophische Bedeutung von Herauskunft und Wesen der Neuzeit im Denken von Ernst Troeltsch. Regensburg, 1982. 382 p.

2.10.24. Bedeschi, Giuseppe Politica e storia in Hegel. Roma—Bari, 1973. 197 p.

2.10.25. Below, Georg von Die deutsche Geschichtsschreibung von den Befreiungskriegen bis zu unseren Tagen. Geschichte und Kulturgeschichte. Leipzig, 1916. 184 p. Second, enlarged edition with Beigabe: Die deutsche wirtschaftsgeschichtliche Literatur und der Ursprung des Marxismus. München—Berlin, 1924. 207 p. The second edition reprinted by "Scientia" publishing house in 1973.

2.10.26. Bendix, Reinhard Max Weber: an intellectual portrait. Garden City (N. Y.), 1960.

2.10.27. Berg, Gunter Leopold von Ranke als akademischer Lehrer. Studien zu seinen Vorlesungen und seinem Geschichtsdenken. Göttingen, 1968. 249 p. (Including the most detailed bibliography on Ranke.)

2.10.28. Berghahn, Volker "Die Fischer–Kontroverse — 15 Jahre danach". Geschichte und Gesellschaft 6 (1980) 403—419 p.

2.10.29. Bergmann, Willfred Zur Analyse und konzeptionellen Kritik neuester Tendenzen in der bürgerlichen Historiographie und "DDR-Forschung" der BRD zur Geschichte der DDR. Berlin, Akademie für Gesellschaftswissenschaften beim ZK der SED. Diss. A., 1978.

2.10.30. Bergsträsser, Arnold "Wilhelm Dilthey and Max Weber. An historical approach to historical synthesis". Ethics LVII (1947) 92—110 p.

2.10.31. Berlekamp, Brigitte Analyse und Kritik der gegenwärtigen Geschichtsauffassungen der CDU und der CSU zur deutschen Geschichte von 1918 bis 1945. Berlin, Akademie für Gesellschaftswissenschaften beim ZK der SED. Diss. A., 1981.

2.10.32. Berthold, Werner "... grosshungern und gehorchen." Zur Entstehung und politischen Funktion der Geschichtsideologie des westdeutschen Imperialismus untersucht am Beispiel von Gerhard Ritter und Friedrich Meinecke. Berlin, 1960.

2.10.33. Berthold, Werner Marxistisches Geschichtsbild — Volksfront und antifaschistisch-demokratische Revolution. Zur Vorgeschichte der Geschichtswissenschaft der DDR und zur Konzeption der Geschichte des deutschen Volkes. Berlin, 1970.

2.10.34. Berthold, Werner—Katsch, Günter—Kinner, Klaus Zur Geschichte der marxistisch-leninischen deutschen Geschichtswissenschaft(1917—1945)Potsdam,1978.

2.10.35. Berthold, Werner—Lozek, Gerhard—Meier, Helmut "Entwicklungstendenzen im historisch-politischen Denken in Westdeutschland". ZfG 4 (1964) 585—602 p.

2.10.36. Berthold, Werner—Lozek, Gerhard—Sysle, Horst "Grundlinien und Entwicklungstendenzen in der westdeutschen Geschichtsschreibung von 1945—1964". Wissenschaftliche Zeitschrift der Karl-Marx Universität Leipzig XIV (1965) 609—622 p.

2.10.37. Berthold, Werner—Katsch, Günter "Zentren historiographischer Forschung in der UdSSR. Zur Bedeutung der sowjetischen Historiographie für die Erforschung der Geschichte der Geschichtsschreibung der DDR und Westdeutschlands". ZfG XV (1967)478—485p.

2.10.38. Berthold, Werner—Lozek, Gerhard—Meier, Helmut— Schmidt, Walter (eds.) Unbewältigte Vergangenheit. Kritik der

bürgerlichen Geschichtsschreibung in der BRD. Berlin, 1970.
Köln, 1977 (revised edition.)

2.10.39. Berthold, Werner—Lozek, Gerhard—Meier, Helmut
Geschichte der Geschichtswissenschaft: Grundlinien und Entwicklungstendenzen in der Geschichtsschreibung der BRD
(1945—1975). Berlin, 1977. 72 p.

2.10.40. Biedermann, Gerd. S. Polen im Urteil der national-
preußischen Historiographie des 19. Jahrhunderts. Nürnberg—
Erlangen, 1967. (Diss.)

2.10.41. Birtsch, G. Die Nation als sittliche Idee. Der National-
staatbegriff in Geschichtsschreibung und politischer Gedankenwelt J. G. Droysens. Köln, 1964.

2.10.42. Blackbourn, David—Eley, Geoff Mythen deutscher
Geschichtsschreibung. Die gescheiterte bürgerliche Revolution
von 1848. Köln, 1980. Revised English edition: The peculiarities
of German history: bourgeois society and politics in nineteenth-
century Germany. Oxford, 1984.
A debate on the book in the review Merkur:
— *Wehler, H. U.* "Deutscher Sonderweg" oder allgemeine
    Probleme des westlichen Kapitalismus? Zur Kritik an
    einigen "Mythen deutscher Geschichtsschreibung". 35
    (May, 1981) 478—487 p.
— *Eley, G.* "Hans Ulrich Wehler". 35 (July, 1981) 757—759
    p.
— *Wehler, H.U.* "Rückantwort an Geoff Eley". ibid. 760 p.
— *Wehler, H. U.* "Der deutsche Sonderweg: Eine Nachle-
    se". 35 (August, 1981) 793—803 p.
Other comments:
— *Kocka, J.* "Der »deutsche Sonderweg« in der Diskussi-
    on". German Studies Review 5 (1982) 365—380 p.
— *Evans, Richard* "The Myth of Germany's missing revo-
    lution". New Left Review 149 (February, 1985).
— *Groh, Dieter* "Le »Sonderweg« de l'histoire Allemande:
    mythe ou realité". Annales 38 (1983) 1166—1187 p.

2.10.43. Boehlich, W. (ed.) Der Hochverrats-Prozeß gegen Gervinus. Frankfurt a. M., 1967.

2.10.44. Boockmann, Hartmut—Esch, Arnold—Heimpel, Hermann—Nipperdey, Thomas—Schmidt, Heinrich Geschichtswissenschaft und Vereinwesen im 19. Jahrhundert. Beiträge zur Geschichte historischer Forschung in Deutschland. Göttingen, 1972. 191 p. Veröffentlichungen des Max-Planck-Instituts für Geschichte. Vol. 1.

2.10.45. Brandi, K. Die Entstehung Leopold von Rankes "Deutsche Geschichte im Zeitalter der Reformation". Nachrichten von der Akademie der Wissenschaften in Göttingen 47 (1946)

2.10.46. Brands, M. C. Historisme als Ideologie. Het "Onpolitieke" en "Anti-Normatieve" Element in de duitse Geschiedwedenschap. Assen, 1965. 275 p.

2.10.47. Braune, Frieda Edmund Burke in Deutschland. Heidelberg, 1917.

2.10.48. Bravo, Benedetto Philologie, histoire, philosophie de l'histoire. Etude sur J. G. Droysen, historien de l'antiquité. Wroclaw, 1968. 409 p.

2.10.49. Bresslau, Harry Geschichte der Monumenta Germaniae Historica. Hannover, 1921. 679 p.

2.10.50. Brocke, Bernhard von Kurt Breysig. Geschichtswissenschaft zwischen Historismus und Soziologie. Lübeck und Hamburg, 1971. 351 p.

2.10.51. Bucholz, Arden Hans Delbrück and the German military establishment. Iowa City, 1985. 191 p.

2.10.52. Burrichter, Clemens "Das Verhältnis von Wissenschaft und Politik in der DDR." Aus Politik und Zeitgeschichte 21 (1971).

2.10.53. Busch, Otto (ed.) Hans Herzfeld, Persönlichkeit und Werk. Berlin (West), 1983. 116 p.

2.10.54. Bussmann, Walter Treitschke. Sein Welt— und Geschichtsbild. Göttingen, 1952. Second edition 1981. 479 p.

2.10.55. Bussmann, Walter "Treitschke als Politiker". HZ 177 (1954)249—279p.

2.10.56. Bussmann, Walter "Heinrich von Sybel". *In:* Bonner Gelehrte. Geschichtswissenschaft. Bonn, 1968.

2.10.57. Butowsky, Harry Allen Leopold von Ranke and the Jewish question. Urbana-Champaign. University of Illinois (Ph.Diss.), 1975.

2.10.58. Buxhoeveden, Christina von Geschichtswissenschaft und Politik in der DDR: das Problem der Periodisierung. Köln, 1980.301p.

2.10.59. Cantillo, Giuseppe Ernst Troeltsch. Napoli, 1979. 286 p.

2.10.60. No entry.

2.10.61. Christ, Karl Römische Geschichte und deutsche Geschichtswissenschaft. München, 1982. 394 p.

2.10.62. Conze, Werner "Die deutsche Geschichtswissenschaft seit 1945". HZ 225 (1977) 1—28 p.

2.10.63. Craemer, R. "Über die völkische Haltung Treitschke's". HZ 158 (1938) 77—105 p.

2.10.64. Cremer, Helmut Analyse und Kritik der in der sozialreformistischen Historiographie der BRD vorherrschenden Auffassungen zur deutschen Geschichte vom Aufkommen des Imperialismus bis zum Ausbruch der kapitalistischen Weltwirtschaftskrise (1897/98 bis 1929/30). Diss. A. Berlin, Akademie für Gesellschaftswissenschaften beim ZK der SED., 1983. 156+82 p.

2.10.65. Czok, Karl "Karl Lamprecht (1856—1915)". *In:* Bedeutende Gelehrte in Leipzig. Vol. 1. Leipzig, 1965.

2.10.66. Czok, Karl "Der Methodenstreit und die Gründung des Seminars für Landesgeschichte und Siedlungskunde 1906 an der Universität Leipzig". *In:* Jahrbuch für Regionalgeschichte (Leipzig), 1967.

2.10.67. Czok, Karl Karl Lamprechts Wirken an der Universität Leipzig. Berlin, 1984. (Sitzungsberichte der sächischen Akademie der Wissenschaften zu Leipzig. Band 124/6.)

2.10.68. Danilov, A. I. "Nemeckie istoriki liberal'nogo napravleniâ vo vremâ pervoj mirovoj vojny i revolûcii 1918—1919 gg". Novaâ i novejšaâ istoriâ 1958/5.

2.10.69. Danilov, A. I. Problemy agrarnoj istorii rannego srednevekov'a v nemeckoj istoriografii konca XIX — načala XX v. M., 1958. 367 p. Important milestone in the development of Soviet historiography.

2.10.70. Danilov, A. I. "Friedrich Meinecke i nemeckij burzoaznyj istorizm". Novaâ i novejsaâ istoriâ 1962/2/43—56 p.

2.10.71. Davis, H. W. C. The political thought of Heinrich von Treitschke. N.Y., 1915.

2.10.72. Dehio, Ludwig F. Meinecke, der Historiker in der Krise. Festrede, gehalten am Tage des 90. Geburtstages. Berlin—Dahlem, 1953.

2.10. 73. Dehio, Ludwig "Ranke und der deutsche Imperialismus". HZ 170 (1950) 307—328. In English: "Ranke and German imperialism". *In: Dehio, L.* Germany and world politics in the twentieth century. N.Y., 1967. 38—71 p.

2.10.74. Deisenroth, Alexander Deutsches Mittelalter und deutsche Geschichtswissenschaft im 19. Jahrhundert. Irrationalität und politisches Interesse in der deutschen Mediävistik zwischen aufgeklärtem Absolutismus und erstem Weltkrieg. Rheinfelden (Shäuble), 1983. 372 p.

2.10.75. Delbrück, Hans—Schäfer, Dietrich—Wolf, Gustav Nationale Ziele der deutschen Geschichtsschreibung seit der französischen Revolution. Gotha,1918.

2.10.76. Deutsch, Robert—Schameres, H. —Peters, C. Eine Studie zum Alltagsleben des Historie. Zeitgeschichte des Faches Geschichte an der Heidelberger Universität 1945—1978. Interdisziplinäre Studien zur Historie und Historiographie. Heft 2. Heidelberg, 1978. 169 p.

2.10.77. Dickerhoh-Fröhlich, Hedwig Das historische Studium an der Universität München im 19. Jahrhundert: vom Bildungsfach zum Berufsstudium. München, 1979. 229 p.

2.10.78. Diether, Otto "L. v. Ranke und J. G. Droysen". Eine Parallele. Preußische Jahrbücher 142 (1910) 1—20 p.

2.10.79. Diether, Otto Ranke als Politiker. Leipzig, 1911. (Diss.)

2.10.80. Docekal, Herta Ursula Ernst von Lasaul. Ein Beitrag zur Kritik des organischen Geschichtsbegriffs. Münster, 1970. 141 p.

2.10.81. Dockham, Karl Deutscher Geist und angelsächische Geistesgeschichte. Ein Versuch zur Deutung ihres Verhältnisses. Göttingen, 1954.

2.10.82. Dorpalen, Andreas "The German historians and Bismarck". Review of Politics 15 (1953) 53—67 p.

2.10.83. Dorpalen, Andreas Heinrich von Treitschke. New Haven, 1957.

2.10.84. Dorpalen, Andreas "Historiography as history: the work of Gerhard Ritter." Journal of Modern History **XXXIV** (1962) 1—18 p.

2.10.85. Dorpalen, Andreas "Die Revolution von 1848 in der Geschichtsschreibung der DDR." HZ 210 (1970).

2.10.86. Dorpalen, Andreas German history in Marxist perspective: The East German approach. L., 1985. 542 p.

2.10.87. Dotterweich, Volker Heinrich von Sybel. Geschichtswissenschaft in politischer Absicht 1817—1861. Schriftenreihe der Historischen Kommission bei der Bayerischen Akademie der Wissenschaften, Vol.16. Göttingen, 1978. 420 p.

2.10.88. Dove, A. Treitschkes "Deutsche Geschichte". In: Ausgewählte Schriften. Leipzig, 1898.

2.10.89. Dow, Earle W. "Features of the new history." AHR 3 (April, 1898). 431—498 p.(On Lamprecht's "Deutsche Geschichte")

2.10.90. Duncker, M. "J. G. Droysen". Preußische Jahrbücher. Vol. 54 (1884).

2.10.91. Eckert, Roland Kultur, Zivilisation und Gesellschaft. Die Geschichtstheorie Alfred Webers, eine Studie zur Geschichte der deutschen Soziologie. Tübingen, 1970. 176 p.

2.10.92. Elsholz, Konrad Das politische und religiöse Moment in der Geschichtsschreibung Rankes (dargestellt am Versuch einer geschichtsphilosophischer Analyse seiner "Deutschen Geschichte im Zeitalter der Reformation".) (phil. Diss.) Marburg, 1967.

2.10.93. Elsner, Dieter Die grosse Französische Revolution im Spiegel der neueren bürgerlichen Historiographie der BRD, dargestellt am Beispiel von Eberhard Schmitt und Rolf Reichardt. Leipzig, (Univ. Diss. A.) 1985.

2.10.94. Engel, Josef "Die deutschen Universitäten und die Geschichtswissenschaft." HZ 189 (1959) 223—378 p.

2.10.95. Engelberg, Ernst "Politik und Geschichtsschreibung. Die historische Stellung und Aufgabe der Geschichtswissenschaft in der DDR." ZfG 6 (1958) 468—495 p.

2.10.96. Engelberg, Ernst Die deutsche bürgerliche Geschichtsschreibung zur Großen Sozialistischen Oktoberrevolution. Berlin, 1967.

2.10.97. Engel-Jánosi, Friedrich The growth of German historism. Baltimore (Md.), 1944. 101 p.

2.10.98. Epstein, F. T. "F. Meinecke in seinem Verhältnis zum europäischen Osten". Jahrbuch für die Geschichte Mittel- und Osteuropas 3 (1955).

2.10.99. Erbe, Michael (ed.) Friedrich Meinecke heute. Berlin, 1981. 258 p. Bericht über ein Gedenk — Colloquium zu seinem 25. Todestag am 5. und 6. April 1979.

2.10.100. Faulenbach, Bernd (ed.) Geschichtswissenschaft in Deutschland: Traditionelle Positionen und gegenwärtige Aufgaben. München, 1974. 201 p.

2.10.101. Faulenbach, Bernd Ideologie des deutschen Weges. Die deutsche Geschichte in der Historiographie zwischen Kaiserreich und Nationalismus. München, 1980. 516 p.

2.10.102. Fehrenbach, E. "Die Reichsgründung in der deutschen Geschichtsschreibung." *In: Schieder, Th.—Deuerlein, E. (ed.)* Reichsgründung 1870/71. Stuttgart, 1970.

2.10.103. Fenske, W. "J. G. Droysen und das deutsche Natio-nalstaatproblem". Erlanger Abhandlungen zur mittleren und neu-eren Geschichte. II (1930).

2.10.104. Finckenzeller, R. Die Darstellung des Zeitalters der Religionskriege bei Ranke. (Diss.) Frankfurt, 1962.

2.10.105. Fischer, Dietrich Die deutsche Geschichtswissen-schaft von J.G. Droysen bis O. Hintze in ihrem Verhältnis zur Soziologie. Köln, 1966.

2.10.106. Fischer, K. Der historische Positivismus Kurt Brey-sigs (1866—1940). Ein Beitrag zur Geschichte der deutschen bürgerlichen »allgemeinen Kulturgeschichtsschreibung« der 1. Hälfte unseres Jahrhunderts. (Phil.Diss.) Rostock, 1969.

2.10.107. Fischer, M. Treitschkes Anschauung über Wesen und Gegenstand der Geschichte. (Diss.) Heidelberg, 1917.

2.10.108. Fleischer, Helmut "Zur Kritik des Historikerstreits". Aus Politik und Zeitgeschichte 40—41 (1988) 3—14 p.

2.10.109. Fletcher, Roger "Recent development in West Ger-man historiography: the Bielefeld school and its critics". German Studies Review 7 (1984) 451—480 p.

2.10.110. Forster, Karl (ed.) Gibt es ein deutsches Geschichts-bild? Würzburg, 1961.

2.10.111. Forschepoth, Josef Reformation und Bauernkrieg im Geschichtsbild der DDR. Zur Methodologie eines gewandelten Geschichtsverständnisses. Berlin, 1976. 170 p.

2.10.112. Frank, Jürgen Die Geschichtsauffassung von J. G. Droysen und ihre geisteswissenschaftlichen Grundlagen. (Diss.) Berlin, 1951.

2.10.113. *Freitag, Grete* Leopold von Ranke und die Römische Geschichte. (Diss.) Marburg, 1966.

2.10.114. *Frick, G.* Der handelnde Mensch in Rankes Geschichtsbild. (Diss.) Affoltern—Zürich, 1953.

2.10.115. *Fuchs, Walter Peter* "Der junge Ranke". In: Ranke, Leopold v. Frühe Schriften. München, 1973. 13—45 p.

2.10.116. *Fuchs, Walter Peter* "Ranke und die Öffentlichkeit". GWU 27 (1976) 9—24 p.

2.10.117. *Fuchs, Walter Peter* "Ranke und Luther". *In:* Lutherjahrbuch 45 (1978) 80—110 p. These studies (2.10.115, 2.10.116, 2.10.117) also in *Fuchs, Walter Peter* Nachdenken über Geschichte. Vorträge und Aufsätze.Herausgegeben von Gunter Berg und Volker Dotterweich.Stuttgart, 1980. 100—118, 54—81, 82—99 p.

2.10.118. Gadamer, H. G. Wahrheit und Methode. Tübingen, 1965. (Two chapters on Ranke and Droysen.)

2.10.119. Gaedeke, Corinna Geschichte und Revolution bei Niebuhr, Droysen und Mommsen. Bonn, 1978. 189 p.

2.10.120.Gall, Lothar(ed.) Das Bismarck-Problem in der Geschichtsschreibung nach 1945. Neue Wissenschaftliche Bibliothek, Vol. 42. Köln—Berlin, 1971. 452 p. An analytical introduction to excerpts from the works of mainly German historians. Useful also for general information on post-World War II German historiography.

2.10.121.Gasparan,Ashot Der Begriff der Nation in der deutschen Geschichtsschreibung des 19. Jahrhunderts. (Diss.) Leipzig, 1916.

2.10.122. Gavrilecev, V. A. "Theoretiko-metodologičeskie osnovy istoričeskih issledovanij G. von Sybela." *In:* Metodologičeskie i istoriograficeskie voprosy istoriceskoj nauki. Vypusk 1., Tomsk,1963.

2.10.123.Gavrilecev,V.A. "Ob idejno-metodologiceskih principah nemeckoj burzuaznoj istoriografii 50—60-h godov XIX.v." *In:* Metodologiceskie i istoriograficeskie voprosy istoriceskoj nauki. Vypusk 5. Tomsk, 1967. ᕒ5Ϥ9Ⅰ9

2.10.124.Gegenbach,ConstanzeN. Ranke: the development of the historian's craft. (Ph. D. Diss.) Chicago, 1977. 399 p.

2.10.125. Geiss, Imanuel Die Habermas-Kontroverse. Ein deutscher Streit. Berlin, 1988. 230 p.

2.10.126.Gerhard,Dietrich "Otto Hintze: his work and his significance in historiography." Central European History 3 (1970)17—48 p.

2.10.127. Geschichte, Ideologie, Politik: Auseinandersetzung mit bürgerlichen Geschichtsauffassungen in der BRD. Berlin, 1983.293p.

2.10.128. Giertz, H. "Das Berliner Seminar für osteuropäische Geschichte und Landeskunde (bis 1920)." In: Jahrbuch für Geschichte der UdSSR und der volksdemokratischen Länder Europas (Berlin), 1967.

2.10.129. Gilbert, Felix Johann Gustav Droysen und die preussisch-deutsche Frage. München, 1931. (Beiheft der Historischen Zeitschrift.)

2.10.130. Gilbert, Felix "German historiography during the Second World War." AHR 53 (October, 1947) 50—58 p.

2.10.131. Gilbert, Felix "The new edition of Johann Gustav Droysen's »Historik«". Journal of the History of Ideas 44 (1983) 327—336p.

2.10.132. Gilbert, Felix "Jacob Burckhardt's student years: the road to cultural history". Journal of the History of Ideas 47 (1986) 249—274p.

2.10.133. Goetz, Walter Die deutsche Geschichtsschreibung des letzten Jahrhunderts und die Nation. Leipzig und Dresden, 1919. Also in *Goetz, Walter* Historiker in meiner Zeit. Köln—Graz,1957.88—111p.

2.10.134. Goetz, Walter "Karl Lamprechts deutsche Geschichte". *In: Goetz, Walter* Historiker in meiner Zeit. 296—307 p.

2.10.135. Goetz, Walter "Karl Lamprechts Stellung in der Geschichtswissenschaft". *In:* Goetz, Walter Historiker in meiner Zeit. 308—312 p.

2.10.136. Gollwitzer, Heinz "Neuere deutsche Geschichtsschreibung". *In:* Deutsche Philologie im Aufriss. 3. Berlin, 1967. 2287—2356p.

2.10.137. Gooch, G. P. "Ranke's interpretation of German history". *In: Gooch, G. P.* Studies in German history. L., 1948.

2.10.138. Gooch, G. P. "Treitschke in his correspondence". *In: Gooch, G. P.* Studies in German History. London, 1948.

2.10.139. Grant, Michael "A great German Historian". The Listener 50. (November 5, 1953). On Theodor Mommsen.

2.10.140. Green, R. W. (ed.) Protestantism and Capitalism. The Weber thesis and its critics. Boston, 1959.

2.10.141. Grote, Adolf Unangenehme Geschichtstatsachen zur Revision des neuen deutschen Geschichtsbildes. Nürnberg, 1960.

2.10.142. Grundmann, Herbert Monumenta Germaniae Historica. München, 1969. 46 p. Bibliography 21—22 p.

2.10.143. Guglia, Eugen Leopold von Rankes Leben und Werke. Leipzig, 1893.

2.10.144. Guilland, A. L'Allemagne nouvelle et ses historiens. Paris, 1899. In English: Modern Germany and her historians. London, 1965. Westport (Conn.). (On Mommsen, Ranke and Treitschke.)

2.10.145. Gur'ev, V. S. J. Burckhardt o socialnom krizise XIX v. *In: Zigalov, B. S.—Mogil'nickij, B. G. (eds.)* Voprosy vseobsej istorii i istoriografii. Tomsk, 1973.

2.10.146. Haferkorn, Folkert Soziale Vorstellungen Heinrich von Sybels. Stuttgart, 1976. 222 p.

2.10.147. Hallgarten, G. W. P. "H. v. Treitschke. The role of the »outsider« in German political tought". History 36 (1951) 227—243 p.

2.10.148. Hallmann, Hans (ed.) Revision des Bismarckbildes: die Diskussion der deutschen Fachhistoriker 1945—1955. Darmstadt, 1972. 493 p.

2.10.149. Hammerow, Theodore S. "Guilt, redemption, and writing German history". AHR 88 (1983). 53—72 p.

2.10.150. Hammerstein, Notker (ed.) Deutsche Geschichtswissenschaft um 1900. Stuttgart, 1988. 355 p.

2.10.151. Handke, Horst "Zur sozialgeschichtlichen Forschung in der DDR". ZfG 34 (1986/4) 291—302 p.

2.10.152. Handl, Herbert Ranke und das revolutionäre Problem. (Phil. Diss.) Wien, 1951.

2.10.153. Harden, J. Kriegsursachen und Kriegsschuld im Urteil Rankes. Hamburg, 1953.

2.10.154. Hardtwig, Wolfgang Geschichtsschreibung zwischen Alteuropa und moderner Welt. Jacob Burckhardt in seiner Zeit. Göttingen, 1974. 405 p.

2.10.155. Hardtwig, Wolfgang Konzeption und Begriff der Forschung in der deutschen Historie des 19. Jahrhunderts. *In: Diener, Alwin* Konzeption und Begriff der Forschung in den Wissenschaften des 19. Jahrhunderts. Meisenheim a.Gl., 1978. 11—31 p.

2.10.156. Harnack, Axel von "Ranke und Burckhardt". Neue Rundschau LXII (1951) 73—78 p.

2.10.157. Hartmann, L. M. Theodor Mommsen. Gotha, 1908.

2.10.158. Hartmann, Volker Die deutsche Kulturgeschichtsschreibung von ihren Anfängen bis W.H. Riehe. Dissertation. Marburg, 1971. (Manuskript)

2.10.159. Hashagen, J. "Historikerpflichten im neuen Deutschland". Zeitwende (1926) 4.

2.10.160. Hastenkamp, Heinrich "Die mittelalterliche Kaiserpolitik in der deutschen Historiographie seit v. Sybel und Ficker". Historische Studien, Heft 255. Berlin, 1934.

2.10.161. Haun, Horst Zur Geschichte der Historiker-Gesellschaft der DDR. Der Gründungsprozeß. Die Gründungskonferenz der Historiker-Gesellschaft der DDR. Wissenschaftliche Mitteilungen der Historiker-Gesellschaft der DDR. /1985/3/9—44p.;/1986/1/5—42p.

2.10.162. Haun, Horst "Der X. Internationale Historikerkongreß 1955 in Rom und die Geschichtswissenschaft der DDR". ZfG34(1986)4/303—314p.

2.10.163. Hauser, H. Rankes protestantisches Geschichtsbild. (Diss.) Affoltern—Zürich, 1950.

2.10.164. Hausrath, Adolf Zur Erinnerung an Heinrich von Treitschke.Leipzig, 1901.

2.10.165. Hausrath, A. Heinrich von Treitschke. Berlin, 1913.

2.10.166. Heffter, H. "Vom Primat der Außenpolitik". HZ 171 (1951).

2.10.167. Heiber, Helmut Walter Frank und sein Reichsinstitut für Geschichte des neuen Deutschlands. Stuttgart, 1967.

2.10.168. Heimpel, Hermann Zwei Historiker. Friedrich Christoph Dahlmann und Jacob Burckhardt. Göttingen, 1962. 84 p.

2.10.169. Heintel, Erich "Wie es eigentlich gewesen ist. Ein geschichtsphilosophischer Beitrag zum Problem der Methode der Historie". *In:Derbolar,Josef—Nicolin,Friedhelm(eds.)* Erkenntnis und Verantwortung, Festschrift für Theodor Litt. Düsseldorf, 1960.

*2.10.170. Heitzer, Heinz—Noack, Karl-Heinz—Schmidt, Walter(eds.)*Wegbereiter der DDR—Geschichtswissenschaft, 24 Biographien.Berlin, 1989. 398 p.

2.10.171. Hellmann, Manfred (ed.) Osteuropa in der historischen Forschung der DDR. 1-2. Düsseldorf, 1972. 360, 406 p.

2.10.172. Helmolt, Hans P. Ranke-Bibliographie, Leipzig, 1910.

2.10.173. Helmolt, Hans F. Leopold Rankes Leben und Wirken.Leipzig,1921.

2.10.174. Hennig, Eike Zum Historikerstreit: was heißt und zu welchem Zweck studiert man Faschismus? Frankfurt am Main, 1988.230p.

2.10.175. Henz, Günter Johannes Leopold von Ranke: Leben, Denken, Wort 1795—1814. (Diss.) Köln, 1968.

2.10.176. Hepner, F. Wie kam Treitschke zu seinen Auffassungen über Staat und Gesellschaft? (Diss.) Berlin, 1918.

2.10.177. Herzberg, Guntolf "Wilhelm Dilthey in der heutigen westdeutschen Philosophie". Deutsche Zeitschrift für Philosophie 1970/1.

2.10.178. Herzberg, Guntolf Wilhelm Dilthey und die bürgerliche Wissenschaftstheorie." Deutsche Zeitschrift für Philosophie 1973/5.

2.10.179. Herzberg, Guntolf Wilhelm Dilthey und die Probleme des Historismus. Diss. A. (Manuskript) Humboldt Univ. Berlin, 1976.

2.10.180. Herzberg, Guntolf "Historismus: Wort, Begriff, Problem und die philosophische Begründung durch Wilhelm Dilthey." Jahrbuch für Geschichte 25 (1982) 259—304 p.

2.10.181. Herzfeld, Hans "Staat und Persönlichkeit bei Heinrich von Treitschke." Preussische Jahrbücher 194 (1923) 267—294 p.

2.10.182. Herzfeld, Hans Politik und Geschichte bei Leopold von Ranke. In: Festschrift für G. Ritter. Tübingen, 1950. 322—341 p.

2.10.183. Herzfeld, Hans "Germany: after the catastrophe". Journal of Contemporary History II (1967) 1/79—92 p. (On West-German historiography.)

2.10.184. Heuss, A. Theodor Mommsen und das 19. Jahrhundert. Kiel, 1956.

2.10.185. Heydemann, Günther Geschichtswissenschaft im geteilten Deutschland: Entwicklungsgeschichte, Organisationsstruktur, Funktionen, Theorie— und Methodenprobleme in der Bundesrepublik Deutschland und in der DDR. Peter Lang: Frankfurt am Main—Bern, 1980. 267 p.

2.10.186. Heydemann, Günther (ed.) Geschichtswissenschaft in der DDR. Band 1: Geschichte der Geschichtswissenschaft, Theorie- und Methodenprobleme. Didaktik der Geschichte, Geschichtsunterricht und historisches Museum. Berlin (West), 1988. 550p.

2.10.187. Hiden, John—Farguharson, John Explaining Hitler's Germany: historians and the Third Reich. L., 1983. 237 p.

2.10.188. Hinrichs, Carl Ranke und die Geschichtstheologie der Goethezeit. Göttingen, 1954.

2.10.189. Hintze, Otto und die moderne Geschichtswissenschaft. Ein Tagungsbericht. *Ed. Busch, Otto—Erbe, Michael.* Einzelveröffentlichungen der Historischen Komission Berlin 38, 1983. 208p.

2.10.190. Historische Forschungen in der DDR. Analysen und Berichte. Berlin, 1960. Sonderheft der ZfG.

2.10.191. Historische Forschungen in der DDR, 1960—1970. Berlin, 1970. Sonderband der ZfG. 836 p.

2.10.192. Historische Forschungen in der DDR. Analysen und Berichte 1970—1980. Berlin, 1980. Sonderband der ZfG.

2.10.193. Die Historische Kommission bei der Bayerischen Akademie der Wissenschaften. 1858—1958. Göttingen, 1958. 266 p.

2.10.194. Hjelholt, Holger Treitschke und Schleswig-Holstein. München—Berlin, 1929.

2.10.195. Hodges, H. A. The philosophy of Wilhelm Dilthey. L., 1952.

2.10.196. Hoeft, Bernhard Rankes Stellungnahme zur Französischen Revolution. (Diss.) Greifswald, 1932.

2.10.197. Hofer, Walther Geschichtsschreibung und Weltanschauung. Betrachtungen zum Werk Friedrich Meineckes. München, 1950. 552 p. Meinecke and the historicist school.

2.10.198. Hofer, Walther "Der mißbrauchte Ranke. Konservative Revolution in der deutschen Geschichtsschreibung." Der Monat 7 (1957) Heft 84.

2.10.199.Hofer,Walther "Normalization or falsification of Nazi-history? A. J. P. Taylor and the »neo-revisionist« school in Germany". *In*: L'historien et les relations internationales. Recueil d'études en hommage à Jacques Fregmond. Textes réunis par *Saul Fridländer, Harish Kapur, André Reszler.* Genéve, 1981. 309-323 p.

2.10.200.Hofmeister,K. Karl Lamprecht. Seine Geschichte als Ideologie und seine Stellung zum Imperialismus. Göttingen, 1956.

2.10.201.Horn,Ingeborg Die Darstellung und Auffassung der neuzeitlichen Revolutionen bei Ranke. (Diss.) Jena, 1952.

2.10.202.Horowitz,A.H. Zur Entwicklungsgeschichte der deutschen Historiographie. Wien, 1865.

2.10.203.Höhle,Th. Franz Mehring. Sein Weg zum Marxismus 1869—1891.Berlin,1958.

2.10.204. Hughes, H. Stuart Oswald Spengler. A critical estimate. N. Y., 1952.

2.10.205.Hübinger,Gangolf Georg Gottfried Gervinus, historisches Urteil und politische Kritik. Göttingen, 1984. 257 p.

2.10.206.Hübinger, Paul Egon "Heinrich von Sybel". *In: Forst, Walter(ed.)* Rheinisch-Westfälische Rückblende. Köln, 1967.

2.10.207.Iggers, Georg G. "The image of Ranke in American and German historical thought". HT 2 (1962) 1/17—40 p.

2.10.208.Iggers, Georg G. The dissolution of German historism. *In:* Ideas in History (*ed. Herr, R.—Parker, H. T.*) Durham (N. C.), 1965.

2.10.209.Iggers, Georg G. The German conception of history. The national tradition of historical thought from Herder to the present. Wesleyan University Press, 1968. 363 p., Second edition 1983. The German version: Deutsche Geschichtswissenschaft. Eine Kritik der traditionellen Geschichtsauffassung von Herder bis zur Gegenwart. München, 1971. 413 p., Second edition 1976.

2.10.210.Iggers, Georg G. —Moltke, K. von (eds.) Leopold von Ranke. The theory and practice of history. N. Y., 1973.

2.10.211.Iggers, Georg G. (ed.) The social history of politics. Critical perspectives in West German historical writing since 1945. Leamington Spa—Dover, N. H.—Heidelberg, 1985. 314 p., N. Y. 1986.

2.10.212. Irmschler, K. "Zum historisch — »sozialwissenschaftlichen« Konzept einer bürgerlichen Gesellschaft im Lichte der Historiographie der BRD". ZfG 28 (1980) 12/1136—1147 p.

2.10.213.Irmschler,K. "Zur Genesis der theoretisch-methodologischen Konzepte von Sozial-, Struktur- und Gesellschaftgeschichte in der bürgerlichen Historiographie der BRD". Jahrbuch für Geschichte 25 (1982).

2.10.214.Jäger,Wolfgang Historische Forschung und politische Kultur in Deutschland. Die Debatte 1914—1980 über den Ausbruch des Ersten Weltkrieges. Göttingen, 1984. 322 p.

2.10.215.*Jennings,W.*German historiography and the evolution of German political ideas in the nineteenth century. Ph. D. thesis, L., London School of Economics, 1949. (Manuscript).

2.10.216.*Jucker,M.* Rankes Idee der Monarchie. (Diss.) Affolten—Zürich, 1954.

2.10.217.*Jung,J.* Julius Ficker. Ein Beitrag zur deutschen Gelehrtengeschichte. Innsbruck, 1907.

2.10.218.*Kaegi,Werner* "Geschichtswissenschaft und Staat in der Zeit Rankes." In:Historische Meditationen Vol. 2. Zürich, 1946,121—171p.

2.10.219.*Kaegi,Werner* Jacob Burckhardt. Eine Biographie. 1-7.Basel,1947—1982.

2.10.220.*Kaegi,Werner* "Jacob Burckhardt zwischen Naturwissenschaft und Philosophie". HZ 224 (1977) 1—16 p.

2.10.221.*Kaerst,J.* "Die Geschichtsauffassung Rankes und Droysens in ihrer nationalen Bedeutung". Vierteljahrschrift für Sozial-und Wirtschaftsgeschichte 20 (1927) 219—242 p.

2.10.222.*Katsch,Günter* "Forschungen zur Geschichte der Geschichtswissenschaft an der Karl-Marx Universität Leipzig: eine Bilanz." Wissenschaftliche Zeitschrift der Karl Marx Universität Leipzig. (Gesellschafts- und Sprachwissenschaften) 32 (1983) 4/413—420p.

2.10.223.*Katsch,Hildegard* Heinrich von Treitschke und die preussisch-deutsche Frage von 1860—1866. München—Berlin, 1919.

2.10.224.*Kehr,Eckart* Neuere deutsche Geschichtsschreibung. *In:* Der Primat der Innenpolitik. Gesammelte Aufsätze zur preussisch-deutschen Sozialgeschichte im 19. und 20. Jahrhundert. Veröffentlichungen der Historischen Kommission zu Berlin beim

Friedrich Meinecke Institut der Freien Universität Berlin. Vol. 19. *Ed. Wehler, Hans-Ulrich* Berlin, 1965. 254—268 p.

2.10.225. Kemiläinen, Aiva Die historische Sendung der Deutschen in Leopold Rankes Geschichtsdenken. Helsinki, 1968. 192 p. Bibliography 181—185 p.

2.10.226. Kende, Oskar Neue Strömungen auf dem Gebiete der deutschen Geschichtswissenschaft. Wien—Leipzig, 1928. 38 p.

2.10.227. Kessel, Eberhard "Rankes Idee der Universalgeschichte." HZ 178 (1954). 269—308 p.

2.10.228. Kessel, Eberhard "Rankes Auffassung der amerikanischen Geschichte." Jahrbuch für Amerikastudien 7 (1962) 19-59 p.

2.10.229. Kinner, Klaus Marxistische deutsche Geschichtswissenschaft 1917 bis 1933. Geschichte und Politik im Kampf der KPD. Berlin, 1982. 526 p.

2.10.230. Kluback, William Wilhelm Dilthey's philosophy of history. N.Y., 1956.

2.10.231. Kluge, Johannes Erhard Von den Reichshistorikern zum Dritten Reich. Eine Untersuchung zu Darstellungsmethoden, Darstellungsmotiven und zur Gegenstandsbildung in Darstellungen deutscher Geschichte. (Diss.) Köln, 1970. 196 p.

2.10.232. Kneppe, Alfred Friedrich Münzer: ein Althistoriker zwischen Kaiserreich und Nationalsozialismus. Bonn, 1983. 310 p.

2.10.233. Kocka, Jürgen "Theory and social history. Recent developments in West Germany". Social Research 47 (1980) 3.

2.10.234. Kocka, Jürgen "Historisch-anthropologische Fragestellungen — ein Defizit der Historischen Sozialwissenschaft?"

In: Süssmuth, H. (ed.) Historische Anthropologie. Der Mensch in der Geschichte. Göttingen, 1984.

2.10.235.Kocka,Jürgen Ciencia social historica versus historia do cotidiano. Novas controversias na ciencia historica da Alemanha Ocidental. In:Sociedade Brasileira de Pesquisa Historia. Anais da VI Reuniao. Sao Paulo, 1987.

2.10.236. Kocka, Jürgen German history before Hitler: the debate about the German "Sonderweg". Journal of Contemporary History 23 (199).

2.10.237. Koehler, W. E. Troeltsch. Tübingen, 1941. Heidelberg,1947.

2.10.238. König, Hartmut Bismarck als Reichskanzler. Seine Beurteilung in der sowjetischen und der DDR-Geschichtsschreibung. Böhlau, Köln, 1978. 294 p.

2.10.239. Koester, Udo Literarische Radikalismus. Zeitbewusstsein und Geschichtsphilosophie in der Entwicklung vom Jungen Deutschland zur Hegelschen Linken. Frankfurt am Main, 1972.174p.

2.10.240. Kohlstrunk, Irene Logik und Historie in Droysens Geschichtstheorie. Eine Analyse der Genese und Konstitutionsprinzipien der Droysenschen "Historik". Wiesbaden, 1980. 182 p.

2.10.241.Kohn,Hans(ed.) German history: some new German views. Boston, 1954. 224 p.

2.10.242.Kornbichler,Thomas Deutsche Geschichtsschreibung im 19. Jahrhundert. Wilhelm Dilthey und die Begründung der modernen Geschichtswissenschaft. Centaurus-Verlagsgesellschaft.Pfaffenweiler, 1984.330 p.

2.10.243.Kosiek,Rudolf Historikerstreit und Geschichtsrevision. Tübingen, 1987.239 p.

2.10.244.Krause,H. Dietrich Schäfer. Vom Schüler Treitschkes zum ideologischen Wegbereiter des ersten Weltkrieges. (Diss.) Halle, 1968.

2.10.245. Kretschmar, H. Heinrich von Treitschke. Dresden, 1938.

*2.10.246.Krieger,L.*Ranke. The meaning of history. Chicago—London, 1977. 402 p.

2.10.247.Krill,Hans-Heinz Die Rankerenaissance. Max Lenz und Erich Marcks. Ein Beitrag zum historisch-politischen Denken in Deutschland 1880—1935. Mit einem Vorwort von Hans Herzfeld. Berlin (West), 1962. 271 p. A review by *Schleier,Hans* in ZfG 12(1964)3/497—500p.

2.10.248.Kuczynski,Jürgen Theodor Mommsen. Porträt eines Gesellschaftswissenschaftlers. Mit einem Kapitel über Mommsen, den Juristen von Hermann Klenner. Studien zu einer Geschichte der Gesellschaftswissenschaften. Bd.9. Berlin, 1978. 238 p.

2.10.249.Kudrna,Jaroslav "Einige Bemerkungen zur älteren deutschen bürgerlichen Geschichtsauffassung". Sbornik Praci Filosoficke Fakulty Brnenské University 1963/10/71—86p.

*2.10.250.Kudrna,Jaroslav*Historie, filosofie, politika v N. S. R. Praha, 1964. (On West German historiography)

2.10.251.Kuhnert,A. Der Streit um die geschichtswissenschaftlichen Theorien Karl Lamprechts. Berlin, 1906.

2.10.252.Kunkel, Wolfgang Geschichte als Prozess?: historischer Materialismus oder marxistische Geschichtstheorie. Hamburg, 1987. 392 p. On East German historiography.

*2.10.253.Kupisch,Karl*Heinrich von Treitschke. Berlin, 1949.

2.10.254.Kupisch,Karl Die Hieroglyphe Gottes. Grosse Historiker der bürgerlichen Epoche von Ranke bis Meinecke. München, 1967. 247 p. (Studies on Ranke, Burckhardt, Treitschke, Theodor Mommsen, Adolf von Harnack, Dilthey, Meinecke.)

2.10.255.Küntzel,G. Niebuhr's Römische Geschichte und ihr zeitgenössischer politischer Gewalt. *In:* Festgabe für C. Ebrard. Frankfurt,1920.181—221p.

2.10.256. Labuda, Gerard "Stare i nowe tendencje w historiografii Zachodnionemeckij". Przegladu zachodniego 1956/7-8/224—252p.

2.10.257.Lave,Theodor Leopold Ranke. The formative years. Princeton,1950.

2.10.258.Leipprand,E. Treitschke im englischen Urteil. Stuttgart,1931.

2.10.259.Leipprand,Ernst Heinrich von Treitschke im deutschen Geistesleben des 19. Jahrhunderts. Stuttgart, 1935.

2.10.260Lenz,Max Heinrich von Treitschke. Preußische Jahrbücher 84 (1896) 526—541 p.; Also *In:* Kleine historische Schriften 1. München—Berlin 1910.

2.10.261.Lenz,Max Ranke und Bismarck. *In:* Kleine historische Schriften. München—Berlin, 1910.

2.10.262.Lenz,Max Rankes biographische Kunst und die Aufgabe der Biographien *In :* Preussische Jahrbücher 149 (1912) 385—397p.

2.10.263. Lenz, Max Die Bedeutung der deutschen Geschichtsschreibung seit den Befreiungskriegen für die nationale Erziehung. (Geschichtliche Abende im Zentralinstitut für Erziehung und Unterricht 9.) Berlin, 1918.

2.10.264.Levine,Norman "The German historical school of law and the origins of historical materialism". Journal of the History of Ideas LXVIII/1987/3/431—451 p.

2.10.265.Levockina, L.P. "Izučenie istorii FRG v sovetskoj i nemeckoj (GDR) istoričeskoj nauke". *In: Kurginan, E. A. (ed.)* Voprosy istoriografii novoj i novejšej istorii. M., 1973.

2.10.266.Lewark,Sybille Das politische Denken Johann Gustav Droysens. (Diss.) Tübingen, 1975. 182 p.

2.10.267. Liebschütz, Hans Ranke. Historical Association pamphlet. L., 1954.

2.10.268.Liebschütz, Hans Das Judentum im deutschen Geschichtsbild vom Hegel bis Max Weber. Tübingen, 1967. 360 p.

2.10.269.Loewenstein,Bedrich "Zur Kritik am Nationalgedanken in der westdeutschen Geschichtsschreibung". *In: Stern, Leo et al.(eds.)* Der Antikommunismus in Theorie und Praxis. Zur Auseinandersetzung mit der imperialistischen deutschen Geschichtsschreibung. Halle, 1963.

2.10.270.Lorenz,L. Treitschke in unserer Zeit. Leipzig, 1916.

2.10.271.Lozek, Gerhard—Sysle, Horst Geschichtsschreibung contra Geschichte. Über die antinationale Geschichtskonzeption führender westdeutscher Historiker. Berlin, 1964. 327 p. Bibliography 289—318 p.

2.10.272.Lozek,Gerhard—Richter,Rolf Legende oder Rechtfertigung? Zur Kritik der Faschismustheorien in der bürgerlichen Geschichtsschreibung. Berlin, 1979. 100 p.

2.10.273.Lozek,Gerhard "Zur Theoriediskussion in der nicht – marxistischen Geschichtswissenschaft Ende des 19., Anfang des 20. Jahrhunderts". ZfG 32 (1984) 395—404 p.

2.10.274. Ludwig, Irmgard Treitschke und Frankreich. München—Berlin, 1934.

2.10.275. Lutze, K. Georg Gottfried Gervinus. Seine politische Ideenwelt bis zur »Einleitung in die Geschichte des neunzehnten Jahrhunderts« 1853. (Diss.) Berlin, 1956.

2.10.276. MacCabe, J. Treitschke and the Great War. L., 1914.

2.10.277. Maclean, Michael J. "Johann Gustav Droysen and the development of historical hermeneutics". HT **XX** (1982) 34–47 p.

2.10.278. Mägdefrau, W. "H. V. Treitschke und die imperialistische »Ostforschung«". ZfG 11 (1963) 8/1444—1465 p.

2.10.279. Maibaum, Werner "Geschichte und Geschichtswissenschaft in der DDR". *In: Ludz, P.Chr.(ed.)* Wissenschaft und Gesellschaft in der DDR. München, 1971.

2.10.280. Markov, Walter "Zur Krise der deutschen Geschichtsschreibung". Sinn und Form 2 (1950) Heft 2.109—155 p.

2.10.281. Markwart, Otto Jacob Burckhardt. Persönlichkeit und Jugendjahre. Basel, 1920.

2.10.282. Märtz, K. Die Methodik der Geschichtswissenschaft nach Ranke, Sigwart und Wundt. (Diss.) Leipzig, 1916.

2.10.283. Masur, Gerhard Rankes Begriff der Weltgeschichte. München—Berlin, 1926. (Beiheft 6, Historische Zeitschrift)

2.10.284. Mauser, Wolfram Karl Hillebrand. Leben, Werk, Wirkung. Dornbirn, 1960. 301 p.

2.10.285. Mayer, J.P. Max Weber and German politics. L., 1956.

2.10.286.McClelland, Ch. E. The German historians and England: a study in nineteenth century views. Cambridge, 1971. 301 p.

2.10.287. McClelland, Ch. E. "Berlin historians and German politics". *In:* Journal of Contemporary History 8 (1973) 3—33 p.

2.10.288. McClelland, Ch. E. State, society and university in Germany 1700—1914. Cambridge, 1980.

2.10.289.Mehring, Franz "H. v. Treitschke; Treitschkes Briefe". *In:* Gesammelte Aufsätze und Schriften 5. Berlin, 1931.

2.10.290.Meier, Christian 40 Jahre nach Auswitz. Deutsche Geschichtserinnerung heute. München, 1987. 96 p.

2.10.291. Meinecke, Friedrich Weltbürgertum und Nationalstaat. München—Berlin, 1908.

2.10.292.Meinecke, Friedrich Die Entstehung des Historismus. München, 1936; München, 1946; München, 1959. Werke, 3. Herausgegeben und eingeleitet von *Carl Hinrichs.* München, 1965. 617p.

2.10.293.Meinecke, Friedrich Schaffender Spiegel. Studien zur deutschen Geschichtsschreibung und Geschichtsauffassung. Stuttgart, 1948.

2.10.294.Meinecke, Friedrich Ranke und Burckhardt. Berlin, 1948.

2.10.295. Meinecke, Friedrich Zur Geschichte der Geschichtsschreibung. München, 1968. 486 p. Herausgegeben und eingeleitet von Eberhard Kessel. Werke, 7. A reprint of 53 articles (written 1888—1951) on 19-20th century German historiography.

2.10.296.Meisner, H. O. "Otto Hintzes Lebenswerk". *In:* HZ 164(1941)66—90p.

2.10.297.Meister,G. "Die geschichtsphilosophischen Voraussetzungen von J. G. Droysens Historik". Historische Vierteljahrsschrift 23 (1926)

2.10.298.Mérei, Gyula "A nemzetekfölötti állam" eszméje a nyugatnémet és az osztrák történetírásban". Századok 96 (1961) 6,97(1962)1-2.

2.10.299.Mérei,Gyula Die Idee der europäischen Integration in der westdeutschen bürgerlichen Geschichtsschreibung. Budapest,1966.206p.

2.10.300. Mérei, Gyula "Strukturgeschichtsforschung in der bürgerlichen Geschichtsschreibung der BRD." Études HistoriquesHongroises 1975.Budapest,1975/I/59—88p.

2.10.301.Metz,Karl-Heinz Grundformen historiographischen Denkens. Wissenschaftsgeschichte als Methodologie: Dargestellt an Ranke, Treitschke und Lamprecht. München, 1979. 737 p.

2.10.302.Michael,W. Ranke und Treitschke und die deutsche Einheit. Berlin, 1922.

2.10.303.Mogil'nickij,B.G. "Ob odnom opyte psichologičeskoj interpretacii istorii srednevekovoj Germanii (kul'turno-istoričeskij metod Karla Lamprechta)". *In:* Metodologičeskie i istoriografičeskie voprosy istoričeskoj nauki. Vypusk 6. Tomsk, 1969.

2.10.304.Momigliano,Arnoldo J. G. Droysen between Greeks and Jews."HT 9 (1970) 2/139—153 p.

2.10.305. Mommsen, Hans "Historical scholarship in transition: the situation in the Federal Republic of Germany". Daedalus 100(Spring, 1971)485—508 p.

2.10.306.Mommsen,Hans Das Ressentiment als Wissenschaft. Anmerkungen zu Ernst Noltes "Der europäische Bürgerkrieg

1917—1945. Nationalsozialismus und Bolschevismus. GWU 14 (1988)4/495—512p.

2.10.307.Mommsen,Wilhelm Stein — Ranke — Bismarck. Ein Beitrag zur politischen und sozialen Bewegung des 19. Jahrhunderts. München, 1954. 304 p.

2.10.308.Mommsen, Wolfgang Max Weber und die deutsche Politik, 1890—1920. Tübingen, 1959. Überarbeitete und erweiterte Auflage, Tübingen, 1974. 586 p.; English version: Max Weber and German politics 1890—1920. Chicago, 1985. The debate on this book in the early 1960s is summarized in the material of the 1964 conference of the German Sociological Association.

2.10.309. Mommsen, Wolfgang J. "Universalgeschichtliches und politisches Denken bei Max Weber." HZ 201 (1965) 557—612p.

2.10.310. Mommsen, Wolfgang J. Die Geschichtswissenschaft jenseits des Historismus. Düsseldorf, 1971. 46 p.

2.10.311. Mommsen, Wolfgang J. Max Weber: Gesellschaft, Politik und Geschichte. Frankfurt am Main, 1974. 280 p.

2.10.312.Mommsen,WolfgangJ. "Gegenwärtige Tendenzen in der Geschichtsschreibung der Bundesrepublik". Geschichte und Gesellschaft 7 (1981) 149—188 p.

2.10.313.Mommsen,WolfgangJ. "Max Weber und die historiographische Methode seiner Zeit." Storia della Storiografia 3 (1983)28—50p.

2.10.314.Mommsen,WolfgangJ.—Schwentker,Wolfgang(eds.) Max Weber und seine Zeitgenossen. Göttingen, 1988. 799 p.

2.10.315.Mordstein,F. "Heinrich von Treitschkes Etatismus." Zeitschrift für Politik 8 (1961) 30—53 p.

2.10.316.Morsey,Rudolf "Geschichtsschreibung und amtliche Zensur. Zum Problem der Aktenveröffentlichung über die spanische Thronkandidatur der Sigmaringer Hohenzollern." HZ 184 (1957)555—572p.

2.10.317. Moses, John A. The war aims of Imperial Germany: Prof. F. Fischer and his critics. University of Queensland Papers I./4.St.Lucia,1968.

2.10.318.Moses, John A. The politics of illusion: the Fischer controversy in German historiography. N.Y.—L., 1975.

2.10.319.Muelbe,Erich Selbstzeugnisse Rankes über seine historische Theorie und Methode im Zusammenhang der zeitgenössischen Geistesrichtungen. Berlin, 1928.

2.10.320. Müller, Karl Alexander von "Treitschke als Journalist." HZ 135 (1926—27) 382—412 p.

2.10.321.Müller,Max Historie und Geschichte im Denken J. G. Droysens. In: *Bauer, C. —Boehm, L. —Müller, M. (eds.)* Speculum historiale. Geschichte im Spiegel von Geschichtsschreibung und Geschichtsdeutung. Festschrift für Johannes Spörl zum 60. Geburtstag. München, 1965.

2.10.322.Muralt,L.von War Ranke ein protestantischer Historiker? Der Historiker und die Gesellschaft. Berlin, 1960.

2.10.323.Nalbandian,Wahan Leopold von Rankes Bildungsjahre und Geschichtsauffassung. (Diss.) Leipzig, 1901.

2.10.324. Neumann, Carl Jacob Burckhardt. München, 1927. 401p.

2.10.325. Neumüller, Michael Liberalismus und Revolution. Das Problem der Revolution in der deutschen liberalen Geschichtsschreibung des 19. Jahrhunderts. Düsseldorf, 1973.

2.10.326.Nitschke,August "German politics and medieval history". Journal of Contemporary History 3 (April, 1968) 75—92 p.

2.10.327.Noack,Karl-Heinz "Das Bild Friedrich II. im bürgerlich-junkerlichen Geschichtsdenken während des Kampfes um die Reichseinigung". *In:Bartel,Hund—Engelberg,Ernst(eds.)* Die großpreußisch-militaristische Reichsgründung von 1871. Voraussetzungen und Folgen. Berlin, 1970. I./202—217 p.

2.10.328.Nolte,Ernst Das Vergehen der Vergangenheit. Antwort an meine Kritiker im sogenannten Historikerstreit. 2. erweiterte Auflage. Berlin, 1988. 244 p.

2.10.329.Nurdin,J. "Jakob Burckhardt et le refus de la modernité". Revue d'Allemagne 14 (1982) 88—96 p.

2.10.330.Oestreich,Gerhard(ed.) Otto Hintzes Lebenswerk. I. Göttingen, 1962; II. Göttingen, 1964; III. Göttingen, 1967.

2.10.331.Oestreich,Gerhard "Die Fachhistorie und die Anfänge der sozialgeschichtlichen Forschung in Deutschland". HZ 208 (1969)320—363 p.

2.10.332. Olszewski, Henryk Nauka historii w upadku: studium o historiografii i ideologii historycznei w imperialistycznych Niemczeh. Poznan, 1982. 656 p. With table of contents in German.

2.10.333. Oncken, Hermann "Wandlungen des Geschichtsbildes in revolutionären Epochen". *In:* Hundert Jahre Historische Zeitschrift 1859—1959. Sonderband HZ 189 (1959) 124—138 p.

2.10.334.Orlova,M.J. "Osnovnye napravleniâ burzuaznoj i social-reformistskoj istoriografii FRG". Novaâ i novejsaâ istoriâ 1977/4/165—181 p.

2.10.335. Ortega y Medina, Juan A. Teoria y critica de la historiografia cientifico-idealista alemana: Guilermo de Humboldt,

Leopoldo Ranke: Mexico, 1980. 273 p. With a selection of Humboldt (1818—21) and Ranke (1830—60) texts.

2.10.336.Ottnad,B. Mensch und Geschichte bei J.G. Droysen. (Diss.) Freiburg, 1952.

2.10.337.Patriaev,K.D. Mify i destwitel'nost' v "kriticeskom peresmotre" prošlogo. Ocerki burzuaznoj istoriografii FRG. Kiev, 1969.247p.

2.10.338. Perpat, Wilhelm Erich Rothacker, Philosophie des Geistes aus dem Geist der Deutschen Historischen Schule. Bonn, 1968.123p.

2.10.339.Patryšev,AleksandrIvanovic Neoliberal'naâ istoriografiâ FRG. Formirovanie, metodologiâ, koncepcii. M., 1981. 146 p.

2.10.340.Petersdorff,Hermannvon Bismarck und Treitschke. Bismarck-Jahrbuch 6 (1898) 271—308 p.

2.10.341. Petrušev, A. I. "Die Tradition des »deutschen Historismus« in der bürgerlichen Geschichtsschreibung der BRD". Sowjetwissenschaft29(1976)3/285—302p.

2.10.342.Petzold,Joachim Die Dolchstosslegende. Eine Geschichtsfälschung im Dienst des deutschen Imperialismus und Militarismus. Berlin, 1963. 148 p.

2.10.343.Pitscher,JohnHarold Heinrich Ritter von Srbik and the evolution of gesamtdeutsch historiography. (Ph. D. Diss.) Tolane University, 1976.292 p.

2.10.344. Pflaum, Chr. D. J. G. Droysens Historik in ihrer Bedeutung für die moderne Geschichtswissenschaft. Geschichtliche Untersuchungen, (ed. *Lamprecht, Karl* Bd. 5. H. 2.) Gotha, 1907. The first analytical appraisal of Droysen's Historik.

2.10.345.Pois,RobertA. Friedrich Meinecke and German politics in the twentieth century. Berkeley—L., 1972. 164 p.

2.10.346.Postel,Rainer Johann Martin Lappenberg. Ein Beitrag zur Geschichte der Geschichtswissenschaft im 19. Jahrhundert. Lübeck—Hamburg, 1972. 352 p.

2.10.347.Pöls,Werner "Bismarck und Sybels »Begründung des Deutschen Reichs durch Wilhelm I". *In:* Historische Studien zu Politik, Verfassung und Gesellschaft. Festschrift für Richard Dietrich. Braunschweig, 1986.

2.10.348.Pufkus,C. Heinrich von Treitschke. Een studie voer politiche apriorismen in de geschiedschrijwing. (Diss.) Assen, 1945.

2.10.349. Ranke, Leopold von A special issue of the Syracuse Scholar (Vol.9. No. 1, 1988) with the following contributions:
— *Powell, James M.* "Introduction: the confusing and ambiguous legacy of Leopold von Ranke"
— *Schulin, Ernst* "Ranke's universal and national history"
— *Gilbert, Felix* "Ranke as the teacher of Jacob Burckhardt"
— *Burke, Peter* "Ranke the reactionary"
— *Ross, Dorothy* "On the misunderstanding of Ranke and the origins of the historical profession in America"
— *Iggers, Georg G.* "The crisis of the Rankean paradigm in the nineteenth century"
— *Weinberg, Gerhard L.* "The end of Ranke's history?"

2.10.350. Rantzau, J. A. von "Das deutsche Geschichtsdenken der Gegenwart und die Nachwirkungen Rankes". GWU 1 (1950).

2.10.351. Rau, H. Geschichtsphilosophische Gedanken bei Treitschke. Stuttgart, 1927.

2.10.352. Raumer, K. von "Ranke als Spiegel deutscher Geschichtsschreibung im 19. Jahrhundert". Die Welt als Geschichte 12(1952).

2.10.353. Reichel, Waltraud Studien zur Wandlung von Max Lehmanns preußisch-deutschem Geschichtsbild. Göttingen— Frankfurt am Main, 1963. 201 p.

2.10.354. Richter, F. J. G. Droysen und seine sittliche Welt. (Diss.) Wien, 1938.

2.10.355. Riedel, M. "Der Staatsbegriff der deutschen Geschichtswissenschaft des 19. Jahrhunderts in seinem Verhältnis zur klassisch-politischen Philosophie". Der Staat 2 (1953) Heft 1. 41—63p.

2.10.356. Riesenberger, Dieter Geschichte und Geschichtsunterricht in der DDR. Göttingen, 1973.

2.10.357. Riesterer, Berthold Philipp Karl Löwith's view of history: a critical appraisal of historicism. The Hague, 1969. 108 p.

2.10.358. Ringer, Fritz The decline of the German Mandarins. The German academic community, 1890—1933. Cambridge (Mass.), 1969. In German: Die Gelehrten. Der Niedergang der deutschen Mandarine 1890—1933. Stuttgart, 1983. A brilliant analysis of the social and intellectual context of German scholarship before 1933.

2.10.359. Rippel-Manß, Irmtraud Selbstverständnis und Selbstreflexion der deutschen Historie zwischen 1914 und 1935 in der "Historischen Zeitschrift". (Diss.) Erlangen—Nürnberg, 1976. 282p.

2.10.360. Ristic, Jovan Leopold Ranke i oslobodjenje Srbije. Beograd, 1892. 29 p.

2.10.361.Ritter, Gerhard Ein politischer Historiker in seinen Briefen. Edited by *Klaus Schwabe* and *Rolf Reichardt.* Boppard am Rhein: Harold Boldt Verlag, 1984. 330 p. Long introduction by *Klaus Schwatz.*

2.10.362. Ritter, Gerhard A. —Vierhaus, Rudolf (eds.) Aspekte der historischen Forschung in Frankreich und Deutschland. Schwerpunkte und Methoden. Aspects de la recherche historique en France et en Allemagne. Deutsch-Französisches Historikertreffen, Göttingen, 1979. Göttingen, 1981. (Veröffentlichungen des Max Planck-Instituts für Geschichte. 69.)

2.10.363.Rittinghaus, W. Die Kunst der Geschichtsschreibung Heinrich von Treitschkes. (Diss.) Leipzig, 1914.

2.10.364.Rose, Günther Grundpositionen und Tendenzen bürgerlicher Weltgeschichtsschreibung in der BRD." ZfG 24 (1976) 133—149p.

2.10.365. Rosenberg, Arhur "Treitschke und die Juden". Die Gesellschaft 7 (1930) 2/78—83 p.

2.10.366.Rossi, Pietro La storicismo tedesco contemporaneo. Torino, 1956. 550 p.

2.10.367. Rothacker, E. "Savigny, Grimm, Ranke." HZ 128 (1923)

2.10.368.Rother, H. Geschichte und Politik in der Gedankenwelt J. G. Droysens. Breslau, 1935.

2.10.369. Rotteck, Carl von "Betrachtungen über Gang, Charakter und heutigen Zustand der historischen Studien in Deutschland (1840)." *In:* Gesammelte und nachgelassene Schriften, herausgegeben von Hermann von Rotteck. Vol. 1., Pforzheim, 1841.

2.10.370. Rotthaus, K. Der dynamische Zusammenhang des äußeren und inneren Staatslebens bei Ranke. (Diss.) Heidelberg, 1915.

2.10.371.Ruch, K.-H. Die »Mitteleuropa«-Idee und die imperialistische deutsche Historiographie zwischen den beiden Weltkriegen. (Diss.) Halle, 1967.

2.10.372.Rüsen, Jörn "Politisches Denken und Geschichtswissenschaft bei J. G. Droysen." *In:* Politische Ideologien und nationalstaatliche Ordnung. Festschrift Theodor Schieder. München, 1968.

2.10.373.Rüsen, Jörn Begriffene Geschichte. Genesis und Begründung der Geschichtstheorie J.G. Droysens. Paderborn, 1969. 174 p. (One of the most important works in the field of historiography in the 1960s).

2.10.374.Rytkönen, Seppo Baerthold Georg Niebuhr als Politiker und Historiker. Zeitgeschehen und Zeitgeist in den geschichtlichen Beurteilungen von B. G. Niebuhr. Helsinki, 1968. 378 p. Bibliography 350—373 p.

2.10.375. Salomon, Albert In praise of enlightenment. Cleveland—New York, 1963. (Includes a good essay on Burckhardt.)

2.10.376.Salov, V.I. Sovremennaâ zapadnogermanskaâ burzoaznaâ istoriografiâ. Nekotorye problemy novejsej istorii. M., 1968. 381 p.

2.10.377. Schaaf, Julius Jakob Geschichte und Begriff, eine kritische Studie zur Geschichtsmethodologie von Ernst Troeltsch und Max Weber. Tübingen, 1946.

2.10.378.Schäfer, D. Deutsches Nationalbewußtsein im Lichte der Geschichte. Akademische Antrittsrede an der Universität Jena. Jena, 1884.

2.10.379. Schallenberg, Horst Untersuchungen zum Geschichtsbild der Wilhelminischen Ära und der Weimarer Zeit. Düsseldorf, 1964. An analysis of school-textbooks.

2.10.380. Schaumkell, Ernst Geschichte der deutschen Kulturgeschichtsschreibung. Preisschriften der Fürstlich Jblonowskischen Gesellschaft zu Leipzig. Nr. XXIV. der Historisch–Nationalökonomischen Sektion. Leipzig, 1905. 320 p.

2.10.381. Schenk, Willy Die deutsch-englische Rivalität vor dem Ersten Weltkrieg in der Sicht deutscher Historiker. Missverstehen oder Machtstreben. Aarau, 1967. 174 p.

2.10.382. Scherer, Emil Clemens Geschichte und Kirchengeschichte an den deutschen Universitäten. Freiburg, 1927.

2.10.383. Schewill, Ferdinand "Ranke. Rise, decline, and persistence of a reputation". *In: Schevill, Ferdinand* Six historians. Chicago, 1956. 125—155 p.

2.10.384. Schieblich, W. Die Auffassung des mittelalterlichen Kaisertums in der deutschen Geschichtsschreibung von Leibniz bis Giesebrecht. Berlin, 1932.

2.10.385. Schieder, Theodor "Das historische Weltbild Rankes". GWU 1 (1950)

2.10.386. Schieder, Theodor Der Typus in der Geschichtswissenschaft. *In: Schieder, Theodor* Staat und Gesellschaft im Wandel unserer Zeit. München, 1958. 172—187 p.

2.10.387. Schieder, Theodor (ed.) Hundert Jahre Historische Zeitschrift 1859—1959. München, 1959.

2.10.388. Schieder, Theodor "Die deutsche Geschichtswissenschaft im Spiegel der Historischen Zeitschrift". HZ 189 (1959) 1—50p.

2.10.389.Schieder,Theodor "Grundfragen der neueren deutschen Geschichte: zum Problem der historischen Urteilsbildung." HZ 197 (1961) 1—16 p.

2.10.390.Schieder,Theodor Begegnungen mit der Geschichte. Göttingen, 1962.

2.10.391.Schiemann,Theodor Heinrich von Treitschkes Lehr- und Wanderjahre 1834—1866. München und Leipzig, 1896. 270 p.

2.10.392.Schiera,Pierangelo Otto Hintze. Napoli, 1974. 238 p. Bibliography 219—230 p.

2.10.393.Schleier,Hans Sybel und Treitschke. Antidemokratismus und Militarismus im historisch-politischen Denken großbourgeoiser Geschichtsideologen. Berlin, 1965. 317 p.

2.10.394.Schleier,Hans "Treitschke, Delbrück und die »Preußischen Jahrbücher« in den 80er Jahren des 19. Jahrhunderts." *In:* Jahrbuch für Geschichte (Berlin), 1967.

2.10.395.Schleier,Hans "Zur Auswirkung der Reichsgründung auf die historisch-politische und methodologische Konzeption der bürgerlichen deutschen Geschichtsschreibung." *In:* Die preussische militaristische Reichsgründung. II. Berlin, 1971.

2.10.396. Schleier, Hans "Zum Verhältnis von Historismus, Strukturgeschichte und sozialwissenschaftlichen Methoden in der gegenwärtigen Geschichtsschreibung der BRD." *In: Engelberg, E. (ed.)* Probleme der Geschichtsmethodologie. Berlin, 1972.

2.10.397.Schleier,Hans Theorie der Geschichte-Theorie der Geschichtswissenschaft. Zu neueren theoretisch-methodologischen Arbeiten der Geschichtsschreibung in der BRD. Berlin, 1975. 113 p.

2.10.398. Schleier, Hans Die bürgerliche deutsche Geschichtsschreibung der Weimarer Republik. Berlin, 1975. 593 p.

2.10.399. Schleier, Hans "DDR-Forschungen über die Geschichte der bürgerlichen Geschichtswissenschaft." Beiträge zur Geschichte der Arbeiterbewegung 21 (1979) 3/358—371 p.

2.10.400.Schleier,Hans"Karl Schmückles Auseinandersetzung mit dem bürgerlichen deutschen Historismus." Jahrbuch für Geschichte 25 (1982) 305—325 p.

2.10.401. Schleier, Hans "Karl Lamprecht als Initiator einer intensivierten Forschung über die Geschichte der Geschichtsschreibung." Storia della Storiografia 2 (1982).

2.10.402. Schleier, Hans Grundlinien der bürgerlichen deutschen Geschichtsschreibung und Geschichtstheorien vor 1945. Hrg. von der Hauptabteilung Lehrerbildung des Ministeriums für Volksbildung. Manuskript. Berlin, 1983. 214 p.

2.10.403.Schleier,Hans"Zum idealistischen Historismus in der bürgerlichen deutschen Geschichtswissenschaft." Jahrbuch für Geschichte 28 (1983) 133—155 p.

2.10.404.Schleier,Hans "A historizmus problémája a német történettudományban." Történelmi Szemle 1985/2/374—384 p.

2.10.405.Schleier,Hans"Die Auseinandersetzung mit der Rankeschen Tradition Ende des 19. Jahrhunderts in Deutschland. Die deutschen Historiker und die Herausforderungen an die Geschichtswissenschaft." Jahrhbuch für Geschichte 32 (1985)

2.10.406.Schleier,Hans "Heinrich von Treitschke. Vom liberalen »Reichspropheten« zum polizeistaatlichen Historiker und »Sozialistentäter« In: *Seeber, Gustav (ed.)* Gestalten der Bismarckzeit. Vol. 2. Berlin, 1986.

2.10.407.Schleier,Hans"Der Kulturhistoriker Karl Lamprecht, der »Methodenstreit« und die Folgen". In: Karl Lamprecht: Alternative zu Ranke. Schriften zur Geschichtstheorie. Leipzig, 1988.7—45p.

2.10.408.Schleifstein,J. Franz Mehring. Sein marxistisches Schaffen 1891—1919.Berlin,1959.

2.10.409. Schmidt, Gustav Deutscher Historismus und der Übergang zur Demokratie. Untersuchungen zu den politischen Gedanken von Meinecke, Troeltsch, Max Weber. Lübeck, 1964. 327p.

2.10.410. Schmidt, Walter "Forschungen zur Geschichte der marxistisch-leninistischen Geschichtswissenschaft der DDR." Beiträge zur Geschichte der Arbeiterbewegung 21 (1979) 358—371 p.

2.10.411.Schmidt,Walter Nation und deutsche Geschichte in der bürgerlichen Ideologie der BRD. Berlin, 1980. 106 p.

2.10.412. Schmidt, Walter "Die Geschichtswissenschaft der DDR in den fünfziger Jahren." ZfG 31 (1983) 291—312 p.

2.10.413.Schmidt,Walter Zur Konstituierung der DDR Geschichtswissenschaft in den fünfziger Jahren. Berlin, 1984. 30 p.

2.10.414. Schmidt-Brücken, Sabine Leopold von Ranke im Spiegel der deutschsprachigen Literatur. (Manuskript) Frankfurt am Main, 1958.

2.10.415.Schmoller,G. Sybel und Treitschke. *In: Schmoller, G.* Charakterbilder. München—Leipzig, 1913.

2.10.416.Schneider,Friedrich Die neueren Anschauungen der deutschen Historiker über die deutsche Kaiserpolitik der Mittelalters und die mit ihr verbundene Ostpolitik. Weimar, 1904. 156 p.

2.10.417. Schneider, Friedrich Universalstaat oder National-staat. Macht und Ende des ersten deutschen Reiches. Die Streit-schriften von Heinrich von Sybel und Julius Ficker zur deutschen Kaiserpolitik des Mittelalters. Innsbruck, 1941.

2.10.418. Schochow, W. Deutsch-jüdische Geschichtswissen-schaft. Eine Geschichte ihrer Organisationsformen unter beson-derer Berücksichtigung der Fachbibliographie. West Berlin, 1969. 327 p.

2.10.419. Schoeps, Julius H. "Treitschke redivivus? Ernst Nolte und die Juden". Zeitschrift für Religions- und Geistesgeschichte 40(1988)2/170—176p.

2.10.420. Schorn-Schütte, Louise Karl Lamprecht: Kulturge-schichtsschreibung zwischen Wissenschaft und Politik. Göttingen, 1984. 373p.

2.10.421. Schönebaum, Herbert Karl Lamprecht. Leben und Werk eines Kämpfers um die Geschichtswissenschaft 1856—1915. Manuskript. Universitätsbibliotheken Leipzig und Bonn.

2.10.422. Schradi, Johannes Die DDR-Geschichtswissenschaft und das bürgerliche Erbe: das deutsche Bürgertum und die Revo-lution von 1848 im sozialistischen Geschichtsverständnis. Frank-furt am Main—Bern—N. Y., 1984. 324 p.

2.10.423. Schurig, E. Entwicklung der politischen Anschau-ungen Heinrich von Treitschkes. (Diss.) Heidelberg, 1909.

2.10.424. Schroeter, Manfred Metaphysik des Untergangs. Ei-ne kulturkritische Studie über Oswald Spengler. München, 1949. 270p.

2.10.425. Schulin, Ernst Die weltgeschichtliche Erfassung des Orients bei Hegel und Ranke. Göttingen, 1958.

2.10.426.Schulin,Ernst Traditionskritik und Rekonstruktionsversuch. Studien zur Entwicklung von Geschichtswissenschaft und historischem Denken. Göttingen, 1979. 299 p. (A collection of studies on German historiography and historical thought.)

2.10.427. Schulin, Ernst "Der Einfluß der Romantik auf die deutsche Geschichtsforschung". GWU 13 (1962) 404—423 p.

2.10.428.Schulin,Ernst "Das Problem der Individualität. Eine kritische Betrachtung des Historismus-Werkes von F. Meinecke". HZ 197 (1963) 102—133 p.

2.10.429. Schultz, W. "Der Einfluß lutherischen Geistes auf Rankes und Droysens Deutung der Geschichte". Archiv für Reformationsgeschichte 39 (1942) 108—142 p.

2.10.430. Schultze, J. "Zur Entstehungsgeschichte der Historischen Zeit". HZ 124 (1921).

2.10.431. Schulze, Winfried Deutsche Geschichtswissenschaft nach 1945. (HZ Beiheft, Neue Folge 10) München, 1988. 352 p.

2.10.432. Schumann, Peter Die deutschen Historikertage von 1893 bis 1937. Die Geschichte einer fachhistorischen Institution im Spiegel der Presse. Göttingen, 1975. 459 p.

2.10.433. Schumann, Peter "Gerhard Ritter und die deutsche Geschichtswissenschaft nach dem Zweiten Weltkrieg". *In:* Mentalitäten und Lebensverhältnisse. Beispiele aus der Sozialgeschichte der Neuzeit. Rudolf Vierhaus zum 60. Geburtstag. Herausgegeben von Mitarbeitern und Schülern. Göttingen, 1982. 399—415p.

2.10.434. Schwabe, K. Wissenschaft und Kriegsmoral 1914—1918.Göttingen,1970.

2.10.435. Schwabe, K. "Zur politischen Haltung der deutschen Professoren im Ersten Weltkrieg". HZ 193 (1961) 601—634 p.

2.10.436. Schwarz, G. M. Political attitudes in German universities during the reign of William II. 1890—1914. (Ph.D.thesis). Oxford,1962.

2.10.437. Seier, Helmut Die Staatsidee Heinrich von Sybels in den Wandlungen der Reichsgründungszeit, 1862—1871. Lübeck,1961.

2.10.438. Seifert, Friedrich Der Streit um K. Lamprechts Geschichtsphilosophie. Augsburg, 1925.

2.10.439. Seuffert, B. Rankes Schrift "Die großen Mächte". Graz,1935.

2.10.440. Sheehan, James "What is German history? Reflections on the role of the *Nation* in German history and historiography". Journal of Modern History 53 (1981) 1—23 p.

2.10.441. Simon, E. Ranke und Hegel. München, 1928. Beiheft 15. Historische Zeitschrift.

2.10.442. Simon, W. M. "Power and responsibility: Otto Hintze's place in German historiography". *In: Krieger, L. — Stern, F.(eds.)* The responsibility of power. N. Y. 1968.

2.10.443. Skalweit, St. "Ranke und Bismarck." HZ 176 (1953).

2.10.444. Smolenskij, N. J. "Leopold von Ranke. Metodologiâ i metodika istoričeskogo issledovaniâ". *In:* Metodologičeskie i istoriografičeskie voprosy istoričeskoj nauki. Vypusk 4. Tomsk, 1966.

2.10.445. Smolenskij, N. J. Princip istorizma v nacionalno-političeskoj istoriografii Germanii XIX v. M., 1978.

2.10.446. Sontag, Raymond J. "Heinrich von Treitschke". Foreign Affairs 18 (1939) 127—139 p.

2.10.447. Spieler, Karl-Heinz Untersuchungen zu J. G. Droysens Historik. Berlin, 1970. 152 p.

2.10.448. Sproemberg, Heinrich Mittelalter und demokratische Geschichtsschreibung. Ausgewählte Abhandlungen. Berlin; 1971. 460p.

2.10.449. Srbik, Heinrich Ritter von Geist und Geschichte vom deutschen Humanismus bis zur Gegenwart. 1-2. München, 1960—61. 436, 421 p.

2.10.450. Srbik, Heinrich Ritter von "Rankes Universalismus und Nationalbewußtsein". Mitteilungen des Österreichischen Instituts für Geschichtsforschung 52 (1968).

2.10.451. Stadelmann, R. "Jacob Burckhardts weltgeschichtliche Betrachtungen". HZ 169 (1949) 31—72 p.

2.10.452. Steinberg, Siegfried Die Geschichtswissenschaft der Gegenwart in Selbstdarstellungen. (Georg von Below, Alfons Dopsch, Heinrich Ficke, Walter Goetz, R.F. Kaindl, Max Lehmann, Georg Steinhausen.) Leipzig, 1925.

2.10.453. Steinbüchel, T. "Ranke und Hegel". *In:* Große Geschichtsdenker. Tübingen, 1949. 173—215 p.

2.10.454. Sterling, Richard W. Ethics in a world of power: the political ideas of Friedrich Meinecke. Princeton, 1958.

2.10.455. Stern, Leo et al. (eds.) Der Antikommunismus in Theorie und Praxis. Zur Auseinandersetzung mit der imperialistischen deutschen Geschichtsschreibung. Halle, 1963.

2.10.456. Streisand, Joachim "Progressive Traditionen und reaktionäre Anachronismen in der deutschen Geschichtswissenschaft".ZfG9(1961)8/1774—1788p.

2.10.457. Streisand, Joachim (ed.) Studien über die deutsche Geschichtswissenschaft I-II. Berlin, 1963—1965. 354, 442 p.

I. Die deutsche Geschichtswissenschaft vom Beginn des XIX. Jahrhunderts bis zur Reichseinigung von oben.

II. Die bürgerliche deutsche Geschichtsschreibung von der Reichseinigung von oben bis zur Befreiung Deutschlands vom Faschismus.

2.10.458. Streisand, Joachim Geschichtliches Denken von der deutschen Frühaufklärung bis zur Klassik. Berlin, 1964.

2.10.459. Sybel, Heinrich von "Über den Stand der neueren deutschen Geschichtsschreibung. Rede zur Feier des Geburtstages des Kurfürsten am 20.8.1856". *In:* Kleine Historische Schriften I. München, 1863. 343—359 p.

2.10.460. Sybel, Heinrich von "Gedächtnisrede auf Leopold von Ranke". HZ 56 (1886).

2.10.461. Tessitore, Fulvio Friedrich Meinecke, storico della idee. Firenze, Le Monnier, 1969.

2.10.462. Tessitore, Fulvio "La svolta dello storicismo negli anni di Weimar". Rivista storica italiana 91 (1979) 591—616 p.

2.10.463. Thimme, Annelise Hans Delbrück als Kritiker der Wilhelminischen Epoche. Düsseldorf, 1955.

2.10.464. Tod, Robert James Niebuhr 1776—1831: an appreciation in honour of the 200th anniversary of his birth. Cambridge, 1977. 14 p.

2.10.465. Tokody, Gy. "Der Weg der grossdeutschen Geschichtsschreibung zum Faschismus." Etudes Historiques Hongroises 1970. Budapest, 1970. 428—453 p.

2.10.466. Tornow, Elisabeth Der Revolutionsbegriff und die späte römische Republik: eine Studie zur deutschen Geschichts-

schreibung im 19. und 20. Jahrhundert. Lang. Frankfurt—Bern—
Nancy,1978.158p.

2.10.467.Tschuppik,Karl "Treitschke und die Folgen". Neue
Rundschau 41 (1930) 1/145—159p.

2.10.468. Vajnštejn, O. L. "Leopold von Ranke i sovremennaâ
buržuaznaâ istoriografiâ." *In: Vajnštejn, O. L. et al. (eds.)* Kritika
novejsejburžuaznojistoriografii.M.—Leningrad,1961.113—149
p. (One of the very few Soviet studies on Ranke.)

2.10.469. Varentrupp, C. "Rankes Historisch-Politische Zeitschrift und das Berliner Politische Wochenblatt". HZ 99 (1907)

2.10.470. Veit-Brause, Irmline "Zur Kritik an der Kritischen
Geschichtswissenschaft". GWU 31 (1984) 1—24 p.

2.10.471. Vierhaus, R. Ranke und die soziale Welt, Münster,
1957.

2.10.472. Vierhaus, R. "Zur Lage der historischen Forschung in
der Bundesrepublik Deutschland". *In:* Jahrbuch der historischen
Forschung in der Bundesrepublik Deutschland. Stuttgart,
1974.17—32p.

2.10.473. Vierhaus, R. "Geschichtswissenschaft: Situation—
Funktion—Aufgabe". *In:*WirtschaftundWissenschaft.1975.Heft
3.3—27p.

2.10.474. Viikari, Matti Die Krise der "historischen" Geschichtsschreibung und die Geschichtsmethodologie Karl Lamp-
rechts.Helsinki, 1977.

2.10.475.Voigt, Gerdt Otto Hoetzsch. 1876—1946. Wissenschaft und Politik im Leben eines deutschen Historikers. Berlin,1978.404p.Bibliography351—389p.

2.10.476.Voigt,Gerdt Die deutschen Rußlandhistoriker. 1843 bis 1933. Diss. B. Akademie der Wissenschaften der DDR. Berlin, 1986.

2.10.477.VomBruch,Rüdiger Wissenschaft, Politik und öffentliche Meinung. Gelehrtenpolitik im Wilhelmischen Deutschland. 1850—1914.Musum,1980.512p.

2.10.478. Vom Bruch, Rüdiger Weltpolitik als Kulturmission: auswärtige Kulturpolitik und Bildungsbürgertum in Deutschland am Vorabend des Ersten Weltkrieges. Paderbaum—München—Wien,1982.232p.

2.10.479.Vorob'ev,A.A. "Ob idejno-metodologičeskih osnovah istoriceskih vzglâdov Georga von Belowa". *In:* Metodologičeskie i istoriografičeskie voprosy istoričeskoj nauki. Vypusk 6. Tomsk, 1969.

2.10.480. Völker, Monika Die Auseinandersetzung mit der Französischen Revolution in der Geschichtsschreibung der »kleindeutschen« Schule (Diss.) Frankfurt am Main, 1974.

2.10.481. Vossler, O. Der Nationgedanke von Rousseau bis Ranke. Berlin, 1937.

2.10.482. Webb, W. P. "The historical seminar: its outer shell and its inner spirit." Mississippi Valley Historical Review 42 (1955) On Ranke's seminar.

2.10.483. Weber, Wolfgang Priester der Klio. Historisch-sozialwissenschaftliche Studien zur Herkunft und Karriere deutscher Historiker und zur Geschichte der Geschichtswissenschaft 1800—1970. Lange. Frankfurt am Main—Bern—N. Y.—Nancy, 1984. 613p.

2.10.484. Weber, Wolfgang Biographisches Lexikon zur Geschichtswissenschaft in Deutschland, Österreich und der Schweiz: die Lehrstuhlinhaber für Geschichte von den Anfängen des

Faches bis 1970. Lange. Frankfurt am Main—Bern—N. Y.—
Nancy,1984.697p.

2.10.485. Wegele, Franz X. von Geschichte der deutschen Historiographie seit dem Auftreten des Humanismus. München—
Leipzig,1885.1093p.

2.10.486. Wehler, Hans-Ulrich (ed.) Moderne deutsche Sozialgeschichte. Köln, 1966.

2.10.487. Wehler, Hans-Ulrich "Probleme der modernen deutschen Wirtschaftsgeschichte". *In:* Krisenherde des Kaiserreichs
1871—1918.Göttingen,1970.

2.10.488. Wehler, Hans-Ulrich (ed.) Deutsche Historiker.
(Kleine Vandenhoeck Reihe). Göttingen, 1971—82. I.—IX.

2.10.489. Wehler, Hans-Ulrich Einleitung. *In: Rosenberg, Arthur* Demokratie und Klassenkampf. Ausgewählte Studien. Herausgegeben und eingeleitet von *Hans-Ulrich Wehler.* Ullsteiner
Buch Nr.3041. Frankfurt am Main—Berlin—Wien, 1974. 307 p.
An introduction to Rosenberg's life-work and place in the development of German historiography.

2.10.490. Wehler, Hans-Ulrich Historische Sozialwissenschaft
und Geschichtsschreibung. Studien zu Aufgaben und Traditionen
deutscher Geschichtswissenschaft. Göttingen, 1980. 409 p.

2.10.491. Wehler, Hans-Ulrich Entsorgung der deutschen Vergangenheit. Ein polemischer Essay zum "Historikerstreit." München,1988.192p.

2.10.492. Weiss, Andreas von Die Diskussion über den historischen Materialismus in der deutschen Sozialdemokratie 1891—
1918.Wiesbaden,1965.

2.10.493. Weissbecker, Manfred Entteufelung der braunen
Barbarei. Zu einigen neueren Tendenzen in der Geschichtsschrei-

bung der BRD über Faschismus und faschistische Führer. Frankfurt am Main, 1975. 112 p.

2.10.494. Weisz, Christoph Geschichtsauffassung und politisches Denken. Münchener Historiker der Weimarer Zeit. Konrad Beyerle, Max Buchner, Michael Doeberl, Erich Marcks, Karl Alexander von Müller, Hermann Oncken. Beiträge zu einer historischen Strukturanalyse Bayerns im Industriezeitalter. Vol. 5. Berlin, 1970.

2.10.495. Wentzke, Paul "Über Treitschkes Deutsche Geschichte. Kritik von Freunden und Fachgenossen." *In:* Archiv für Politik und Geschichte, Monatschrift, Neue Folge der Hochschule, Vol. 2., 1924. 252—279 p.

2.10.496. Wenzel, Johannes Jacob Burckhardt in der Krise seiner Zeit. Berlin, 1967.

2.10.497. Werner, F. Geschichtswissenschaft. Freiburg, 1951. With a rich bibliography on the history of German historical writing.

2.10.498. Werner, Karl Ferdinand Das NS-Geschichtsbild und die deutsche Geschichtswissenschaft. Stuttgart—Berlin—Köln—Mainz, 1967. 123 p.

2.10.499. Wesendonck, H. Die Begründung der neueren deutschen Geschichtsschreibung durch Gatterer und Schlözer. Leipzig, 1876.

2.10.500. Westphal, O. "Der Staatsbegriff Henrich von Treitschkes." *In:* Deutscher Staat und deutsche Parteien. Beiträge zur deutschen Partei- und Ideengeschichte, F. Meinecke zum 60. Geburtstag dargebracht. München und Berlin, 1927. 155—200 p.

2.10.501. Wickert, Lothar Theodor Mommsen: eine Biographie. 1-4. Frankfurt am Main, 1959—1980.

2.10.502.Wilharm,Heiner Politik und Geschichte. Jakobinismusforschung in Deutschland. Frankfurt am Main—Bern—N. Y.
1. DDR, 1984. 207 p.
2. Bundesrepublik, 1984. 249 p.

2.10.503.Willey, Thomas E. Back to Kant: the revival of Kantianism in German social and historical thought, 1860—1914. Detroit, 1974.

2.10.504.Wines,Roger(ed.) Leopold von Ranke. The secret of world history. N. Y., 1981. (A study on Ranke + selection of Ranke-texts.)

2.10.505. Wittenberg, Erich Bismarcks politische Persönlichkeit im Bilde der Weimar-Republik. Eine ideengeschichtliche Betrachtung einer politischen Tradition. Vol. 1.: Geschichte und Tradition von 1918—1933 im Bismarckbild der deutschen Weimar-Republik. Ideengeschichtliches zum Aufkommen des totalitären Staates. Lund, 1969. 319 p.

2.10.506. Wittichen, Carl "Briefe von Gentz an Ranke". HZ 98 (1907) 329—336 p.

2.10.507. Wittichen, Paul "Briefe Rankes an Gentz". HZ 93 (1904). 876—888 p.

2.10.508. Wolandt, Ursel Die Einheit des christlichen Abendlandes als Leitidee in der Geschichtsschreibung Leopold von Rankes. (Diss.) Würzburg, 1950.

2.10.509. Wolf, Gustav Dietrich Schäfer und Hans Delbrück. Nationale Ziele der deutschen Geschichtsschreibung seit der französischen Revolution. Gotha, 1918.

2.10.510. Wolf, Heinz Deutsch-Jüdische Emigrationshistoriker in den USA und der Nationalsozialismus. Bern — N. Y. P. Lang, 1988. 557 p.

2.10. 511. Wolfson, Philip J. "Friedrich Meinecke (1862—1954)." Journal of the History of Ideas XVII (1956) 511—525 p.

2.10.512. Wucher, A. Theodor Mommsen. Geschichtsschreibung und Politik. Göttingen, 1956;

2.10.513. Wunderlich, Paul Die Beurteilung der Vorreformation in der deutschen Geschichtsschreibung seit Ranke. Erlangen, 1930.

2.10.514. Zeisler, K. Theodor Schiemann als Begründer der deutschen imperialistischen Ostforschung. (Diss.) Halle, 1963.

2.10.515. Zemlin, Michael-Joachim Geschichte zwischen Theorie und Theoria. Untersuchungen zur Geschichtsphilosophie Rankes. (Diss.) Köln, 1985.

2.10.516.Zemlin,Michael-Joachim "Zeigen, wie es eigentlich gewesen". Zur Deutung eines berühmten Rankewortes. GWU 33/1986/6/333—350p.

2.11. Great Britain

2.11.1. Abott, W. C. Adventures in reputation. Cambridge (Mass.), 1935. A chapter on Macaulay.

2.11.2. Altholz, Josef C. Newman and History. Victorian Studies, 7 (March, 1964).

2.11.3.Anderle, Othmar Das universalhistorische System A. J. Toynbees. Frankfurt, 1955.

2.11.4.Anderson, Ollive "The political uses of history in mid-19th century England". Past and Present 36 (1967) 88—105 p.

2.11.5.Angus-Buttersworth, L.M. Ten master historians. Aberdeen, 1961. Hume, Smith, Goldsmith, Gibbon, Southey, Prescott, Macaulay, Froude, Green, Churchill.

2.11.6.Ashley, Maurice Churchill as historian. L., 1968.

2.11.7. Auchmuty, James Johnston Lecky. A biographical and critical essay. Dublin, 1945. 134 p.

2.11.8.Aaroyn, Giles St. Victorian eminence. Life and works of Thomas Henry Buckle. L., 1958.

2.11.9. Ausubel, H.—Brebner, J.B.—Hunt, E. H. (eds.) Some modern historians of Britain. Essays in honour of R. L. Schuyler. N.Y., 1951. Essays on Hallam, Carlyle, Froude, Tawney, Namier, Fower, Heldsworth, Andrews, Trevelyan, Churchill, Beer, Lecky.

2.11.10. Bann, Stephen The clothing of Clio. A study of the representation of history in 19th century Britain and France. Cambridge, 1984. 196 p.

2.11.11. Beatty, Richmond Croom Lord Macaulay: Victorian liberal. University of Oklahoma Press, 1938. 381 p.

2.11.12.Bell, H.E. Maitland. A critical examination and assessment. L., 1965.

2.11.13.Ben-Israel, Hedvah English historians on the French Revolution. Cambridge, 1968. 321 p.

2.11.14.Berlin, I. "L. B. Namier. A personal impression". Journal of Historical Studies 1 (Winter, 1968) 117—136 p.

2.11.15.Blaas, P.B.M. Continuity and anachronism. Parliamentary and constitutional development in whig historiography and in the anti-whig reaction between 1890 and 1930. The Hague—Boston—L., 1978. 441 p.

2.11.16.Bockhorn,Klaus Der deutsche Historismus in England. Göttingen, 1950.

2.11.17.Brasher,N.H. Argumentation in History: Britain in the nineteenth century. L., 1968.

2.11.18.Brentano,R. "The sound of Stubbs." Journal of British Studies VI/2 (May 1967).

2.11.19.Brooke,John "Namier and Namierism." HT III (1964) 331—347p.

2.11. 20. Brooke, John "Namier and his critics." Encounter February 1965. 7—49 p.

2.11.21.Brown,D. Walter Scott and the historical imagination. L.,1979.

2.11.22.Buckley,Jerome H. The triumph of time. A study of the Victorian concepts of time, history, progress and decadence. Cambridge (Mass.), 1966.

2.11.23.Burrow,J.W. "The village community" and the uses of history in late nineteenth century England. *In: N. McKundrick (ed.)*Historical perspectives. Studies in English thought and society in honour of J. H. Plumb. L., 1974.

2.11.24. Burrow, J. W. A liberal descent. Victorian historians and the English past. Cambridge University Press, 1981. 308 p.

*2.11.25.Butterfield,Herbert*The whig interpretation of history. L.,1931.

2.11.26.Butterfield,Herbert The Englishman and his history. 2 vols. Cambridge, 1944.

2.11.27.Butterfield,Herbert Lord Acton. L., 1948.

2.11.28.Butterfield, Herbert "The originality of the Namier school". Cambridge Review 25 May, 1957.

2.11.29.Butterfield, Herbert "Sir Lewis Namier as historian." The Listener 18 May 1961/873—876p.

2.11.30.Butterfield, Herbert George III. and the historians. L., 1957. Rev.ed. N.Y., 1959.

2.11.31. Cairns, J.C. "Sir Lewis Namier and the history of Europe". Historical Reflections 1 (1974)

2.11.32. Cam, Helen "Stubbs seventy years after." Cambridge Historical Journal IX(1948) no. 2.

2.11.33. Canning, Albert S.G. Macaulay, essayist and historian. L., 1913. 288 p.

2.11.34.Carpenter,L.P. G.D.H. Cole: an intellectual biography. L., 1973. 271 p.

2.11.35. Chadwick, Owen Acton and Gladstone. L., 1976. (Creighton lectures in history, 1975) 56 p.

2.11.36. Clark, G. Kitson "A hundred years of the teaching of history at Cambridge, 1873—1973" Historical Journal XVI (1973)

2.11.37. Clark, G.N. "The origins of the Cambridge Modern History." Cambridge Historical Journal VIII (1945) 57—64 p.

2.11.38. Clive, John Leonard "British history 1870—1914 reconsidered: recent trends in the historiography of the period" AHR 68 (July 1963) 987—1009p.

2.11.39.Clive,J.L. Thomas Babington Macaulay. The shaping of the historian. L., 1973. 499 p.

2.11.40.Cobb, Richard Charles Modern French history in Britain. L., 1974. (Raleigh lectures on history.)

2.11.41. Colbourn, H. Trevor The lamp of experience: whig history and the intellectual origins of the American Revolution. Chapel Hill, 1965.

2.11.42.Cronin, James "Creating a Marxist historiography: the contribution of Hobsbawm." Radical History Review 19 (1979) 87—109p.

2.11.43.Deakin, Frederick William Dampier Churchill, the historian. Zürich, 1970. 19 p. (Winston Churchill memorial lectures, 1969)

2.11.44.Dockhorn, Klaus Der deutsche Historismus in England: ein Beitrag zur englischen Geistesgeschichte des 19. Jahrhunderts. Göttingen—Baltimore, 1950. 230 p.

2.11.45. Dunn, Waldo Hilary James Anthony Froude. A biography. I (1818—1856), Oxford, 1961., II., Oxford, 1964.

2.11.46.Edwards, Owen Dudley Macaulay. N.Y., 1988. 182 p.

2.11.47. Elton, G. R. Modern historians on British history 1485—1945: a critical bibliography 1945—1969. L.—Ithaca, N.Y., 1970.

2.11.48. Elton, G. R. "Herbert Butterfield and the study of history." Historical Journal 27 (1984) 3/729—743 p.

2.11.49. Elton, G. R. F.W. Maitland. New Haven—L.—Yale University Press, 1985. 18 p.

2.11.50. Engel, A. J. From clergyman to don: the rise of the academic profession in nineteenth-century Oxford. Oxford, 1983.

2.11.51.Erdmann,KarlDietrich "Das Problem des Historismus in der neueren englischen Geschichtswissenschaft." HZ 170 (1950)73—89p.

2.11.52.Erofeev,N.A."Lewis Namier and his place in bourgeois historiography." Soviet Studies in History 15 (1976—77)3/26—50

2.11.53.Eyck,Frank G.P.Gooch, a study in history and politics. L.,1982.498p.

2.11.54. Fahey, David M. "Henry Hallam. A conservative as whig historian". The Historian 28 (1966) no.4.

2.11.55.Fahey,DavidM. "Gardiner and Usher in perspective". Journal of Historical Studies I (1968), 137—150p.

*2.11.56.Fielding, K.J.—Tarr, R.L. (eds.)*Carlyle past and present.L.,1976.

2.11.57. Firth, C.H. Modern history in Oxford. 1841—1918. Oxford,1920.

2.11.58. Firth, C. H. A commentary on Macaulay's history of England.L.,1938.

2.11.59.Fischer,H.A.L. The whig historians. L., 1928.

2.11.60.Forbes,Duncan "Historismus in England". Cambridge Journal IV (1951), 387-400. p. (On the limited impact of Historismus in England.)

2.11.61.Forbes, Duncan The liberal Anglican idea of history. Cambridge, 1952.

2.11.62.Frédericq, Paul The study of history in England and Scotland. Baltimore, 1887.

2.11.63. Furber, E. Ch. (ed.) Changing views of British history. Essays on historical writing since 1939. For the conference on British studies. Cambridge (Mass.), 1966.

2.11.64. Gargan, Edward T. (ed.) The intent of Toynbee's history. Chicago, 1961.

2.11.65. Garside, P.B. "Scotland: the philosophical historians." Journal of the History of Ideas XXXVI (1975)

2.11.66. George, G. H. "Puritanism as history and historiography". Past and Present no. 41. (1968) 77–104.p.

2.11.67. Goldberg, A.L. "Istoriâ Rossii v krugu »lokalnyh civilizacij« (koncepciâ russkoj istorii v trudah A. Toynbee". *In: Vajnštein, O. L. (ed.).* Kritika noveǰsej burzuaznoj istoriografii. Leningrad, 1967. 177—205 p.

2.11.68. Goldstein, Doriss "The professionalization of history in Britain in the late nineteenth-early twentieth centuries". Storia della Storiografia no.3., 1983. 3—27 p.

2.11.69. Grant, A.J. (ed.) English historians. L., 1906. Reprint: Port Washington (Kennikat Press), 1971. 251 p. (Selection from historians illustrating methods)

2.11.70. Gutnova, E.V. "Rodzers i vozniknovenie istoriko-ekonimičeskogo napravleniâ v anglijskoj medievistike". Srednie veka. Vypusk XVII. M., (1960)

2.11.71. Hale, J.R. (ed.) The evolution of British historiography: from Bacon to Namier. Cleveland, 1964—L., 1967. (A cogent introductory essay, followed by brief extracts). A critical review: *Butterfield, Herbert* "Narrative history and the spade-work behind it". History 53 (June, 1968) 165—180 p.

2.11.72. Hamburger, Joseph Macaulay and the whig tradition. Chicago, 1976. 274 p.

2.11.73.Harrold,C.F. Carlyle and German thought. New Haven,1934.

2.11.74.Hart,Jennifer "Nineteenth century social reform. A Tory interpretation of history." *In: Flinn, M. W.—Smaut, T. C. (eds.)*Essays in social history. Oxford, 1974.

2.11.75.Hartman,M.P. Contemporary explanations of the English Revolution. Cambridge, Ph.D. dissertation. 1977.

*2.11.76.Harvie,Christopher*The lights of liberalism. University liberals and the challenge of democracy 1860—1886. L., 1976.

2.11.77. Herman, Joseph H. "The last whig historian and consensus history". AHR LCXXI (1976) 166—197 p. (On G.M. Trevelyan)

2.11.78.Hexter,J.H. "Storm over the gentry. The Tawney-Trevor-Roper controversy." Encounter No. 56 (May, 1958) 23—34 p.

2.11.79.Heyck, T. W. The transformation of intellectual life in Victorian England. L., 1981.

2.11.80.Hill,Christopher"The Norman yoke." In his Puritanism and revolution. L., 1958.

2.11.81. Himmelfarb, Gertrude Lord Acton. A study in conscience and politics. Chicago, 1952.

2.11.82.Himmelfarb, G. Victorian minds. (Four essays on Froude and Acton) L., 1966.

2.11.83. Hinton, R. W. K. "History Yesterday: five points about whig history". History Today 9 (November 1959) 720—728 p.

2.11.84.Holloway,John The Victorian Sage. Norton, 1965.

2.11.85.Hoskins, W.G. Local history in England, L., 1959.

2.11.86.Houghton, WalterE. The Victorian frame of mind. New Haven (Conn.), 1957.

2.11.87.Hurstfield,Joel "That arch-liar Froude". The Listener 50 (July 9, 1953)

2.11.88.Hurstfield,J. The historian as moralist: reflections on the study of Tudor England. L., 1975. (John Coffin memorial lecture), 37 p.

2.11.89.Huth,AlfredH. The life and writings of Henry Thomas Buckle. N. Y., 1980.

2.11.90.Irmschler,Konrad Analyse und Kritik einiger theoretisch-methodologischer Entwicklungstendenzen in der bürgerlichen Historiographie der 80er Jahre. Diss. B. Berlin, Akademie für Gesellschaftswissenschaften beim ZK der SED, 1983. 154 p. (Mainly England)

2.11.91. Jann, Rosemary "From amateur to professional: the cases of the Oxbridge historians". Journal of British Studies 22 (1983)2/122—147p.

2.11.92. Jann, Rosemary The art and science of Victorian history. Columbus, Ohio State University Press, 1985. 272 p.

2.11.93.Jeffares,A.N.(ed.) Scott's mind and art. L., 1969.

2.11.94. Jones, Thomas Martin The Becket controversy. N. Y., 1970.Cambridge,1984.

2.11.95. Kaplan, Fred Thomas Carlyle: a biography. Ithaca, N. Y., 1983. 614 p.

2.11.96. Kaye, Harvey J. The British Marxist historians. Cambridge, 1984. 316 p.

2.11.97.Kenyon, John The history men. The historical profession in England since the Renaissance. L., 1983. 322 p.

2.11.98.Koch, DorothyA. English theories concerning the nature and use of history. Yale, 1946. Ph. D. dissertation

2.11.99.Kochan, L. Acton on history. L., 1954.

2.11.100.Lehman, B.H. Carlyle's theory of the hero. Its sources, development, history and influence on Carlyle's work. A study of a nineteenth century idea. L., without date.

2.11.101.Levine, G. The boundaries of fiction. Carlyle, Macaulay, Newman. L., 1968.

2.11.102. Lottenburger, H. Die Geschichtsphilosophie H. T. Buckles. München, 1912. Diss.

2.11.103. Mac Elrath, Damian Lord Acton. The decisive decade, 1864—1874. Essays and documents. Louvain, 1970. 275 p.

2.11.104.Maitland, FredericWilliam William Stubbs, bishop of Oxford. Selected historical essays (*ed. Carr, H.*) L., 1957.

2.11.105.Maitland, Frederic William Selections from his writings. Ed. with an introduction by Robert Livingston Schuyler. Berkeley, University of California Press, 1960.

2.11.106.Manbi, L.M. "Nekotorye voprosy razvitiâ progressivnojistoriografii v Anglii" VI 1963/5/76—90 p.

2.11.107."Marxism and history. The British contribution". Radical History Review 19 (Winter 1978—1979)

2.11.108. Mason, Henry L. Toynbee's approach to world politics. New Orleans, 1958.

2.11.109.Masur, Gerhard "Arnold Toynbees Philosophie der Geschichte". HZ CLXXIV (1952) 269—286 p.

2.11.110.Mathew,David Acton. The formative years. L., 1946.

2.11.111.Mathew,David Lord Acton and his times L., 1968.

2.11.112.McCartney,Donal "W. E. H. Lecky". Irish Historical Studies 14 (1964) 119—141 p.

2.11.113.McLachlon,J. "The origin and early development of the Cambridge historical tripos". Cambridge Historical Journal 9 (1947).

2.11.114.McNeill, William H. (ed.) Lord Acton. Essays in the liberal interpretation of history. Chicago, 1966.

2.11.115.Mechta,Ved. Fly and the Fly-battle: encounters with British intellectuals. L., 1963.

2.11.116.Messerschmidt,Manfred Deutschland in englischer Sicht. Die Wandlungen des Deutschlandbildes in der englischen Geschichtsschreibung. Düsseldorf, 1955. 191 p.

2.11.117.Mitchell,H. "Hobson revisited". Journal of the History of Ideas 26 (1966) no.3.

2.11.118.Montagu, M.F.A. (ed.) Toynbee and history. Critical essays and reviews. Boston, 1956.

2.11.119.Montpensier, Roy Stone de "Maitland and the interpretation of history". American Journal of Legal History X (1966)

2.11.120.Mossner,E.C. "Was Hume a Tory historian?" Journal of the History of Ideas 2 (1941)

2.11.121.Mowat,CharlesLoch Great Britain since 1914. Ithaca, N. Y., 1971. 224 p. (The sources of history: studies in the uses
of historical evidence.)

2.11.122.Namier,JuliaLady Lewis Namier: a biography. L.—
N. Y.—Toronto. Oxford University Press, 1971. 347 p.

2.11.123.Newman, Bertram (ed.) English historians. Selected
passages.L.,1957.

*2.11.124.Nurser,J.S.*The idea of conscience in the work of Lord
Acton. Ph. D. thesis, Cambridge, 1958.

2.11.125.Owen, John "Professor Butterfield and the Namier
school". Cambridge Review 10 May 1958.

2.11.126.Owen, John "The Namier way". New Statesman 26
Jan.1962.

2.11.127. Palmer, D. Bryan The making of E. P. Thompson.
Marxism, humanism, and history. Toronto, 1981. 145 p.

*2.11.128.Parker,Christopher*The development of history cour-
ses in British universities 1850—1945. A dissertation. Exeter,
1976.

2.11.129.Parker,Christopher"English historians and the oppo-
sition to positivism." HT 22 (1983) 2/120—145 p.

2.11.130. Parker, Irene Dissenting academics in England.
Cambridge (Mass.), 1914.

2.11.131.Paul,Herbert Life of Froude. L., 1905.

2.11.132. Peardon, T.P. The transition in English historical
writing,1760—1830.N.Y.,1933.Reprint 1966.340p.

2.11.133.Perkin,Harold "Social history in Britain". Journal of Social History 10 (1976) 2/129—143 p.

2.11.134.Plumb, J.H. "The atomic historian". New Statesman 1 Aug. 1969. (On Namier.)

2.11.135.Plumb, J.H. G. M. Trevelyan. L., 1951.

2.11.136.Preyer,Robert Bentham, Coleridge and the science of history. Bochum, 1958.

2.11.137.Price,JacobM. "Party, purpose and pattern: Sir Lewis Namier and his critics". Journal of British Studies I (1961) 71-81 p. The ensuing debate on Namier in the Journal: *Mansfield,Harvey C.* "Sir Lewis Namier considered". II (1962) 28-35 p. *Walcott, Robert* "Sir Lewis Namier considered". III (1964) 85 p. *Mansfield, HarveyC.* "Sir Lewis Namier again considered". III (1964) 109-115 p.

2.11.138.Rabinowicz, OskarKwasnitt Arnold Toynbee on Judaism and Zionism. A critique. L., 1974. 372 p.

*2.11.139.Rein,Adolf*Sir John Robert Seeley. Eine Studie über den Historiker. Langensalza, 1912. 112 p.

2.11.140. Robertson, J. G. Buckle and his critics. A study in sociology.L.,1895.

2.11.141. Rose, Norman Lewis Namier and Zionism. Oxford, 1980. 182 p. (Covers numerous aspects of Namier's career, not only the problem of Zionism.)

2.11.142.Rosenberg, JohnD. Carlye and the burden of history. Cambridge (Mass.), 1985. 209 p.

*2.11.143.Rotenstreich,Nathan*Philosophy, history and politics. Studies in contemporary English philosophy of history. The Hague, 1976.

2.11.144.Rothblatt,Sheldon The revolution of the dons. Cambridge,1968.

2.11.145.Saleh,Zaki Trevor-Roper's critique of Arnold Toynbee. A symptom of intellectual chaos. Baghdad, 1958.

2.11.146.Sarifzanov,I.I."Idejno-metodologičeskie osnovy istoričeskich vzglådov Lorda Actona". *In:* Metodologičeskie i istoriografičeskie voprosy istoričeskoj nauki. Vypusk 6. Tomsk, 1969.

2.11.147. Schlatter, Richard (edited by for a conference on British studies.) Recent views on British history: essays on historical writing since 1966. New Brunswick (N. J.), 1984. 525 p.

2.11.148. Schuetinger, Robert L. Lord Acton. Historian of liberty. Open Court. La Salle (Illinois), 1976.

2.11.149. Schuyler, Robert Livingston "Macaulay and his history: a hundred years after". Political Science Quarterly no. 63. (1948)161—193p.

2.11.150. Schuyler, Robert Livingston "J. R. Green and his short history". Political Science Quarterly 1949.

2.11.151. Schuyler, Robert Livingston "The historical spirit incarnate Frederic William Maitland". AHR LVII (1952) 303—322 p.

2.11.152.Sedgwick,Romney "The Namier revolution". History Today 10 (1960) 723—34 p.

2.11.153.Semenov,U.N. Social'naâ filosofiâ A. Toynbee. Kriticesky ocerk. M., 1980. 200 p.

2.11.154.Skinner,Quentin "History and ideology in the English Revolution". History Journal 8 (1965) 151—178 p.

2.11.155. Smith, A. L. Frederic William Maitland. Oxford, 1968. 71 p.

2.11.156.Smith,E.J. "Sir Lewis Namier and British eighteenth-century history". Parliamentary Affairs 17 (1963—64) 465—469 p.

2.11.157. Smith, Lacey Baldwin "A study of textbooks on European history during the last fifty years". Journal of Modern History XXIII (September, 1951) 250—256 p.

2.11.158. Stephens, W. R. W. The life and letters of E. A. Freeman. L., 1895. I-II.

2.11.159.Street,Pamela Arthur Bryant: portrait of an historian. L.—Sidney—Toronto, 1979. 232 p.

2.11.160. Stromberg,Roland Nelson Arnold J. Toynbee: historian for an age in crisis. With a preface by Moore, Henry Thomson. L.—Amsterdam, 1972. 152 p.

2.11.161.Stubbs,William Two lectures on the present state and prospects of historical study. Oxford, 1876.

2.11.162. Sutherland, L. Sir Lewis Namier. Proceedings of the British Academy 48 (1962).

2.11.163.Taine,H. L'idealisme anglais. Etude sur Carlyle. Paris—L.—N.Y., 1864. 187 p.

2.11.164. Taylor, Arthur "History at Leeds 1877—1974: the evolution of a discipline". Northern History X (1975) 141—164 p.

2.11.165.Terrill,Ross R.H. Tawney and his times. Socialism as fellowship. L., 1974. 373 p.

2.11.166. Times Literary Supplement, 6 Jan. 1956. Special edition on the 50th anniversary of the Historical Association: Historical Writing.

*2.11.167.*Toynbee and history. Critical essays and reviews. *Ed. M. F. Ashley Montagu.* Boston, 1956.

*2.11.168.*Toynbee on Toynbee. A conversation between Arnold J. Toynbee and G. R. Urban. N.Y.—Oxford University Press, 1974.113p.

2.11.169.Toynbee,A.J. "Lewis Namier. Historian". Encounter January 1961.

2.11.170. Trevelyan, Sir George Otto The life and letters of Lord Macaulay. N.Y., 1875.

2.11.171. Uhner, R. G. A critical study of the historical method of Samuel Rawson Gardiner. St. Louis, 1915.

2.11.172.Vinogradov,K.B. Ocerki angliskoj istoriografii novovo i novejševo vremeni. Leningrad, 1959. 96 p. 1975

2.11.173. Wash, W. H. "History and Theory" Encounter 18 (June 1962) 50—54 p. An essay on why British historians are disinterested in the philosophy of history.

2.11.174.Ward,Addison "The Tory view of Roman history". Studies in English Literature 4 (Summer 1964) 413—456 p.

2.11.175. Watson, Charles A. The writing of history in Britain. A bibliography of past 1945 writings about British historians and biographers. N.Y., 1982. 726 p.

2.11.176.Wellek,René "Carlyle and the philosophy of history". Philological Quarterly 23 (1944) 55—76 p.

2.11.177. Wells, G.A. The critics of Buckle. Past and Present no.9. (1956) 75—89 p.

2.11.178.White,F.James The Cambridge movement. The ecclesiologists and the Gothic revival. Cambridge, 1962.

2.11.179.Winkler,H.R. "Sir Lewis Namier". Journal of Modern History 35., no. 1. (March, 1963) 1—19 p.

2.11.180. Woodward, E. L. "British Historians". *In: Turner, W. J. (ed.)* Impressions of English literature. L., 1944. 143—184 p.

2.11.181.Woodward,E.L. "Some considerations on the present state of historical studies". *In: Sutherland, Lucy (ed.)* Studies in history. British Academy Lectures. Oxford, 1966.

2.11.182. Woodward, E.L. "The rise of the professional historian in England." *In: Bourne, K.—Watt, A. C.* Studies in international history. Essays presented to W.N. Medlicott. L., 1967.

2.11.183. Wormell, Deborah Sir John Seeley and the uses of history. Cambridge, 1980. 233 p.

2.11.184. Yoder, E. M. "Macaulay revisited". South Atlantic Quarterly 63 (1964) no. 4.

2.11.185. Young, L. M. Thomas Carlyle and the art of history. Philadelphia, 1939.

2.11.186. Zahn, Ernst, F. J. Toynbee und das Problem der Geschichte: eine Auseinandersetzung mit dem Evolutionismus. Köln, 1954.

2.11.187.Zimilcina, L.A. "Sovetskaâ i anglijskaâ progressivnaâ istoriografiâ poslevoennoj istorii Anglii (1945—1971)". *In: Kurginân, E. A. (ed.)* Voprosy istoriografii novoj i novejšej istorii. M., 1973.

2.12.Greece

2.12.1.Augustinus, Gerasimos Consciousness and history: nationalist critics of Greek society 1897—1914. N.Y., 1977.

2.13.Hungary

2.13.1.Arató,Endre "Die ungarische Geschichtschreibung nach 1945 und ihre Aufgaben." *In*: Jahrbuch für Geschichte der UdSSR und der volksdemokratischen Länder Europas. 8 (1964) 375—424 p.

2.13.2. Baráth, Tibor "L'histoire en Hongrie". Revue Historique, 177 (1936) 84—144 p. and 178 (1936), 25—74 p. Also as an offprint.

2.13.3. Baráth, Tibor A külföldi magyarság ideológiája. Történetpolitikai tanulmányok. Montreal, 1975.

2.13.4. Bellér, Béla "A Dózsa-parasztháború történetpolitikai koncepciója és történeti képe 1945 előtti történetirásunkban." Történelmi Szemle 1974 (17) 3/289—325 p.

2.13.5.Borsody,Stephen "Modern Hungarian Historiography". Journal of Modern History 24 (December, 1952) 398—405 p.

2.13.6. Dénes, Iván Zoltán A "realitás" illuziója. A historikus Szekfű Gyula pályafordulója, Budapest, 1976. 190 p.

2.13.7. Domanovszky, Sándor L'organisation des historiens en Hongrie. Bulletin of the international comittee of historical sciences II.

2.13.8. Fischer, Holger Politik und Geschichtswissenschaft in Ungarn. Die ungarische Geschichte von 1918 bis zur Gegenwart in der Historiographie seit 1956. München, 1982. 179 p. (Untersuchungen zur Gegenwartskunde Südosteuropas Bd. 19)

2.13.9.Flegler,Sándor A magyar történetírás történelme. Budapest, 1877. 303 p. First published as *Flegler, Alexander* "Beiträge zur Würdigung der ungarischen Geschichtsschreibung". HistorischeZeitschrift17—19(1875—1877)319—,236—282,265—346

p. Published together with *Sayous, Éduard* A magyar történelem kútforrásai.

2.13.10.Glatz,Ferenc "Historiography, cultural policy and the organization of scholarship in Hungary in the 1920s". Acta Historica 16 (1970) 273—293 p.

2.13.11.Glatz, Ferenc "Domanovszky Sándor helye a magyar történettudományban". Századok 112/12 (1978) 211—234 p.

2.13.12.Glatz Ferenc Domanovszky Sándor (1877—1955) *In: Domanovszky Sándor* Gazdaság és társadalom a középkorban. Válogatta, sajtó alá rendezte, szerkesztette és a bevezető tanulmányt írta *Glatz, Ferenc*. Budapest, 1979. 371 p.

2.13.13. Glatz, Ferenc Történetíró és politika. Szekfü, Steier, Thim és Miskolczy nemzetről és államról. Budapest, 1980. 267 p.

2.13.14.Glatz, Ferenc "Der Zusammenbruch der Habsburger Monarchie und die ungarische Geschichtswissenschaft". Etudes Historiques Hongroises 1980. Budapest, 1980. II/575—593 p.

2.13.15.Glatz, Ferenc "A marxizmus poziciói a magyar történettudományban." Magyar Tudomány (24) 1983 8/518—528 p.

2.13.16. Glatz, Ferenc "Történetíró, nemzet, társadalom". *In:* Szekfű, Gyula Forradalom után. Sajtó alá rendezte, és a bevezető tanulmányt írta Glatz Ferenc. Budapest, 1983. 244 p.

2.13.17.Glatz,Ferenc Ungarische Historiker — Historiker der Habsburgermonarchie. *In: Glatz, Ferenc—Mellville, Ralph (eds.)* Gesellschaft, Politik und Verwaltung in der Habsburgermonarchie 1830—1918. Stuttgart, 1987. 1—21 p.

2.13.18.Gunst,Péter Acsády Ignác történetírása. Budapest, 1961. 314 p.

2.13.19.Gunst,Péter Marczali Henrik. Budapest, 1983. 202 p.

2.13.20.Gunst, Péter Marczali Henrik (1856—1940) *In: Marczali, Henrik* Világtörténelem — magyar történelem. Válogatta, sajtó alá rendezte és a bevezető tanulmányt írta *Gunst, Péter.* Budapest, 1982. 662 p.

2.13.21. Hóman, Bálint (ed.) A magyar történetírás új útjai. Budapest, 1931. 463 p.

2.13.22. Irinyi, Károly "Hajnal István szociológiai történetszemlélete". Annales Instituti Historici Universitatis Scientiarum Debreciensis de Ludovico Kossuth nominetae, 1962. 167—183p.

2.13.23. Léderer, Emma A magyar polgári történetírás rövid története. Budapest, 1969. 197 p.

2.13.24.Lékai,Lajos A magyar történetírás, 1790—1830. Budapest,1942.

2.13.25. Lékai, Louis J. "Historiography in Hungary, 1790—1848". Journal of Central European Affairs 14 (1954) 3—18 p.

2.13.26.Litván,György Szabó Ervin, a történetíró. *In: Szabó Ervin* történeti írásai. Válogatta, a sajtó alá rendezte és a bevezető tanulmányt írta *Litván,György.* Budapest, 1979. 714 p. 5—19 p.

2.13.27.Lukinich,Imre Histoire de la Sociéte Historique Hongroise 1876—1917. Budapest, 1918. L'Academie Hongroise et les sciences historiques en Hongrie. Revue des études hongroises IV (1926).

2.13.28. Mályusz, Elemér A magyar történettudomány. Budapest, 1942. 156 p.

2.13.29. Márki, Sándor Történet és történetírás. Budapest, 1914. 138 p.

2.13.30.Márki,Sándor Horváth Mihály. Budapest, 1917.

2.13.31. Márkus, László A szociáldemokrata történetfelfogás fejlődéséhez. (A kezdettől 1918-ig) Budapest, 1963. 210 p.

2.13.32. Pach, Zsigmond Pál "Marxista történettudományunk fejlődésének problémái." Századok 98 (1964) 5—6/1011—1052 p.

2.13.33. Pach, Zsigmond Pál "A történetíró Molnár Erik." Történelmi Szemle 24 (1981) 4/513—520 p.

2.13.34. Pach, Zsigmond Pál Történetszemlélet és történettudomány. Budapest, 1977. 565 p.

2.13.35. Pach, Zsigmond Pál — Pamlényi, Ervin Les sciences historiques en Hongrie. Budapest, 1975. 22 p. (Studie Historica Academiae Scientiarum Hungaricae. 87.) Published also in Russian: Istoriceskaâ nauka v Vengrii. Budapest, 1975. 24 p. (Studia Historica Academiae Scientiarum Hungaricae 88.)

2.13.36. Pajewski, J. Sociétes historiques en Hongrie. Bulletin d'Information des sciences historiques en Europe Orientale V (1933).

2.13.37. Pál, Lajos Horváth Mihály (1809—1878) *In: Horváth, Mihály* Polgárosodás, liberalizmus, függetlenségi harc. Válogatott írások. Válogatta, sajtó alá rendezte és a bevezető tanulmányt írta *Pál, Lajos.* Budapest, 1986. 511 p.

2.13.38. Pamlényi, Ervin Horváth Mihály. Budapest, 1954. 101 p.

2.13.39. Pamlényi, Ervin "Szalay László: Magyarország története." A Magyar Tudományos Akadémia Társadalmi–Történeti Tudományok Osztályának közleményei XIV/1965/29—40 p.

2.13.40. Pók, Attila "A Huszadik Század körének történetfelfogása" *In:* A Huszadik Század körének történetfelfogása. Válogatta, sajtó alá rendezte, szerkesztette és a bevezető tanulmányt írta *Pók, Attila* Budapest, 1982. 436 p.

2.13.41.Pók,Attila "Rankes Einfluß auf Geschichtschreibung und Geschichtsdenken in Ungarn — ein historisierter Historiker". *In: Mommsen, Wolfgang J. (ed.)* Leopold von Ranke und die moderne Geschichtswissenschaft. Köln, 1988. 201-214 p.

2.13.42.Rottler,Ferenc "Beiträge zur Kritik der Historiographie des frühen Mittelalters. Über die Geschichtsanschauung László Erdélyis". *In: Oroszlán, Zoltán (ed.)* Annales Sectio Historica. III.Budapest,1961.121—152p.

2.13.43. Rottler, Ferenc "Beiträge zum Versuch der Bildung einer Gruppe von kirchlichen Geschichtsschreibern in Ungarn der 1860-er Jahre". Acta Historica Academiae Scientiarum Hungaricae 19 (1973) 1—53 p.

2.13.44.Rottler,Ferenc "Katolikus történetírók a kiegyezés korában". *In:* Egyház, műveltség, történetírás. Excerpts from the works of *Rómer, Flóris—Ipolyi,Arnold—Fraknói, Vilmos* Válogatta, sajtó alá rendezte, szerkesztette és a bevezető tanulmányt írta *Rottler, Ferenc*. Budapest, 1981. 389 p.

2.13.45. R.Várkonyi Ágnes Thaly Kálmán és történetírása. Budapest,1961.

2.13.46. R. Várkonyi Ágnes "Buckle and Hungarian bourgeois historiography". Acta Historica Academiae Scientiarum Hungaricae 10 (1963) 49—86 p.

2.13.47.R.Várkonyi Ágnes "The impact of scientific thinking on Hungarian historiography about the middle of the 19th century". Acta Historica Academiae Scientiarum Hungaricae 14 (1968) 1—20p.

2.13.48. R. Várkonyi Ágnes A pozitivista történetszemlélet a magyar történetírásban. 1—2. Budapest, 1973. 308, 521 p.

2.13.49. Steinmüller, Éva "Zehn Jahre neue ungarische Geschichtsschreibung". ZfG 4 (1956) 369—376 p.

2.13.50. Szendrey Th. L. The ideological and methodological foundations of Hungarian historiography, 1750-1970. St. John's University, Jamaica, N. Y. Ph. D. 1972. Microfilm-xerography 1981.

2.13.51. Thienemann, Tivadar. "A pozitivizmus és a magyar történettudományok". Minerva 1922.

2.13.52. Valjavec, Fr. "Das neue ungarische Geschichtsbild". Ungarische Jahrbücher 1934.

2.13.53. Vancura J. "O nejnovejsi historiografii madarské" Ceske Historicky Casopis 1985.

2.13.54. Várdy, Steven Béla Modern Hungarian historiography. N.Y., 1976. 333 p. Reviews: *Niederhauser, Emil* Századok 11 (1977) 826—827 p. *Szendrey, Thomas* The Canadian-American Review of Hungarian Studies VI/1979/2/107—114 p.

2.13.55. Várdy, Steven Béla Clio's art in Hungary and in Hungarian America. East European monographs distributed by Columbia University Press, No. CLXXIX., 1985. 327 p. A collection of studies:
-The social and ideological make-up of Hungarian historiography in the age of Dualism
-The foundation of the Hungarian Historical Association and its impact on Hungarian historical studies
-The birth of the Hungarian *Kulturgeschichte* school.
-The Hungarian economic history scool: its birth and development
-The development of East European historical studies in Hungary to 1945
-Antal Hodinka: A pioneer of Slavic historical studies in Hungary
-The Ottoman Empire in European historiography. A reevaluation by Sándor Takáts
-The changing image of the Turks in twentieth-century Hungarian historiography

-Trianon in interwar Hungarian historiography
-Hungarian historiography and the *Geistesgeschichte*school
-Elemér Mályusz and the Hungarian ethnohistory school
-Research in Hungarian-American history and culture.
Achievement and prospects (with Ágnes Huszár Várdy).

2.13.56.Wagner, Ferenc A magyar történetírás új útjai 1945—
1955. Washington D.C., 1956.

2.14.Ireland

2.14.1. Lee, Joseph Irish historiography 1970—1979. Cork,
1981.238p.

2.14.2. Martin, Francis Xavier—Byrne, Francis John (eds.) The
scholar revolutionary: Eoin MacNeill, 1867—1945., and the making of the new Ireland. Shannon, 1973. 429 p.

2.14.3. Moody, Theodore William (ed.) Irish historiography
1936—1970. Dublin, 1971. 155 p. A report prepared for CISH.

2.15.Italy

2.15.1.Barbagallo, Corrado "The conditions and tendencies of
historical writings in Italy today". Journal of Modern History I
(1929) June 236—244 p.

2.15.2.Baum, Hans-Reiner Analyse und Kritik der bürgerlichen
Historiographie Italiens über den italienischen Faschismus. Diss.
A. Berlin, Akademie für Gesellschaftswissenschaften beim ZK
der SED. 265+205 p. 1981.

2.15.3.Berengo, Marino "Italian historical scholarship since the
Fascist era". Daedalus 100 (Spring, 1971) 469—484 p.

2.15.4.Bulferetti,Luigi Introduzione alla storiografia socialistica in Italia. Firenze, 1949. 154 p.

2.15.5.Bulferetti,Luigi La storiografia italiana dal romanticismo a oggi. Milano, 1957. 214 p.

2.15.6. Caponigri, A. Robert History and liberty. The historical writings of Benedetto Croce. L., 1955.

2.15.7. Caracciolo, Alberto L'unita del lavoro storico. Napoli, 1967. 204 p.

2.15.8. Casali, Antonio Storici italiani fra le due guerre: la "Nuova rivista storica" 1917—1943. Napoli, 1980. 212 p.

2.15.9.Chabod,Federico "Croce storico." Rivista storica italiana LXIV (1952) 473—530 p.

*2.15.10.*Congresso la storia dell'Italia unita storiographia del secondo dopoguerra. (1978 Palermo) Milano, 1981. 407 p.

2.15.11.Croce,Benedetto Storia della storiografia italiana nel secolo decimono. I-II. Bari, 1947.

2.15.12. de Felice, Franco Manacorda, Gastone et alia. La ricerca storica marxista in Italia. A cure di Ottavio Cecchi. Roma, 1974. 150 p.

2.15.13. de Felice, Renzo "La storiografia contemporaneistica italiana dopo la seconda guerra mondiale." Storia contemporeana 10(1979) 91—108 p.

2.15.14. Ghibaudi, Silvia Rota Giuseppe Ferrari. L'evoluzione del suo pensiero (1938—1860). Firenze, 1969.

2.15.15.Granata,Ivano Il socialismo italiano nella storiografia del secondo dopoguerra. Roma-Bari, 1980. 199 p.

2.15.16.Lapeyre,Henri De Machiavel a Benedetto Croce. Geneve, 1970.239 p.

*2.15.17.*La storiografia italiana negli ultimi vent' anni. Atti congresso nazionala di scienze storiche. Milano, 1970.

2.15.18. Manselli, Raul La nazione italiana nelsuo sviluppo storico e nella discussione storiografica. Torino, 1979. 107 p.

2.15.19.Marcelli, Umberto Interpretazioni del Risorgimento. Bologna, 1970.176 p.

2.15.20.Masella,Luigi Passato e presente nel dibattito storiografico: storici marxisti e mutamenti della societa italia. 1955—1970: antologia critika. Bari, 1979.

2.15.21. Miozzi, U. Massimo Storici italiani tra'800 e '900: appunti e note. Roma, 1976. 263 p.

2.15.22. Miozzi, U.Massimo La scuda storica romana, 1926—1943.1—2.Roma, 1982.39—84,255,315p.

*2.15.23.Pepe,Gabriele*Il Mezzogiorno d'Italia sotto gli spagnoli, la tradizione storiografia. Firenze, 1952. 277 p.

2.15.24.Romano,Ruggiero La storiografia italiana oggi. Milano, 1978.127p.

2.15.25.Sasso,Genaro Il Guardia della storiografia: „Profilo di Frederico Chabod" e altri staggi. Napoli, 1985. 364 p.

2.15.26.Sorge,Giuseppe Interpretazioni italiane della rivoluzioni francesse nel secolo decimonono. Roma, 1973. 170 p.

2.15.27.Spriggo,J.S. Benedetto Croce, man and thinker. New Haven, 1952.

2.15.28.Tholfsen, Trygve "What is living in Croce's theory of history?" Historian XXIII (1961) 283—302 p.

2.15.29.Tranfaglia,Nicola L'Italia unita nella storiografia del secondo dopoguerra. Roma, 1980.

2.15.30. Valiani, Leo L'historiographie de l'Italie contemporaine, Genève, 1968. 170 p.

2.15.31.Volpe,Giocchino Storici e maestri. Firenze, 1967. 509 p.

2.15.32.White,Hayden "The abiding relevance of Croce's idea of history." Journal of Modern History XXXV (1963) 2.

2.16. Luxembourg

2.16.1.Kellen,Tong Die luxemburgische Geschichtsschreibung, ein Rückblick und ein Ausblick, zugleich ein bibliographischer Führer für die luxemburgische Geschichtswissenschaft und ihre Hilfswissenschaften.Luxembourg, 1933. 107 p.

2.17. The Netherlands

2.17.1. Besauw, van F. Ced. Balans en perspectiet: Visies op de geschiedwetenochop in Nederland. Groningen, 1987. 296 p.

2.17.2.Blok, PieterJohannes Geschichtsschreibung in Holland. Beigegeben ist *Ziehen, Julius* Die Geschichte der Niederlande in Deutschland. Heidelberg, 1924. 50 p.

2.17.3.Boogman, J. C. "Die historikus Pieter Geyl: aktivistisch Strijder en reformatief Konservatief" *In*: Ons Erfdeel 16 (1973) 54—58p.

2.17.4.Colie,RosalieL. "Johan Huizinga and the task of cultural history". AHR LII (April, 1964).

2.17.5. Duke, A. C. — Tamse, C. A. (eds.) Clio's mirror: historiography in Britain and the Netherlands. Zutphen, 1985. 238 p. Paper delivered to the eighth Anglo-Dutch historical conference.

2.17.6. Dunk, H. W. von der "Johann Huizinga:prophet of dram or counsellor to man". Delta 16 (1972—73) 17—27 p.

2.17.7. Geurts, P. A. M. — Janssen, A. E. M. (eds) Geschiedschrigving in Nederland: studies orer de historiografie van de Nieuwe Tijed 1—2 The Hague, 1981. 382,275 p.

2.17.8.Kossmann—Putta, J.—Witte, (eds.) Historical research in the Low Countries 1981—83:a critical survey.Leiden, 1985. 117 p.

2.17.9.Mijnhardt, W. W. (ed.) Kontelend Geschiedbeeld. Nederlandse historiografie sinds 1945. Utrecht, 1983.

2.17.10.Schöffer,I. Het nationaal — socialistische beeld van de geschiedenis der Nederlanden. Een historiografische en bibliografische studie. Arnhem, 1956.

2.17.11.Vermeulen,EgidiusEligiusGerardus Frain en Huizinga over de wetenschap der geschiedenis. Arnhem, 1956.

2.18.Norway

2.18.1. Dahl, Otmar Norsak hitorieforskning i 19. og 20. arhundre. Oslo, 1959. 282 p. A review VI 1962/3.

2.18.2.Falnes,OscarJ. National romanticism in Norway. N. Y., 1968.

*2.18.3. Smith, Leslie F.*Modern Norwegian historiography. Oslo,1962.116p.

2.19. Poland

2.19.1. Adamus, Jan Monarchizm i republikanizm w syntezie dziejów Polski. Łódź, 1961.177 p.

2.19.2.Adamus, Jan O kierunkach w polskiej myśli historycznej. Łódź,1964.

2.19.3. Arnold, Udo — Biskup, Marian (eds.) Der Deutschordenstaat Preussen in der polnischen Geschichtsschreibung der Gegenwart. Marburg, 1982.

2.19.4. Ascheraden, Konstanze von Probleme der Theorie und Methodologie der Geschichtswissenschaft in der VR Polen (Diss.) Köln, 1978. 354 p.

2.19.5. Barycz, Henrik Stanislaw Smolka w zyciu i nauce. Kraków,1975.410p.

2.19.6. Bromke, Adam The meaning and uses of Polish history. N.Y., 1987. 244 p. Boulder East European monographs no. 212.

*2.19.7.*Spór o historyczna szkóle krakowska. W stulecie katedry historii Polski UJ. 1869—1969. (Praca zbiorowa pod redakciją *Celiny Bobinskiej i Jerzego Wyrozumskiego.*) Kraków, 1972. 374 p.

2.19.8. Bronowski, Franciszek Idea gminowładztwa w polskiej historiografii. (Geneza i formowanie się syntezy republikańskej Lelewela) Łódź, 1969. 158 p.

2.19.9. Feldman, J. "Historical studies in Poland". The Slavonic Review II (1923)

2.19.10.Finkel,L. "Die polnische Geschichtsschreibung". Mitteilungen des Instituts für österreichische Geschichte. 1887, 1890 and Jahresberichte der Geschichtwissenschaft 1895, 1896, 1898, 1900,1902,1906.

2.19.11.Forst–Battaglia,O. "Die polnische Historiographie der Gegenwart". Mitteilungen des Instituts für Österreichische Geschichte 39 (1923).

2.19.12. Golczewski, Frank Das Deutschlandbild der Polen 1918—1939. Eine Untersuchung der Historiographie und der Publizistik. Düsseldorf, 1974. 316 p.

*2.19.13.Górski,Jan*Pogranicze historii. Szkize i felietony. Warszawa,1974.375p.

2.19.14.Grabski,AndrzejFeliks Orientacje polskiej mysli historycznej. Studia i rozwazania. Warszawa, 1972. 429 p.

*2.19.15.Grabski,AndrzejFeliks*Myśl historyczna polskiego Oswiecenia.Warszawa, 1976. 485 p.

2.19.16. Grabski, Andrzej Feliks "The Warsaw school of history". Acta Poloniae Historica 26 (1972) 153—169. p.

2.19.17. Grabski, Andrzej Feliks Historiografia i polityka. Dzieje konkursu historycznego im. Juliana Ursyna Niemcewicza 1897—1922.Warszawa,1979,447p.

2.19.18.Grabski,AndrzejFeliks "Karl Lamprecht i historiografia polska". Kwartalnik Historii Nauki i Techniki 26 (1981) 2/315-334p.

2.19.19.Grabski,AndrzejFeliks Perspektywy przestości. Studia i szkice historiograficzne. Lublin, 1983. 540 p.

2. 19. 20. Halecki, Oskar "Die Geschichtswissenschaft im heutigen Polen". Slavische Rundschau II (1930).

2. 19. 21. Halecki, Oskar "Problems of Polish historiography". Slavonic and East European Review 21 (March 1943) 223—239 p. On Polish historians since the mid-19th century.

2.19.22. Handelsman, Marceli "La méthodologie de l'histoire dans la science polonaise". Revue de synthese historique **XXXVI** (1922).

2.19.23. Handelsman, Marceli "Les études d'histoire polonaise et les tendances actuelles de la pensée historique en Pologne". Revue de synthese historique **XXXIX** (1925).

2.19.24. Handelsman, Marceli Historycy, portrety i profile. Warszawa, 1937. 187 p. 19—20th century Polish historians.

2.19.25. Herbst, Stanislaw — Pietrzak-Pawlowska, Irena (eds.) Polskie Towarzystwo Historyczne 1886-1956. Warszawa, 1958. 281 p. With French and Russian summaries.

2.19.26. Kareev, M.J. Najnowszy zwrot w historiografii Polskiej 1861—1886. Petrohrad, 1888.

2.19.27. Kieniewicz, Stefan Historyk a świadomość narodowc. Warszawa, 1982. 357 p.

2.19.28. Korzec, Pawel "Etudes de l'historiographie de la Pologne populaire, concernant l'histoire contemporaine". Revue de l'Est 4 (1973) 3/258—274. p.

2.19.29. Krasuski, Jerzy — Labuda, Gerard — Maczak, Antoni W. (eds.) Stosunki polsko-niemeckie w historiografii. 1 cz. Studia z dziejów historiografii polskiej i niemeckiej. Poznan, 1974. 533 p.

2.19.30. Kulczykowska, Anna Programy nauczania historii w Polsce, 1918—1932. Warszawa, 1972. 226 p.

2.19.31. Lazuga, Waldemar Michal Bobrzynski: Myśl historyczna a działalność polityczna. Warszawa, 1982. 278 p.

2.19.32. Lesnodorski, Boguslaw "Les sciences historiques en Pologne au cours des années 1945—1955". *In*: Congresso Internazionale di scienze storiche. Roma, 4-11 Settembre 1955. Relazioni VI.457—515p.

2.19.33.Ludat,Herbert Die polnische Geschichtswissenschaft. Entwicklung und Bedeutung. Schneidemühle, 1939.

2.19.34.Ludat,Herbert Deutsch-slawische Frühzeit und modernes polnisches Geschichtsbewusstsein. Ausgewählte Aufsätze. Köln-Wien, 1969.363 p.

2.19.35.Madurowicz-Urbanska,Helena Historia gospodarcza w Polsce jako dyscyplina uniwersytecka (Okres organizacyjny: 1905/6—1921/22,Koncepcja i program.)Studia historica 1974/a. 17.fasc.4.609-626p.

2.19.36. Manteuffel, Tadeusz Historyk wobec historii: Rozprawy nieznané, pisma drobne, wspomnienia (Opracowal i poslowem opatrzyl Stanislaw Trawkowski) Warszawa, 1976. 427 p.

2.19.37.Maternicki, Jerzy Warszawskie srodowisko historyczne,1832—1869.Warszawa,1970.312p.

2.19.38.Maternicki,Jerzy Idee i postawy. Historia i historycy polscy,1914—1918. Studium historiograficzne. Warszawa, 1975. 544p.

2.19.39.Maternicki,Jerzy Dydaktyka historii w Polsce, 1773—1918.Warszawa,1974.453p.

2.19.40.Maternicki,Jerzy Historiografia polska XX. wieku. Cz. 1.1900—1918.Warszawa,1982.

2.19.41.Mrówczynski, Jerzy Ks. Walerian Kalinka. Zycie i dzialalnosc.Poznan,1972.694 p.

2.19.42.Pietrzak-Pawlowska,Janina "Les études historiques en Pologne au début de 1960". Revue historique 84 (tom 224) (1960) 1.

2.19.43. Popkov, B. S. Polskij ucenyj i revolûcioner Joachim Lelewel. Russkaâ problematika i kontakty. M., 1974. 209 p.

2.19.44.Przelaskowi,Ryszard(ed.) Historiografia polska w dobie pozytywizmu (1865—1900). Kompendium dokumentacyjne. Warszawa,1968.257p.

2.19.45.Rappaport,J. "M. Bobrzyński et la science historique polonaise". Le monde Slave 1931.

*2.19.46.Rederowa,Danuta (ed.)*Materialy działalnosci Komisji Historycznej Akademii Umiejetnosci w Krakowie w latach 1873—1918.Wroclaw,1974.346p.WithEnglishandRussiansummaries.

2.19.47. Rose, William J. "Polish historical writing". The Journal of Modern History II/4 (December 1930) 596—985 p.

2.19.48.Rose,WilliamJ. "Realism in Polish history". Journal of Central European Affairs II (October 1942) 233—249 p. A reflection: *Halecki, Oskar* "What is realism in Polish history?" Journal of Central European Affairs III (October 1943) 322—328 p.

2.19.49.Ryszka,Franciszek "Poland: some recent reevaluations". Journal of Contemporary History 2 (January 1967) 107—123p.

2.19.50. Semkowicz, Wladyslaw Rozwój nauk pomocniczych historii w Polsce. Kraków, 1948. 49 p. (PAU Historia nauki polskiej w monografiach 20)

2.19.51.Serejski,MarianHenryk Koncepcja historii powszechnej Joachima Lelewela. Warszawa, 1958.

2.19.52. Serejski, Marian Henryk "Miejsce Joachima Lelewela we wspólczesnej nauce historycznej". Kwartalnik Historyczny 1961.

2.19.53. Serejski, Marian Henryk "Joachim Lelewel (1768—1861)". Acta Poloniae Historica 6 (1962) 35—54 p.

2.19.54. Serejski, Marian Henryk Historycy o historii. Od Adama Naruszewicza do Stanislawa Ketrzynskiego 1775—1918. Warszawa, 1963. 665 p.

2.19.55. Serejski, Marian Henryk Historycy o historii. 1918—1939. Warszawa, 1966. 705 p.

2.19.56. Serejski, Marian Henryk Naród a panstwo w polskiej mysli historycznej. Warszawa, 1973. 338 p.

2.19.57. Serejski, Marian Henryk Europa rozbiory Polski. Studium historiograficzne. Warszawa, 1970. 518 p.

2.19.58. Serejski, Marian Henryk "L'école historique de Cracovie et l'historiographie Européenne". Acta Poloniae Historica 26(1972) 127—151 p.

2.19.59. Skrzypek, J. — Wlodarski, B. Sociétés historiques en Pologne. Bulletin d'information des sciences historiques en Europe orientale V. 1933.

2.19.60. Skurnowicz, Joan S. Romantic nationalism and liberalism: Joachim Lelewel and the Polish national idea. Boulder East European Monographs no. 83. N. Y., 1981. 202 p.

2.19.61. Smolenski, Wladislaw Szkoly historyczne w Polsce. Warszawa, 1886, Reprinted in 1952. 156 p.

2.19.62. Sobieski, W. Optymizm i pesymizm w historyografii polskiej. Studja historika. 1912.

2.19.63. Soós, István "A második világháború utáni lengyel historiográfiáról". Történelmi Szemle 20 (1978) 3—4/601—608 p.

2.19.64.Srowikowski,Tadeusz Joachim Lelewel. Krytyk i autor podreczników historii. Warszawa, 1974. 196 p.

2.19.65. Szafran—Szadkowska, Lucyna Zagadnieinie etnoge-nezy Słowian w historiografii polskiej w okresie od średniowiecza do konca XIX stulecia. Opole, 1983. 143 p.

2.19.66.Topolski,Jerzy "Moralizatorstwo czy wyjasnienie — głównym motywie polskiej historiografii poswieconej rozbiorom". PH 1962/615—625 p. A comment by *Michalski,Jerzy* "Kilka uwag na marginesie artykufu Jerzego Topolskiego." PH 1962/627—628 p.

2.19. 67. Tymieniecki, Kazimierz Zarys dziejów historiografii polskiej. Kraków, 1948. 143 p. (Historia nauki polskiej w monog-rafiach 19/a).

2.19.68.Tyszkowski,K. "Die polnischen Historikerkongresse". Slavische Rundschau 1935.

*2.19.69.Wierzbicka,Maria*Dawne syntezy dziejów Polski. Roz-wój i przemiany koncepcyj metodologicznych. Wrocław, 1974. 159p.

2.19.70. Wierzbicka, Maria Władyslaw Smolenski, Warszawa, 1980.171p.

2.19.71.Wierzbicki,Andrzej Naród-państwo w polskiej myśli historycznej dwudziestolecia międzywojennego. Wroclaw, 1978. 173p.

2.19.72. Wodzynska, Maria Adam Mickiewicz i romantyczna filozofia w College de France. Warszawa, 1976. 280 p.

2.19.73.Wyczański,Andrzej (ed.) La recherche historique en Pologne 1945—1968. Varsovie, 1970. 254 p. (Volume 1 of La Pologne au XIIIe Congres International des Sciences Historiques a Moscov)

2.19.74.Zarnowski,Janusz "Wege und Erfolge der polnischen Historiographie1945—1974".ZfG25/1977/8/958—966p.

2.19.75. Zarys historii historiografii polskiej. 1— 3. Łódź, 1954—1959.110,103,278p.

2.19.76. Zerneck, Klaus (Protokollauszüge und Kommentare von) Zwischen Kritik und Ideologie. Methodologische Probleme der polnischen Geschichtswissenschaft auf dem VII. polnischen Historikerkongress in Breslau 1948. Köln-Graz, 1964. 86 p. (Quellenhefte zur Geschichtswissenschaft in Osteuropa nach dem Zweiten Weltkrieg im Auftrage des Johann Gottfried Herder-Forschungstrates—Marburg, Reihe I. Polen 2)

2.19.77.Ziffer,Bernard Poland, history and historians. Three bibliographical essays. N.Y., 1952. 107 p.

2.20. Portugal

2.20.1. Figueiredo, Fidelino de "Historiografia portuguêsa do sèculo XX.". Revista de História (Sao Paulo) 9 (1954) 333—349 p.

2.20.2. Godinko, Vitorino Magalhaes "A Historiografia portuguêsaor orientacoes, problemas i perspectivas." Revista de História (Sao Paulo) 10 (janerja — junho 1955) 3—21 p.

2.20.3.Marques,Oliveira (ed.) Antologia da historiografia portuguêsa.
1. Des origans a Herculano. Lisboa, 1974. 256 p.
2. De Herculano aos nossos dias. Lisboa, 1975. 289 p.

*2.20.4.*Historiografia portuguesa anterior a herculano: actas do [2⁰] colóqui [organizado pela] Academia potuguêsa da história. Lisboa, 1977. 494 p.

2.20.5. Serrao, Joaquim Verissimo Historia breve da historiografia portuguesa. Lisboa, 1962. 316 p.

2. 21. Roumania

2.21.1.Albu, Corneliu Alesandru Papiu Ilarian.Bucureşti, 1977. 32 p.

2.21.2. Alexandrescu-Dersca Bulgaru, Maria Matilda Nicolae Iorga — a Romanian historian of the Ottoman Empire. Bucharest, 1972.190p.

2.21.3. Andrescu, Stefan "Premières formes de la littérature historique roumaine en Transylvanie". Revue des Etudes Sud-Est Européenne,1975/511—524p.

2.21.4.Berza,Mihai Stiinta si metoda istorica în gîndirea lui N. Iorga. Bucuresti, 1945.

2.21.5.Berza, Mihai "L'historien Andrei Otetea". Revue roumaine d'histoire 8 (1969) 3/407—434 p.

2.21.6.Bodin,D. Scoala noua de istorie. Raspuns dlui N. Iorga. Bucureşti, 1936.

2.21.7.Bogdan,J. Istoriografia româna si problemele ei actuale. Academie rom. discursion de receptiune. Bucureşti, 1905.

2.21.8. Boia, Lucian—Zub, Al. (eds.) A. D. Xenopol: studii privitoare la viata si opera sa. Bucuresti, 1972. 443 p. With a summary in French.

2.21.9.Boia,Lucian Evolutia istoriografiei române. Bucuresti, 1976. 377 p. With a most important bibliography of Roumanian historiography.

2.21.10.Boia,Lucian(Coord.scient.) Théorie et méthode dans l'historiographie roumaine (1965—1979). Bibliographie sélective annotée. Bucarest, 1980.

2.21.11.Boia,Lucian "Romantisme et esprit critique dans l'historiographie roumaine à la fin du XIXe et au début du XXe siècle." Storia della Storiografia 1 (1982) 26—36 p.

2.21.12.Boia,Lucian(ed.) Études d'historiographie. Bucarest, 1985.

2.21.13.Boldur,Alexandru, V. Stiinta istorica romana in ultimi 25 ani. Iasi, 1946. 98 p. Roumanian historical scholarship 1921—1946.

2.21.14.Botez,Octav Alexandru Xenopol teoretician si filosof al istoriei. Bucuresti, 1928. 223 p.

2.21.15. Bucur, Marin (ed.) Jules Michelet si revolutionarii romani: in documente si scrisori de epoca. Cluj—Napoca, 1982. 266p

2.21.16. Cherestesiu, V.—Stănescu, Eugen—Ionasco, I. "Über die Entwicklung der Geschichtswissenschaft in der rumänischen Volksrepublik in den Jahren 1944-1954". ZfG 4 (1956) 143—153

2.21.17. Ciobanu, Radu Stefan Pe urmele stolnicului Constantan Cantanzine. București, 1982. 336 p.

2.21.18. Ciorănescu, Al. Opera istorica a lui Budai-Deleanu. Cercetári literare II/1936, 192—128 p.

2.21.19. Condurachi, Emil L'archéologie Roumaine au XXe siècle. Bucarest, 1963. 104 p.

2.21.20.Condurachi, Emil "Un grand archéologue et historien Roumain de l'antiquité: Vasile Parvan (1882—1927)". Revue Roumaine d'Histoire (1965) 2/183—205 p.

2.21.21.Constantinescu-Iasi, P. Realizaile historiografiei Romane intre anii 1945—1955. Bucureşti, 1955. 195 p.

2.21.22.Cristian, Vasile Contributia istoriografiei pregjatirea ideologica a revolutiei Romane de la 1848. Bucureşti, 1985. 205 p.

2.21.23.Cristian, Vasile Istoria la universitaeia din Iasi. Iasi, 1985.172p.

2.21.24.Curato,Federico "Storiografia Rumena d'oggi". Risorgimento 25 (1973) 42—51., 129—137p.

2.21.25. Curticapeanu, V. "L'historiographie Roumaine, facteur dynamique de la conscience historique et nationale fin du XIXe s. — début du XXe s.". Acta Univ.Bucureşti 32 (1983) 35—50 p.

2.21.26. Deutsch, Robert—Schröder, Wilhelm Heinz Quantitative Analyse der rumänischen Historiographie. Eine quantitative Analyse zur Wissenschaftsforschung. Köln, 1976. VI., 71 p.

2.21.27. Domanovszky, Alexandre [Sándor] La methode historique de N. Iorga. Budapest, 1938. 323 p.

2.21.28.Dragan,Mihai B. P. Hasdeu. Iasi, 1972.

2.21.29.Duicu,Serafim Pe urmele ui Gheorghe Sincai. Bucureşti, 1983.253p.

2.21.30.Duicu,Serafim Pe urmele lui Samuel Micu-Clain. Bucureşti, 1986. 342 p.

2.21.31.Elekes,Lajos "A román történetírás válsága". Századok LXXIV (1940) 30—83 p.

2.21.32.*Gáldi,László* "Iorga". Magyar Szemle XL (1941) 43—47p.

2.21.33. *Gavanescu, Ed. I.* Ioan Monorai. Scurta cunostinta a lucruilor Dachiei. Bucureşti, 1939. 48 p.

2.21.34.*Ghermani,Dionisie* Die kommunistische Umdeutung der rumänischen Geschichte unter besonderer Berücksichtigung des Mittelalters. München, 1967. 189 p.

2.21.35. *Giurescu, C. C.* "Consideratii asupra istoriografiei romanesti in ultimii douazeci de ani". Revista istorica 1926/7-9/137—185p.

2.21.36.*Giurescu, C.C.* In legătură cu istoria romanilor. Bucureşti, 1936.57 p.

2.21.37. *Giurescu, C. C.* Pentru "Vechea scoala de istorie". Raspuns dlui N. Iorga. Bucureşti, 1937.

2.21.38. *Gogoneata, Nicolae—Ornea, Z.* A.D. Xenopol. Bucarest, 1967.93 p.

2.21.39. *Henry, Paul* "Histoire de Roumanie". Revue Historique (Paris) LX (1935) t.176. 486—537 p.; LXVIII (1944) t. 194. 42—65,132—150,233—252.p.

2.21.40.*Holban,Th.* "Societes historiques en Roumanie". Bulletin d'information des sciences historiques en Europe Orientale V (1933).

2.21.41.*Hunfalvy,Pál* "A román történetírás". Századok XII (1878)78—93,183—197p.

2.21.42. *Hurezeanu, Damian—Badea, Marin* "Le marxisme et le developpement de l'historiographie roumaine contemporaine". Revue Roumaine d'Histoire (1970) 4/571—595 p.

2.21.43.Iorga, Nicolae "Les etudes d'histoire en Roumanie pendant le XIX.s.". Revue du Sud Est Europeen X (1933).

2.21.44.Iorga,Nicolae Scoala noua de istorie. O lamurire definitiva. Bucuresti, 1936.

2.21.45.Iorga, Nicolae — istoric al Bizantului. Culegere de studii. *Ed. Stanescu, Eugen.* Bucuresti, 1971.

2.21.46.Jakab, Elek "A román történetírás újabb jelenségei". Századok XXII(1888)841—851,932—947p.

2.21.47.Lapedatu,Alex Activitatea istorica a lui Nic. Densusianiu(1846—1911)Bucuresti, 1912. 63 p.

2.21.48.Lapedatu,Alex Istoriografia romana ardeleană in legătura cu desfásurarea vietii politice a neamului románesc de peste Carpati. Bucuresti, 1923. 40 p.

2.21.49.Lipcsey,Ildikó "Alexandru Dumitrie Xenopol 1847—1920".Világtörténet(1979)4/115—131p.

2.21.50.Lupas,I. Nicolae Popea si Ioan M. Moldovanu. Bucuresti,1920.53 p.

2.21.51.Lupas,I. "L.Ranke und M. Kogalniceanu". Jahrbücher für die Geschichte Osteuropas IV (1939)

2.21.52.Maciu, Vasile—Pascu, Stefan—Berindei, Dan—Constantinescu, Miron—Liveanu, V.—Panaitescu, P. P. Introduction a l'historiographie roumaine jusqu'en 1918. Bucarest, 1964. 98 p. English version: Outline of Rumanian historiography until the beginning of the 20th century. Bucharest, 1964. 96 p.

2.21.53. Makkai, László "A román történetírás új iskolája". Századok LXXII (1938) 60—65 p.

2.21.54.Makkai, László "L'historiographie roumaine dans les dernieres dizaines d'années." Revue d'histoire comparée XXI (1943) No. 3-4, 469—504 p.

2.21.55.Marica, GeorgeEm. George Barițiu — istoric. Cluj-Napoca, 1980. 253 p.

2.21.56.Marinescu, Beatrice "Nicolae Iorga and England" Revue roumaine d'histoire 21 (1982) 135—146 p.

2.21.57.Michelson, Paul E. "The master of synthesis: Constantin C. Giurescu and the coming of age of Romanian historiography: 1917—1947." *In: Fischer-Galati, Stephen et al. (eds.)* Romania between East and West: historical essays in memory of Constantin C. Giurescu. Boulder (Colo.), 1982. 414 p. (East European Monographs, 103.)

2.21.58.Michelson, Paul E. "The birth of critical historiography in Romania: the contributions of Ioan Bogdan, Dimitrie Onciul and Constantin Giurescu." *In*: Analele Universitatii Bucuresti, s. istorie XXXII (1983) 59—76 p.

2.21.59. Miskolczy, Ambrus "Über die historische Rolle des rumänischen Bürgertums. Der Entwicklungsstreit der 1920er Jahre und dessen Nachleben in Rumänien." *In: Bácskai, Vera (ed.)* Bürgertum und bürgerliche Entwicklung in Mittel- und Osteuropa. Studia historiae Europae Medio-Orientalis. Budapest, 1986. 819—878 p.

2.21.60.Netea, Vasile "Simion Barnutiu, combattant pour les droits du peuple roumain." Revue roumaine d'histoire 3 (1964) 501—524 p.

2.21.61.Netea, Vasile "La personalité et l'activité de Nicolas Iorga." Revue roumaine d'histoire 4 (1965) 41—54 p.

2.21.62. Neumann, Victor Vasile Maniu. Monografie istorica. Timisoara, 1984. 212 p.

2.21.63.Niederhauser, Emil Nicolae Iorga. Szigetvári Kelet-Európa konferenciák 1980—83. Edited by Polányi Imre. Pécs, 1984. 132—145p.

2.21.64. Oldson, William O. The historical and nationalist thought of Nicolae Iorga. N. Y., 1973. 185 p. East-European Monographs 5.

2.21.65.Otetea,Andrei. "Kogălniceanu, istoric". *In:* Kogălniceanu, Mihail, Opere. I. Scrieri istorice. Bucuresti, 1946. 7—42 p.

2.21.66. Otetea, Andrei "Les problèmes de l'histoire marxiste roumaine". Revue roumaine d'histoire 4 (1965) 373—383 p.

2.21.67. Otetea, Andrei "N .Iorga historien des Roumains". Revue romaine d'histoire 4 (1965) 1069—1082 p.

2.21.68.Panaitescu,P.P. "Rumänische Geschichtsschreibung". Südostforschungen (München) 8 (1943) 69—109 p.

2.21.69. Panaitescu, P. P. "Inceputurile istoriografiei în Tara Romînesca." Studii si materiale da istorie medie 5 (1962) 195—255p.

2.21.70. Pancratz, Arnold "Der siebenbürgisch-sächsische Anteil an der rumänischen Geschichts- und Sprachforschung". Akademie der Rumänischen Volksrepublik. Zweigstelle Klausenburg. Sektion für Gesellschaftswissenschaften. Forschungen zur Volks- und Landeskunde 2 (1959) 19—44 p.

2.21.71.Pascu,Ştefan "Nicolas Iorga, historien du moyen age roumain." Revue roumaine d'histoire 4 (1965) 1151—1176 p.

2.21.72.Pascu,Ştefan "La condition des historiens roumains a la fin du XIXe siècle et au début du XXe siècle". M. Sectiei Siinte ist. Acad. R. S. Roumania. 8 (1983) 53—62 p.

2.21.73.*Pascu, Stefan—Stanescu, Eugen* Istoriografia moderna a Romîniei. Incercare de periodizare si fixare a principalelor curente si tendinte. Studii 17 (1964) 1. 133—158 p.

2.21.74.*Pascu, Stefan* Gindirea istorica in Academia Romana. Bucuresti, 1975. 29 p.

2.21.75. *Philippi, Paul (ed.)* Geschichtsschreibung und Geschichtsbewußtsein bei den Siebenbürger Sachsen. Studien zur Geschichtsschreibung im 19. und 20. Jh. Köln—Graz, 1967.

2.21.76. *Pippidi, D. M. (ed.)* Nicolae Iorga — l'homme et l'oeuvre. Bucuresti, 1972. 44 p. With a bibliography of Iorga's writings on South-East Europe.

2.21.77. *Popescu-Teinsan, Ilie — Netea, Vasile* August Treboniu Lanvian. Bucuresti, 1970. 303 p.

2.21.78.*Radutiu, Aurel* Incursiuni în istoriografia vietii sociale. Cluj, 1979. 202 p.

2.21.79. *Rura, Michael J.* Reinterpretation of history as a method of furthering communism in Rumania. A study in comparative historiography. Washington, 1961. 123 p.

2.21.80. *Rusu, Dorina N.* Cercetari istorice. 1925—1947. Bibliografie. Bucuresti, 1982. 141 p.

2.21.81. *Stanescu, Eugen* "Les débuts d'un grand historien: Nicolas Iorga (les années 1890—1894)". Revue roumaine d'histoire 4 (1965) 1115—1139 p.

2.21.82.*Stefanescu, Stefan* "Conceptia si metoda istorica a lui Dimitrie Onciul (1865—1923)". Studii 6 (1963) 1237—1253 p.

2.21.83.*Stefanescu, Stefan* "Nicolae Iorga, historien de la paysannerie". Revue romaine d'histoire 4 (1965) 1201—1223 p.

2.21.84.Ştefănescu,Stefan "La formation des États roumains dans la conception de Dimitrie Onciul". Revue Roumaine d'Histoire 11 (1973) 1.5-19 p.

2.21.85.Ştefănescu,Stefan"L'historiographie roumaine dans le contexte international de la fin du XIXe siècle et du début du XXe siècle." A. Univ.Bucureşti. Ist. 32 (1983) 77—90 p.

2.21.86.Ştefănescu,Stefan(coord.stiintific) Enciclopedia istoriografiei romanesti. Bucuresti, 1978. 469 p.

2.21.87.Stoy,Manfred "Politik und Geschichtswissenschaft in Rumänien 1965—1980". Südostforschungen (München) XLI (1982)219—259p.

2.21.88.Sulica, Sz. "Történetírás és történelmi segédtudományok Romániában". Turul, 1936.

2.21.89. Tamás, Lajos "Az oláh történetírás régi és új arca". Magyar Szemle XXII (1923).

2.21.90.Teodor,Pompiliu Evolutia gîndirii istorice românesti. Cluj, 1970. 476 p. German version: Die Entwicklung des historischen Denkens in der rumänischen Geschichtsschreibung. Cluj, 1972.297p.

2.21.91.Teodor,Pompiliu Din gîndirea materialist-istorică romaneasca. (1921—1944). Bucuresti, 1972.

2.21.92. Theodorescu, Barbu Biografia scolara a lui N. Iorga. Studiu si documente. Bucureşti, 1970.

*1.21.93.*Theorie et methode dans l'historiographie roumaine: 1965—1979. Bibliographie sélective annotée. Bucurest, 1980. 134 p.

2.21.94.Toma, Gheorghe Xenopol despre logica istoriei. Bucureşti,1971.261 p.

2.21.95. Valota Cavalotti, Bianca Nicola Iorga. Napoli, 1977. 312p.

2.21.96. Zamfirescu, Dan. N. Iorga. Etape čatre o monografie. Bucureşti, 1981. 188 p.

2.21.97. Zane, Gheorghe "Nicolas Iorga et les problemes sociaux de son époque". Revue roumaine d'histoire 4 (1965) 1189—1199p.

2.21.98. Zub, Al. Mihail Kogalniceanu, biobibliografie. Bucureşti, 1971. LXXXII + 638 p.

2.21.99. Zub, Al. Mihail Kogalniceanu, istoric. Iaşi, 1974. 852 p. With a French summary.

2.21.100. Zub, Al. Vasile Pârvan, biobibliografie. Bucureşti, 1975. LXXXIV + 402 p.

2.21.101. Zub, Al. Junimea: implicatii istoriografice. Iaşi, 1976. 384p.

2.21.102. Zub, Al. "L'historiographie roumanie au service de la lutte pour l'independance". Revue Roumaine d'Histore 16 (1977) 2/259-277p.

2.21.103. Zub, Al A scrie si a face istorie: istoriografia romana post pasoptista. Iasi, 1981. 368 p.

2.21.104. Zub, Al. "Nicolae Iorga et l'évolution de l'esprit critique". Revue roumaine d'histoire 21 (1982) 119—134 p.

2.21.105. Zub, Al. Pe urmele lui Vasile Pârvan. Bucureşti, 1983.

2.21.106. Zub, Al. L'historiographie roumaine à l'âge de la synthese: A.D. Xenopol. Bucurest, 1983. 101 p.

2.21.107.Zub,Al. Biruit-au gindul (note despre istorismul romanesc) Iaşi, 1983. 383 p.

2.21.108.Zub,Al. Les dilemmes d'un historien: Vasile Parvan (1882—1927).Bucarest,1985.157p.

2.21.109.Zub,Al. Critical school in Romanian historiography: genetic model and strategy. *In: Zub, Al. (ed.)* Culture and society, Structures, interferences, analogies in the modern Romanian history. (On behalf of the »A. D. Xenopol« Institute of History and Archeology of Iasi for the 16th International Congress of Historical Sciences) Iaşi, 1985. 113—126 p.

2.21.110.Zub,Al. De la istoria critica la criticism (Istoriografia românâ la finele secolului XIX. si începutul secolului XX.) Bucureşti, 1985. 322 p.

2.22. Russia, Soviet Union

2.22.1.Afanasev,O.A. "Kandidatskie i doktorskie dissertacii po istoriografii, zasisennye v 1964—1973 gg.". Istoriâ i istoriki (Istoriografičeskij ežegodnik) M., 1974. 354—365 p.

2.22.2. Akademiâ nauk ukrainska RSR. Institut Istorii. Razvitok istoričnoj nauki na Ukraini za pozi Radânskoj vladi. Kiev, 1973. 255 p.

2.22.3.Alatorceva,A.I. "Struktura i osnovnye napravleniâ deâtel'nosti žurnala »Istorik marksist« 1926—1941 gg.". *In*: Istoriâ i istoriki (Istoriografičeskij ežegodnik). M., 1971.

*2.22.4.Alatorceva, A. I.*Žurnal"Istorik-marksist".1926—1941. M.,1979.285 p.

2.22.5.Alatorceva, A. I.—Alekseeva, G. D. 50 let sovetskoj istoriceskoj nauki. Hronika naučnoj žizni 1917—1967. M., 1967. 526 p.

2.22.6. Alekseeva, G. D. Oktâbrskaâ revoluciâ i istoričeskaâ nauka v Rossii (1917—1923). M., 1968. 301 p.

2.22.7. Alekseeva, G. D. "Iz istorii razrabotki teoretičeskich problem v sovetskoj istoričeskoj nauke (20-e i načalo 30-h goda XX v.)." *In:* Istoriâ i istoriki (Istoriografičeskij ezěgodnik). M., 1971.

2.22.8. Alekseeva, G. D. "Iz istorii sozdania obšestva istorikov-marksistov pri Kommunističeskoj Akademii CK SSSR". *In: Salinova, É. A. (ed.)* Voprosi istoriografii i istočnikovedeniâ. Kazán, 1974.

2.22.9. Alpatov, M. A. Russkaâ istoričeskaâ mysl' i zapadnaâ Evropa XII—XVII. vv. M., 1973.

2.22.10.Anderle,Alfred(ed.) Entwicklungsprobleme der marxistisch-leninistischen Geschichtswissenschaft in der UdSSR und in der DDR. Im Auftrag der Kommission der Historiker der DDR und der UdSSR. (Protokoll der 31. Wissenschaftlichen Konferenz der Kommission der Historiker der DDR und der UdSSR 1982 in Halle) Halle/Saale, 1983. 357 p.

2.22.11. Anderle, Alfred—Donnert, Erich (eds.) Forschungen zur Geschichte und internationalen Wirksamkeit der sowjetischen Historiographie. Halle/Saale, 1984. 232 p.

2.22.12.Astakhov,V.I. Kurs lekcij po russkoj istoriografii — do konca XIX v. Har'kov, 1965. 581 p.

2.22.13. Badja, L.V. "Sovetskie istoriki na meždunarodnych kongressah (20-50e gody)". Istoriâ SSSR 1974 (3) 33—71. p.

2.22.14. Barber, John Soviet historians in crisis. 1928—1932. (Studies in Soviet history and society.) L.—Basingstoke—Birmingham, 1981. 194 p.

2.22.15. *Batemen, Hermann E.—Mazour, Anatole G.* "Recent conflicts in Soviet historiography." Journal of Modern History XXIV (1952) 56—68 p.

2.22.16.*Behrendt,Lutz-Dieter*Pokrovskij und Deutschland. Zur internationalen Wirksamkeit der sowjetischen Geschichtswissenschaft. *In*: Oktoberrevolution und Wissenschaft. Berlin, 1967.

2.22.17.*Behrendt,Lutz-Dieter* Die internationalen Beziehungen der sowjetischen Historiker (1917-Mitte der dreißiger Jahre.) Zur internationalen Wirksamkeit der sowjetischen Geschichtswissenschaft in ihrer ersten Entwicklungsperiode. (Phil.Diss.B.) Leipzig, 1977.

2.22.18.*Behrendt,Lutz-Dieter* "Das erste Auftreten der sowjetischen Geschichtswissenschaft in der internationalen Arena. Die sowjetische Historikerwoche 1928 in Berlin". Jahrbuch für Geschichte (Berlin) 17 (1977) 237—265 p.

2.22.19. *Behrendt, Lutz-Dieter—Berthold, Werner* Zur Geschichte der sowjetischen Geschichtswissenschaft. (1917 bis zur Gegenwart.) (Hrg. von der Hauptabteilung Lehrerbildung des Ministeriums für Volksbildung.) Berlin, 1978. 137 p.

2.22.20. *Berthold, Werner—Katsch, G.* "Zentren historiographischer Forschung in der UdSSR". ZfG 3 (1967)

2.22.21.*Beyerly,Elizabeth*The Europecentric historiography of Russia. An analysis of the contribution by Russian emigré historians in the U.S.A. 1925—1955, concerning 19th century Russian history. The Hague and Paris, 1973. 385 p.

2.22.22. *Biron, A.K.—Biron, M.F.* Stanovlenie sovetskoj istoriografii Latvii, 20-e i 30-e gody XX veka. Riga, 1981. 322 p.

2.22.23. *Black, C.E. (ed.)* Rewriting Russian History. Soviet interpretations of Russia's past. N.Y., 1956. 413 p.

2.22.24. Black, Joseph L. "Interpretations of Poland in nineteenth century Russian nationalist-conservative historiography". Polish Review (New York) 17 (1972) 4/20—41 p.

2.22.25. Black, Joseph L. "The State School interpretation of Russian history: a re-appraisal of its genetic origins". Jahrbücher für Geschichte Osteuropas. N.F. 21 (1983) 509—530 p.

2.22.26. Black, Joseph L. (ed.) Essays on Karamzin: Russian man-of-letters, political thinker, historian, 1766—1826. The Hague and Paris, 1975. 232 p.

2.22.27. Buzeskul, V. P. Vseobšaâ istoriâ i eë predstaviteli v Rossii v XIX — načale XX v. 1-2. Leningrad, 1929—1931.

2.22.28. Camutali, A. N. Očerki demokratičeskogo napravleniâ v russkoj istoriografii 60—70h godov XIX.v. Leningrad, 1971. 250 p.

2.22.29. Camutali, A. N. Borba tečenij v russkoj istoriografii vo vtoroj polovine XIX. veka. Leningrad, 1977. 287 p.

2.22.30. Camutali, A. N. Borba napravlenij v russkoj istoriografii v period imperializma. Leningrad, 1986. 332 p.

2.22.31. Capkevic, E.J. Evgenij Viktorovič Tarle. M., 1977. 125 p.

2.22.32. Carson, George Barr. "Changing perspective in Soviet historiography". South Atlantic Quarterly XLVII (April 1948) 186—195p.

2.22.33. Cerepnin, L.V. Russkaâ istoriografiâ do XIX veka. Kurs lekcij. M., 1957. 308 p.

2.22.34. Cox, Terry Peasants, class, and capitalism: the rural research of L.N. Kritsman and his school. N.Y.-Oxford, 1986. 271 p.

2.22.35. Cumacenko, Erika Georgievna V. O. Klŭčevskij — istočnikoved. M., 1970. 222 p.

2.22.36. Davies, R. W. Soviet History in the Gorbachev revolution. Indiana University Press, 1989. 232 p.

2.22.37. Donnert, E. "Pokrovskijs Stellung in der sowjetischen Geschichtswissenschaft". *In*: Jahrbuch für Geschichte der UdSSR und der volksdemokratischen Länder Europas. Berlin, 1963.

2.22.38. Donnert, Erich—Anderle, Alfred (eds.) Studien zur Geschichte und Theorie der Geschichtswissenschaft in der UdSSR. Halle/Saale, 1981. 203 p.

2.22.39. Dowshenko, Dmytro A survey of Ukrainian historiography. N.Y., 1957. 262 p.

2.22.40. Dudzinskaâ, Eugeniâ Aleksandrovna Mezdunarodnye naučnye svâzi sovetskih istorikov. M., 1978. 289 p. Bibliography 252—272p.

2.22.41. Dunaevski, V. A. Sovetskaâ istoriografiâ novoj istorii stran zapada 1917—1941 gg. M., 1974. 375 p.

2.22.42. Efimov, A.V. "Izučenie v SSSR novoj istorii za sorok let (1917—1957)". VI/1957/10/201—220p.

2.22.43. Enteen, George M. "Soviet historians review their own past. The rehabilitation of M. N. Pokrovsky". Soviet Studies 20/1969/3.306—320p.

2.22.44. Enteen, George M. "Marxists versus non-marxists. Soviet historiography in the 1920s". Slavic Review 35 (1976) 1/91—110p.

2.22.45. Enteen, George M. The Soviet scholar-bureaucrat: M. N. Pokrovsky and the Society of Marxist Historians. University Park and London, 1978. 236 p.

2.22.46. Enteen, George M.—Gorn, Tatiana—Kern, Cheryl Soviet historians and the study of Russian imperialism. University Park and London, 1979. 60 p.

2.22.47. Epstein, Fr. "Die Marxistische Geschichtswissenschaft in der Sovietunion seit 1927". Jahrbücher für Kultur und Geschichte der Slaven. Neue Folge. Band VI, 1930. Heft 1.

2.22.48. Erickson, Ann K. "E. V. Tarle: the career of a historian under the Soviet regime". American Slavic and East European Review19(1960)2/202-216p.

2.22.49. Filippov, R. V.—Alekseev, V. A. Očerki sovetskoj istoriografii Baskirskoj ASSR. Ufa, 1975. 221 p.

2.22.50. Gapanovitch, Ivan Ivanovich Introduction a l'histoire de la Russie. Historiographie russe hors de la Russie. Paris, 1946. 215 p. (First published in English in China in 1935.)

2.22.51. Gefter, M. J.—Malkov, V. L. "Reply to a questionnaire on Soviet historiography." HT 6 (1967)

2.22. 52. Geyer, Dietrich "Kommunistisches Geschichtsverständnis". *In: Besson, Waldemar (ed.)* Geschichte. Frankfurt am Main, 1961.

2.22.53. Geyer, Dietrich Klio in Moskau und die sowjetische Geschichte. Heidelberg, 1985. 46 p. (Sitzungsberichte der Heidelberger Akademie der Wissenschaften. Phil.-hist. Klasse. 1985, Bericht 2)

2.22.54. Giterman, Valentine "The study of history in the Soviet Union". *In:* Science and Freedom. Congress for Cultural Freedom. L., 1955.

2.22.55. Govorkov, A. A. M. N. Pokrovskij o predmete istoričeskoj nauki. Tomsk, 1976. 263 p.

2.22.56.*Grejtane,R.S.(ed.)* Istoričeskaâ nauka Sovetskoj Latvii na sovremennom étape. Riga, 1983. 229 p.

2.22.*57. Grekov, B. D.* Itogi izučeniâ istorii SSSR za dvadcat' let. M., 1937.

2.22.*58. Grosul, A.S.—Mohov, N.A.* Istoričeskaâ nauka Moldavskoj SSR. M., 1970. 127 p.

2.22.*59. Grothausen, Klaus-Peter* Die historische Rechtschule Russlands. Giessen, 1962.

2.22.*60. Gusev, K.V. (ed.)* Problemy istorii otečestvennoj istoričeskoj nauki. Voronez, 1981. 170 p.

2.22.*61. Halin, H.* "Achtzig Jahre russischer Geschichtsforschung ausserhalb Russlands". Jahrbücher für Geschichte Osteuropas 1957 (5) 9—42 p.

2.22.*62. Halylev, L. N.* Problemy metodologii istorii v russkoj buržyaznoj istoriografii konca XIX — načala XX v. Tomsk, 1978. 172p.

2.22.*63. Harper, Samuel N.* "A communist view of historical studies". Journal of Modern History 1 (March 1929) 77—84 p. (On the Sixth International Congress of Historical Studies.)

2.22.*64. Hecker, Hans* Russische Universalgeschichtsschreibung von den vierziger Jahren des 19. Jahrhunderts bis zur sowjetischen "Weltgeschichte"(1955—1965). München—Wien, 1983. 376p.

2.22.*65. Heer, N. W.* Politics and history in the Soviet Union. Cambridge (Mass.), 1971. 319 p.

2.22.*66. Heinen, Heinz (ed.)* Die Geschichte des Altertums im Spiegel der sowjetischen Forschung. Darmstadt, 1980. 407 p.

*2.22.67.Heller,Ilse*Die Entstehung und Entwicklung der neuen geschichtswissenschaflichen Institutionen in der Sowjetunion (von 1917 bis zur Mitte der dreissiger Jahre). Halle, Univ. Diss.B. 1984.

2.22.68.Hoetzsch, O. (ed.) Aus der historischen Wissenschaft der Soviet-Union. Vorträge ihrer Vertreter während der "Russischen Historikerwoche" veranstaltet in Berlin 1928. Osteuropäische Forschungen. Neue Folge. Band 6, 1929.

2.22. 69. Holmes, Larry E.—Burgess, William "Scholarly voice or political echo? The Soviet party history in the 1920s". Russian History 9 (1982) 378—398 p.

2.22.70.Hösch,E. E. V. Tarle (1875—1955) und seine Stellung in der sowjetischen Geschichtswissenschaft. Wiesbaden, 1964.

2.22. 71. Illerickij, V. E. Istoriâ Rossii v osvešenii revoljucionnych demokratov. M., 1963.

*2.22.72.Illerickij,V.E.*Revolûcionaâ istoričeskaâ mysl' v Rossii. Domarsksistskij period. M., 1974. 348 p.

2.22.73.Illerickij,V.E. Sergej Mihajlovič Solov'ev. M., 1980. 192p.

2.22.74. Illerickij, V. E.—Kydravcev, I. A. Istoriografiâ istorii SSSR drevnejsich vremen do Velikoj Oktâbrskoj Socialističeskoj Revolûcii. M., 1971. 457 p. (A university coursebook.)

2.22. 75. Ivanova, L.V. U istokov sovetskoj istoričeskoj nauki.(Podgotovka kadrov istorikov-marksistov v 1917—1929 gg.) M., 1968.

2.22.76. Istoriâ istoričeskoj nauki v SSR. Dooktâbrskoj period. Bibliografiâ. M., 1965.

2.22.77. Istoričeskaâ nauka v Sibirii za 50 let, osnovnie problemi istorii sovetskoj Sibirii. Novosibirsk, 1972. 276 p.

2.22.78. *Jonas, H.* "Entwicklung der Geschichtsforschung in der Sovjetunion seit dem Ausgang des Weltkrieges". Zeitschrift für Osteuropäische Geschichte V. Neue Folge I. (1931)

2.22.79. *Kalenycenko, P.M. (ed.)* Rozvytek istoriycnoj nauky na Ukrajini za roky radanskoji vlady. Kiev, 1973. 252 p.

2.22.80. *Kireeva, R.A.* V.O. Klûčevskij kak istorik istoričeskoj nauki. M., 1966. 232 p.

2.22.81. *Kireeva, R.A.* Izučenie otečestvennoj istoriografii v dorevolûcionnoj Rossii s serediny XIX v. do 1917 g. M., 1983. 214 p.

2.22.82. *Korffmann, Frank* Die sowjetische Geschichtswissenschaft auf den Weltkongressen der Historiker. Entwicklung, Leistungen und internationale Wirksamkeit, von Rom 1955 bis San Francisco, 1975. (Diss. A.) Halle, 1983. 206+123 p.

2.22.83. *Koval'cenko, I. D.—Siklo, A. E.* "Krizis russkoj buržuaznoj istoričeskoj nauki v konce XIX — nacale XX veka". VI 1982/1/18—35p.

2.22.84. *Kravcenko, I. S.—Kopysskij, Z.U.* Dostiženia istoričeskoj nauki v BSSRZ a 50 let (1919—1969 gg). Minsk, 1970. 94 p.

2.22.85. *Krausz, Tamás* "Pokrovszkij és az orosz abszolutizmus vitája az Októberi Forradalom után." TSZ 23 (1980) 4. 627—648 p.

2.22.86. *Laptin, P. F.* Obščina v russkoj istoriografii poslednej treti XIX. — nacala XX v. Kiev, 1971.

2.22.87. *Laqueur, Walter* The fate of the revolution: interpretations of Soviet history. L.—N.Y., 1967.

2.22.88.Laul, Endel' (ed.) Leninskij etap v estonskoj istoričeskoj nauke. Tallin, 1970. 448 p. A collection of studies with German and Russian summaries.

2.22. 89. Levandovskij, A. A. Iz istorii krizisa russkoj buržuazno-liberalnoj istoriografii. A.A. Kornilov. M., 1982. 178 p.

2.22. 90. Magkov, G.P. "O meste i roli «russkoj istoričeskoj skoly» v idejno-političeskoj borbe v Rossii v načale XX veka". *In: Sofman, A. S. (ed.)* Kritika buržuaznyh koncepcij vseobšej istorii. Kazan', 1973. Vypusk 3.

2.22.91.Marko, Kurt Sowjethistoriker zwischen Ideologie und Wissenschaft. Aspekte der sowjetrussischen Wissenschaftspolitik seit Stalins Tod, 1953—1963. Köln, 1964. 108 p.

2.22.92. Mavrodin, V.V. et al. (ed.) Voprosy istorii istoričeskoj nauki. Leningrad, 1984. 149 p. (A collection of studies published on the occasion of the 50th anniversary of the establishment of the Historical Faculty at Leningrade University on the history of the faculty.)

2.22.93.Mazour, A. G. Modern Russian historiography. Princeton, 1958 New edition in 1975 224 p. Original version: An outline of modern Russian historiography. No place of publication given, 1939.

2.22. 94. Mazour, A. G. The writing of history in the Soviet Union. Stanford (Cal.), 1971.

2.22. 95. Mazour, A. G. "V. O. Kluchevsky. The making of a historian". Russian Review 31 (1972) 345—359 p.

2.22. 96. Mazour, A. G. "V.O. Kluchevsky. The scholar and teacher". Russian Review 32 (1973) 15—27 p.

2.22.97.Mehnert, Klaus Stalin versus Marx. The Stalinist historical doctrine. L., 1952.

2.22.98. Mendel, A.P. "Current Soviet theory of history. New trend or old?" AHR 62 (1966) 1. 50—73 p.

2.22.99. Menzel, Wolfgang Grundprobleme der Entwicklung der sowjetischen Geschichtswissenschaft und der ideologischen Arbeit der KPdSU (B) in den Jahren des Großen Vaterländischen Krieges 1941—1945. (Diss.A.) Halle, 1983. 355 + 9 p.

2.22.100.Meschkat, Klaus Die Pariser Kommune von 1871 im Spiegel der sowjetischen Geschichtsschreibung. Berlin—Wiesbaden, 1965. 267 p.

2.22. 101. Milukov, P.N. Glavnye teceniâ russkoj istoričeskoj mysli. Sentpetersburg, 1897.

2.22.102.Mogil'nickij,B.G. Političeskie i metodologičeskie idei russkoj liberalnoj medievistiki serediny 70h godov XIX v. — načala 900-h godov. Tomsk, 1969. 408 p.

2.22. 103. Mogil'nickij, B. G.—Plotnikova, M. E. "O metodologičeskich i istoriografičeskich issledovoniâch v zapadnosibirskom regione". *In: Mogil'nickij, B. G. (ed.)* Voprosy metodologii istori i istoriografii. Tomsk, 1984. Vypusk 2.

2.22. 104. Munzer, Egbert "Solovjev and the meaning of history". Review of Politics XI (1949). 281—293 p.

2.22. 105. Naumov, V. P. Letopis' geroičeskoj borby. Sovetskaâ istoriografiâ graždanskoj vojny i imperialističeskoj intervencii v SSSR. M., 1972. 471 p.

2.22. 106. Neckina, M.V. et al. (eds.) Očerki istorii istoričeskoj nauki v SSSR. 1-4. M., 1955, 1960, 1963, 1966.

2.22. 107. Neckina, M.V. "K itogam diskussii o periodizacii sovetskoj istoričeskoj nauki". Istoriâ SSSR 1962/2.

2.22.108.Neckina, M.V. (ed.) V. I. Lenin i istoričeskaâ nauka. M., 1968. 551 p.

2.22.109.Neckina, M.V.—Gorodeckij, E.N. (eds.) 50 let sovetskoj istoričeskoj nauki 1917—1967. Hronika, M., 1971.

2.22. 110. Neckina, M.V. Vasilij Osipovic Klûčevskij. Istoriâ žizni i tvorčestva. M., 1974. 635 p.

2.22.111.Neckina, M.V. (ed.) Istoriâ istoričeskoj nauki v SSSR. Dooktâbrskij period. Bibliografiâ. M., 1965. 702 p.

2.22.112.Neckina, M.V. (ed.) Istoriâ istoričeskoj nauki v SSSR. Sovjetskij period. Oktâbr 1917—1967 g. Bibliografiâ. M., 1980. 732 p.

2.22. 113. Niederhauser, Emil "A szlavofilek történetszemléletéhez". Acta Universitatis Debreceniensis de Ludovico Kossuth nominatae. Series historica 5 (1966) 27—42 p.

2.22.114. Oberländer, E. Sowjetpatriotismus und Geschichte. Köln, 1967.

2.22.115. Okladnikov, A.P. (ed.) Istoričeskaâ nauka v Sibiri za 50 let. Novosibirsk, 1972. 275 p.

2.22.116.Pfitzner, J. Die Geschichtswissenschaft in der Sowjetunion. Bolschewistische Wissenschafts- und Kulturpolitik. Ein Sammelwerk herausgegeben von B. Richthofen. Berlin, 1938.

2.22.117.Picht, Ulrich M. P. Pogodin und die slawische Frage. Ein Beitrag zur Geschichte des Panslawismus. Stuttgart, 1969. 294 p.

2.22.118.Piontkovskij, A. "Velikorusskaâ buržuaznaâ istoriografiâ poslednogo desatiletiâ". Istorik Marksist, 1930.

2.22.119.Pokrovskij,M.N. Borba klassov i russkaâ istoričeskaâ literatura. Leningrad, 1927. 123 p.

2.22.120.Pokrovskij,M.N.(ed.andpreface) Russkaâ istoričeskaâ literatura v klassovom osvešenii. 1-2. M., 1927—1930.

2.22.121.Pokrovskij,M.N. Istoričeskaâ nauka i borba klassov (Istoriografičeskie očerki, kritičeskie stat'i i zametki). Vypusk 1-2. M.—Leningrad, 1933.

2.22.122.Pundeff,Martin(ed.) History in the USSR. Selected readings. Stanford (Calif.), 1967.

2.22.123.Raleigh, Donald J.(ed.) Soviet historians and perestroika: the first phase. N.Y., 1989. 291 p. Articles translated from the Russian.

*2.22.124.Rosenfeld,NielsErik*Kapitalismens genesis. Et periodiseringsproblem i sovjetisk historieskrivnung. En analyse av sovjetisko historikers debat 1947—1951 on historiens periodisering, med saerligt henblik pa sporgsmalet om kapitalismens opstáen i Rusland. Kobenhavn, 1971. 176 p. (English summary.)

2.22.125.Rubinstejn,N.L. Russkaâ istoriografiâ. M., 1941. 659 p.

2.22.126. Saharov, A. N. Russkaâ istoriografiâ do 1917 g. M., 1957.

2.22.127.Sapiro,A.L. Russkaâ istoriografiâ v period imperializma. Leningrad, 1962. 234 p. (A series of lectures)

2.22.128.Sarbej,Vitalij Grigorovic V. I. Lenin i gozovtneva spadsina istoriografii Ukrajni. Kiev, 1972. 288 p. Ukrainian historiography during the 19th and early 20th centuries.

2.22.129. Schelting, Alexander von Russland und Europa im russischen Geschichtsdenken. Bern, 1948.

2.22. 130. Schlarp, Karl Heinz Ursachen und Entstehung des Ersten Weltkrieges im Lichte der sowjetischen Geschichtsschreibung. Hamburg, 1971. 289 p.

2.22. 131. Serstobitov, V. P.—Orozaliev, K. K.—Vinnik, D .F. Očerk istorii istoričeskoj nauki v sovetskom Kirgizistane (1918—1960 gg.) Frunze, 1961. 145 p.

2.22. 132. Shteppa, Konstantin F. Russian historians and the Soviet state. New Brunswick (N.J.), 1962.

2.22. 133. Sidorov, A. L. Osnovnye problemy i nekotorye itogi razvitii sovetskoj istoričeskoj nauki. M., 1955. 274 p. The works of Soviet historians for the Xth International Congress of Historical Sciences in French, English, German and Russian.

2.22. 134. Skerpon, Alfred A. "Modern Russian historiography". Kent State University Bulletin, Research Series 1 (1952), 37—60 p.

2.22. 135. Šmidt, S. O. "O metodach vyâvleniâ i izučeniâ materialov po istorii sovetskoj istoričeskoj nauki". *In*: Trudy Moskovskogo istoriko-archivnogo instituta. 22. M., 1965.

2.22. 136. Sokolov, O. D. M.N. Pokrovskij i sovetskaâ istoričeskaâ nauka. M., 1970. 274 p.

2.22. 137. Sporea, Constantin "Die sowjetische Umdeutung der rumänischen Geschichte". Saeculum 1960 (11) 220—246 p.

2.22. 138. Sternkopf, Joachim Sergej und Vladimir Solov'ev. Eine Analyse ihrer geschichtstheoretischen und geschichtsphilosophischen Anschauungen. München, 1973. 667 p.

2.22. 139. Straube, F. "Der Aufschwung der sowjetischen Geschichtswissenschaft nach dem XX. Parteitag der KPdSU". *In*: Jahrbuch für Geschichte der UdSSR und der volksdemokratischen Länder Europas. Berlin, 1964.

2.22.140. Szvák, Gyula "Vaszilij Oszipovics Kljucsevszkij (1841—1911)".Világtörténet 1981(4)111—117p.

2.22.141.Thompkins, Stuart R. "Trends in communist historical thought". Slavonic Review 13 (January 1935) 294—319 p.

2.22.142.Tillett, Lowell The great friendship. Soviet historians on the non-Russian nationalities. Chapel Hill, University of North Carolina Press, 1969. 468 p.

2.22. 143. Vajnstejn, O. L. Stanovlenie sovetskoj istoričeskoj nauki (20-e gody) VI 1966/7/32-47 p. English summary on p.221.

2.22.144.Vajnstejn,O.L. Istoriâ sovetskoj medievistiki (1917—1966).M.,1967.

2.22. 145. Valk, S. N. Istoriceskaâ nauka v Leningradskom universitete za 125 let. Trudy ûbilejnoj naučnoj sessii LGU Sekciâ istoriceskih nauk. Leningrad, 1948.

2.22.146.Veber, Boris Georgievic Istoriografičeskie problemy. M., 1974. 334 p. (On 19—20th century Russian and German historiography. Reviewed by *Dalin, V. M.* Novaâ i novejsaâ istoriâ 1974/5/186—188 p. and *Kantor, P. E.—Kolpakov, A. P.* VI 1975/3/ 180—184p.)

2.22.147.Vernadsky,George Russian historiography. A history. Belmont (Mass.), 1978. 575 p. With a bibliography 538—559 p.

2.22. 148. Vipper, R. U. Krizis istoričeskoj nauki. Kazan, 1921. 37 p. A review by *Pokrovskij, M. N.* "Prof. R. Vipper o krizise istoričeskoj nauki". Pod znamenem marksizma. 1922/3. 33—36 p.

2.22. 149. Volgin, V.P. (ed.) Očerki po istorii Akademii Nauk — Istoričeskie nauki. M.—Leningrad, 1945. 42 p.

2.22. 150. Volgin, V, N.—Tarle, E.V.—Pankratova, A. M. (eds.) Dvadcat' pat' let istoričeskoj nauki v SSSR. M.—Leningrad, 1942.

2.22.151.Vucinich,Alexander Social thought in Tsarist Russia. The quest for a general science of society, 1861—1917. Chicago—London, 1976. IX., 294 p.

2.22.152.Vucinich,Alexander "Soviet Marxism and the history of science". Russian Review 41 (1982/2) 123—143 p.

2.22.153.Warth, Robert D. "Leon Trotskij, writer and historian". Journal of Modern History XX (1948) 27—41 p.

2.22.154.Willisch,Jürgen Aufbau und Entwicklung der sowjetischen Geschichtswissenschaft (1917—1924). (Diss.A.) Halle, 1981. 199 + 13 p.

2.22.155. Zilin, P. A. Zaroždenie i razvitie sovetskoj voennoj istoriografii 1917—1941. M., 1985. 182 p.

2.22. 156. Zimmermann, Manfred Dmitrij M. Petrusevskij (1863—1942) und die Geschichtswissenschaft in der UdSSR am Ende der zwanziger Jahre. (Diss.A.), Halle, 1983. 263 + 9 p.

2.22.157. Žukov, Evgenij Mihailovic (ed.) Razvitie sovetskoj istoričeskoj nauki 1970—1974. M., 1975. 478 p.

2.22.158.Žukov, E.M. 60 let sovetskoj istoričeskoj nauki. *In:* *Aleksandrov, A.P. (ed.)* Oktabr' i nauka. M., 1977. 593—609 p.

2.23. Spain

2.23.1. Alonso, Benito Sanchez Historia de la historiografia espanola.
1. Hasta la publicacione de la cronica de Ocampa. Madrid, 1947.
2. De Sobis al final des siglo 18. Con breve epilogo sobre la historiografia posterier. Madrid, 1950.

2.23.2. Bravo Arosenewa, Daniel La Antiquedad clàsica en el pensamiento historiografia espanol del Siglo XIX. Panama, 1970. 316p.

2.23.3.Ceplecha,Christian The historical thought of Jose Ortega y Gasset. Washington, 1958.

2.23.4. Cirujano Marin, Paloma Historiografia y nacionalismo espanol (1834—1868) Madrid, 1985. XIV, 206 p.

2.23.5.Forner, Juan Pabic Discurso sebre el mode de escribir y mejorar la historia de Espana. Informe fiscol. Edicion, prologo y notas de François López. Barcelona, 1973. 237 p.

*2.23.6.*Historiografia espanola contemporanea; balance y resdumen. X. Coloquio de investigaciones hispanicas de la Universidad de Pain. Madrid, 1980. 498 p.

2.23.7. Monroe, James T. Islam and the Arabs in Spanish scholarship, sixteenth century to the present. Leiden, 1970. 297 p.

2.23.8. Moreno Alonso, Manuel Historiografia romantica espanola: introduccion al estudio de la historia en el siglo XIX. Sevilla, 1979.594p.

2.23.9. Payne, Stanley G. "James Vicens Vives and the writing of Spanish history". Journal of Modern History 34 (1962) 2.

2.23.10.Schmidt,Bernhard: Spanien im Urteil spanischer Autoren. Kritische Untersuchungen zum sogenannten Spanienproblem 1709—1936. [Berlin] Erich Schmidt, 1975. 353 p.

2.23.11. Topia, Francisco Xavier Historiadores sobre Espana. Madrid, Edit. Nacional. 1973. T.1. 435 p., T.2. 500 p.

2.24. Sweden

2.24.1.Åmark, Klas "Några drag i den svenska historieforskningens utveckling under 1960–och 1970–talen". *In:* Åmark, Klas (ed.) Teori- och metodproblem i modern svensk historieforskning Stockholm, 1981. 7—36. p.

2.24.2.Björk, Ragnar Den historiska argumenteringen. Konstruktion, narration och kolligation – förklaringsresonemang hos Nils Ahnlund och Erik Lönnroth. Uppsala, 1983. 340 p. (English summary).

2.24.3.Björk, Ragnar "Survey and bibliography about History of Historiography in Sweden". Storia della Storiografia 4/1983/ 145—151.p.

2.24.4.Björk, Ragnar "Teaching and Learning the Profession. Schools of Thinking in Swedish Historical Research at the Turn of the Century". *In: Cho, S. and Runeby, N. (eds.),* Traditional Thought and Ideological Change. Sweden and Japan in the Age of Industrialization. Stockholm, 1988. 57—67 p.

2.24.5. Hatton, Ragnhild "Some notes on Swedish historiography".History XXXVII (1952) 97—113 p.

2.24.6.Hettne, Björn "Ekonomisk historia i Sverige under 50 ár. Institutionell utveckling och forskningsinriktning". Historisk tidskrift 1980.

2.24.7. Odén, Birgitta Lauritz Weibull och forskarsamhället, Lund, 1975. 280 p. (summary).

2.24.8.Odén,Birgitta "Det moderna historisk-kritiska genombrottet i svensk historisk forskning". Scandia 1975/5—28 p. (summary).

2.24.9.Odén,Birgitta "Forskande kvinnor inom svensk historievetenskap".Historisk tidskrift 1980/244—265 p. (summary).

2.24.10. Schück, Herman "Centralorgan för den svenska historiska forskningen. Historisk tidskrift från sekelskiftet till 1960—talets början". Historisk tidskrift 1980/92—139 p. (summary).

2.24.11.Sjödell,Ulf "Det historiografiska 1930—talslandskapet i Sverige. Ett perspektiv". Lychnos 1981—82/145—174 p. (summary).

2.24.12.Torstendahl,Rolf Källkritik och vetenskapsyn i svensk historisk forskning 1820—1920. Uppsala, 1964. 426 p. (Zusammenfassung).

2.24.13.Torstendahl, Rolf "Minimum Demands and Optimum Norms in Swedish Historical Research 1920—1960". Scandinavian Journal of History 1980/117—141.p.

2.24.14.Torstendahl,Rolf "Stat och samhälle i svensk historievetenskap under 1800–och 1900–talen". Historisk tidskrift 1982/2—9 p. (summary).

2.24.15. Torstendahl, Rolf "En historiker och hans tid. F. F. Cahson, historikerna och tidsbegreppet". *In: Torstendahl, Rolf-Nybom, Thorsten* Historievetenskap som teori, praktik, ideologi. Stockholm, 1988. 25—38 p.

2.25. Switzerland

2.25.1. Feller, R.—Bonjour, E. Geschichtsschreibung der Schweiz vom späten Mittelalter zur Neuzeit. 1-2. Basel-Stuttgart, 1962. 903 p. 2. durchgesehene und erweiterte Auflage, Basel, 1979. 860p.

2.25.2.König,Paul Die Schweiz im Licht der Geschichtsschreibung. Zürich, 1966. 278 p.

2.25.3.König, Paul (ed.) Die Schweiz unterwegs, 1798— Ausgewählte Geschichtschreibung und Deutung. Zürich, 1969. 278 p.

2.25.4. Stiefel, Kurt Werte in der schweizerischen Geschichtsschreibung des 19. Jahrhunderts. Zürich, 1942. 106 p.

2.25.5. Vischer, Eduard "Zur schweizerischen Geschichtsschreibung im 1. Drittel des 20. Jahrhunderts". Schaffhauser Beiträge zur vaterländischen Geschichte 50 (1973) 8—38 p.

2.25.6. Vischer, Eduard Zur Geschichte der Geschichtsschreibung: eine Nachlese. Bern, 1985. 310 p.

2.25.7. Wyss, Georg Geschichte der Historiographie in der Schweiz. Zürich, 1985. 338 p.

2.26.Turkey

2.26.1. Karal, E. Z. "Historiography in Turkey today". Middle Eastern Affairs X (1959).

2.26.2. Key, Kerim K. An outline of modern Turkish historiography. Istambul, 1954. 16 p.

2.26.3. Maxim, Mihai "Atatürk si inceputurile istoriografiei turcesti moderne". Revue Istorii 35 (1982) 105—113 p.

2.26.4. Strohmeier, Martin Seldschukische Geschichte und türkische Geschichtswissenschaft: die Seldschuken im Urteil moderner türkischer Historiker. Berlin, 1984. 273 p.

2.26.5. Tveritinova, A.S. "Falsifikaciâ istorii srednevekovoj Turcii v Kemalistskoj istoriografii". Vizantijskij vremennik VII (1953).

2.26.6. Werner, E. "Panturkismus und einige Tendenzen moderner türkischer Historiographie". ZfG 13 (1965) 8/1342—1354.

2.27.Yugoslavia(Croatia,Serbia,Slovenia)

2.27.1.Djordjević,Dimitrij "Contemporary Yugoslav historiography". East European Quarterly 1 (1967) 75—86 p.

2.27.2.Djurdjev, Branislav et al. "Problemi jugoslavenske istorijske nauke". Jugoslovenski istorijski časopis 3 (1964) 3/57—94, 4/93—107p.

2.27.3. Kos, M. "Pregled slovenske historiografije". Jugoslavenski istorijski časopis I (1935)

2.27.4. Petrovich, Michael B. "The rise of modern Slovenian historiography". Journal of Central European Affairs 22 (1962/63) 440—467p.

2.27.5.Popović,Dalen "Pedesetogodišnij rad Nikole Radojčića na razvitku srpske istoriografije". Zbornik Društva inženjera i tehnicara u Splitu 13/14 (1956) 193—208. With a German summary.

2.27.6.Rački,Fr. Nacrt hrvatske historiografije od 1835 do 1885. Rad. jugoslav. Akad., Zagreb, 1885.

2.27.7.Radojčić,N. "Ideja našeg narodnog jedinstva u srpskoj i hrvatskoj istoriografie". Njiva I (1921)

2.27.8.Radojčić,N. "Kratky prehled moderni srbské historiografie". CCH 1925.

2.27.9.Radojičić,DjordjeSp. "Ruvarcevo mesto u srpskoj istoriografiji". Zbornik Matice srpske. Serija društvenih nauka. Novi Sad,13/14(1956)193—208p.

2.27.10.Šišić,Ferdo Priručnik izvora hrvatske historije. D. I. C. 1. Zagreb, 1914. 653 p. The introduction of this standard book (37—107 p.) gives a detailed survey of Croatian historiography from 16th century beginnings to Stojan Novaković (1842—1915.)

2.27.11.*Šišić,Ferdo* Hrvatska historiografija od **XVI** do **XX** stoljeca. Jugoslavenski istorijski casopis I-II (1935—1936).

2.27.12.*Tadić,Jorjo(ed.)*Ten years of Yugoslav historiography 1945—1955. Beograd, 1955. 685 p. Available also in French. Dix années d'historiographie Yougoslave 1945—1955. Beograd, 1955. 688 p.

2.27.13.*Tadić,Jorjo(ed.)*Historiographie Yougoslave, 1955— 1965. Beograd, 1965.528 p.

2.27.14. *Vucinich, Wayne S.* "Postwar Yugoslav historiography". Journal of Modern History 23 (March 1951) 41—57 p.

2.27.15. *Vucinich, Wayne S.* "Local history in Yugoslavia's historiography". Actes du I. Congrès international des études balkaniques et sud-est européennes. 5. Sofia, 1970. 311—331 p.

2.27.16.*Zagorsky,V.* Francois Rački et la renaissance scientifique et politique de la Croatie 1828—1894. Paris, 1909.

3
America

3. 1. Latin America in general

3. 1. 1. Cline, Howard (ed.) Latin American history. Essays on its study and teaching. 1-2. Austin, 1967.

3. 1. 2. Esquenazi-Mayo, Roberto and Meyer, Michael C. (eds.) Latin-American scholarship since World War II.: trends in history, political science, literature, geography, and economics. Lincoln, University of Nebraska Press, 1971.

3. 1. 3. Rama, Carlos M. Nacionalismo e historiografia en América latina. Madrid, 1981. 175 p.

3.1.4. Stein, Stanley "The tasks ahead Latin American Historians". Hispano-American Historical Review 40 (1960) no. 2.

3. 1. 5. Thomas, Jack Ray Biographical dictionary of Latin American historians and historiography. Westport (Conn.)—L., 1984. 420 p. Bibliography 403-411 p.

3. 1. 6. Wilgus, A. Curtis Histories and historians of Hispanic America. New York, 1942. 144 p.

3. 2. South America in general

3. 2. 1. Carbonell, Diego Escuales de historia en America. Buenos Aires, 1943.

3. 2. 2. Gutierrez del Arroyo, Isabel — Posada, German — Gonzélez y Gonzélez — Chinchilla Aguilar, Ernest — Cavallini, Ligia — etc. Estudios de historiografia americana. Mexico, no date. 487 p.

3.3. Argentina

3. 3. 1. Acuna, Angel Mitre, historiador. Buenos Aires, 1936. 1-2.

3. 3. 2. Barreiro, José P. El Espiritu de mayo el revisionismo historico. Buenos Aires, 1955. 479 p. Argentinian historiography of the 19-20th centuires.

3. 3. 3. Carbia, Raulo D. Historia critica de la historiografia argentina. La Plata — Buenos Aires, 1939. 467 p.

3. 3. 4. Etchepareborda, Roberto Rosas [Juan Manuel Jose Domingo Ortiz de]; controvertida historiografia. Buenos Aires, 1972. 324 p.

3. 3. 5. Halperin, Donghi (Tulio) El revisionismo historico argentino. Mexico, 1971. 95 p.

3. 3. 6. Robinson, John L. Bartolome Mitre: historian of the Americas. Washington, D. C., 1982. 117 p.

3.4. Bolivia

3. 4. 1. Abecía Baldivreso, Valentin Historiografía boliviana. La Paz, 1973. 588 p.

3. 4. 2. Saavedra, Carlos Conzalo El Deon Fumes. La Paz, 1972. 119p.

3.5.Brazil

3. 5. 1. Conrad, Robert "Brazilian Historian". (Joao capistrano de Abreu). Revue de Historica de America (Mexico) no. 59 (1965).

3. 5. 2. Ferreira, Manoel Rodrigues A revisao da historia do Brasil. Sao Paolo, 1983. 169 p.

3. 5. 3. Glenisson, Jean Iniciaco aos estudos históricos. Rio de Janeiro, 1977. 370 p. On Brazilian historiography.

3. 5. 4. Lacombe, Amèrico Jacobina Introduçao ao estudo da história do Brasil. Sao Paolo, 1974. 208 p.

3. 5. 5. Lopes, Luis Carlos O espelho e a imagem: o escravo na historiografia brasileira (1808—1920). Rio de Janeiro, 1987. 126 p.

3. 5. 6. Rodrigues, José Honório Teoria da história do Brasil. Introducao metodológica. Sao Paolo, 1949. 493 p.

3.5.7. Rodrigues, José Honório A Pesquisa histórica no Brasil, sua evolucao e problemas atvais. Rio de Janeiro, 1952.

3.5.8. Rodrigues, José Honório História e historiografia. Vozes, 1970.306p.

3. 5. 9. Rodrigues, Jose Honório Historia da historia do Brasil. Sao Paolo, 1979.

3. 5. 10. Rodrigues, Jose Honório Historia combatente. Rio de Janeiro, 1982. 407 p.

3.5.11.Segismundo, Fernando Joao Francisco Lisboa, historiador. Rio de Janeiro, 1983. 63 p.

3. 5. 12. Skidmore, Thomas E. "The historiography of Brazil, 1889-1964". Hispano-American Historical Review 55/1975/ 4/716-748;56/1976/1/81-109p.

3. 5. 13. Stein, Stanley "The historiography of Brazil, 1808—1899." Hispano-American Historical Review 41/1961/ no. 3.

3.6.Canada

3.6.1. Berger, Carl The writing of Canadian history. Aspects of English-Canadian historical writing. 1900-1970. Toronto-Oxford University Press, 1976. 300 p. Toronto—Buffalo (N.Y.), 1986. 364 p.

3. 6. 2. Morton, Desmond E. P. Thompson dans les arpents de neige: les historiens canadiens-anglais et la classe ouvriere. Revue Historique Amerique Française 37/1983/ 165-184 p.

3.6.3. Robert, Jean-Claude "Quelques réflexions sur l'historiographie récente". Canadian Historical Review 63/1982/ 46-59 p.

3. 6. 4. Taylor, M. Brook Promoters, patriots, and partisans: historiography in nineteenth–century English Canada. University of Toronto Press, 1989. 294 p.

3. 6. 5. Winks, Robin W. Recent trends and new literature in Canadian history. Washington, 1966. 56 p.

3.7.Chile

3. 7. 1. Feliu Cruz, Guillermo Historiografia colonial de Chile. Santiago de Chile, 1958.

3.7.2. Feliu Cruz, Guillermo Francisco A. Encina, historiador. Santiago, 1967. 268 p. Bibliography 211-246 p.

3.7.3. Woll, Allen "The Catholic historian in nineteenth century Chile". Americas 33 (1977) 3/470-489 p.

3. 7. 4. Woll, Allen L. A functional past: the uses of history in nineteenth–century Chile. Baton Rouge, Lousiana State University Press, 1982. 211 p. (Chile: historiography 1824-1920.)

3.8.Cuba

3.8.1. Pérez Cabrera, José Manuel Fundamentos de una historia de la historiografia cubana. Le Habana, 1959. 71 p.

3. 8. 2. Pérez Cabrera, José Manuel Historiografia de Cuba. Mexico, 1962. 395 p.

3.8.3. Pez, Louis A. Historiography in the Revolution: a bibliography of Cuban scholarship, 1959—1979. N.Y., 1982.

3.9.Ecuador

3. 9. 1. Barrera, Isaac J. Historiografia del Ecuador. Mexico, 1956.125p.

3.9.2. Carrasco, Adrian Estado, nacion y cultura: los proyectos historicos en el Ecuador. Cvenca, 1988.

3.10.Mexico

3. 10. 1. Gonzalez Navarro, Moises Sociologia e historia en Mexico. Barreda, Sierra, Parra, Molina Enriquez, Gamio, Caso. Mexico, 1970. 86 p.

3. 10. 2. Ortega y Medina, Juan Antonio Polemicus y ensayos mexicanos en torno a la historia. Mexico, 1970. 475 p.

3.11.Paraguay

3. 11. 1. Cardozo, Efraim Historiografia paraguaya. Mexico, 1959. A general introduction.

3.12.USA

3. 12. 1. Adams, Henry The tendency of history. Annual report of the American Historical Association, 1894. 19 p. (Presidential address).

3. 12. 2. Adams, Henry The study and teaching of history. Richmond, 1898.

3. 12. 3. Allen, Harry C. "F. J. Turner and the frontier in American history". *In: Allen, Harry C. — Hill, Charles F. (eds.)* British essays in American history. L., 1957. 145—166 p.

3. 12. 4. Alvord, C. W. The "new history". Nation, May 9, 1912, 457—459 p. A useful review of J. H. Robinson's The New History; offers comments on contemporary trends in historical inquiry and finds little "news" in Robinson's work.

3. 12. 5. "American historical writing, 1900—1950: A symposium". Mississippi Valley Historical Review 40 (March, 1954) 607—628 p.

3. 12. 6. Andersen, Per Sveas Westward in the course of the Empire. A study in the shaping of an American idea: Turner's frontier. Oslo, 1956.

3. 12. 7. Alpatov, Semen Josifovic SŠA i Evropa. Obššie problemy amerikanskoj kontinentalnoj politiki. Kritičeskij analiz buržuaznoj istoriografii SŠA. M., 1979. 236 p.

3. 12. 8. Ausubel, Herman Historians and their craft. A study of presidential addresses of the American Historical Association. 1884—1945. N.Y., 1950.

3. 12. 9. Baker, Susan Stout Radical beginnings: Richard Hofstadter and the 1930s. Westport(Conn.), 1985. 268 p.

3.12.10. Barnes, Harry E. "James Harvey Robinson." *In: Odum, H. W.* (ed.) American masters of social science. N. Y., 1927.

3.12.11. Barnes, H.E. "American historians and the war—guilt controversy" *In: Barnes, H. E.* World politics in modern civilization. N.Y., 1930.

3.12.12. Bass, H.I. (ed.) The state of American history. Chicago, 1970.

3. 12. 13. Beale, Howard K. Charles A. Beard: An appraisal. Lexington, 1954.

3. 12. 14. Bean, W. E. "Revolt among the historians". Sewance Review XVII (1939)/330—341 p. (On American historiography).

3.12.15. Beard, Ch.A. "Written history as an act of faith". AHR 30/1933/34/.

3. 12. 16. Beck, Roland H. Die Frontiertheorie von Frederick Jackson Turner. Zürich, 1955.

3.12.17. Detachment and writing of history. Essays and letters of *Carl L. Becker*, Edited by Phil. L. Snyder. Cornell Unversity Press. Ithaca (N. Y.), 1958.

3.12.18.Becker, Carl L. "What is the good of history?" Selected letters of Carl L. Becker, 1900—1945. Edited, with an introduction, by Michael Kammen. Ithaca — L., 1973. 372 p.

3. 12. 19. Beckman, Alan C. "Hidden themes in the frontier thesis. An application of pychoanalysis to historiography". Comparative Studies in Society and History VIII (April, 1966) 361—382 p.

3.12.20. Bellot, H. Hale American history and American historians. A review of recent contributions to the integration of the history of the United States. Norman, University of Oklahoma Press, 1952. 336 p.

3.12.21. Bennett, James D. Frederick Jackson Turner. Boston, 1975. 138 p.

3. 12. 22. Benson, Lee Turner and Beard: American historical writing reconsidered. Glencoe (Ill.), 1960.

3. 12. 23. Berg, Ellios The historical thinking of Charles A. Beard. Stocholm, 1957.

3. 12. 24. Beringause, Arthur F. Brooks Adams: A biography. N.Y., 1955.

3. 12. 25. Berkhofer, Robert F. Clio and the culture concept. Some impressions of changing relationship in American historiography. Social Science Quarterly 50 (1972) 297—320 p.

3. 12. 26. Bernstein, Barton Jansen (ed.) Towards a new past. Dissenting essays in American history. N. Y., (Pantheon Books), 1968. 364 p.

3.12.27. Billias, George Athon — Grob, Gerald N. (eds.) American history: retrospect and prospect. Riverside (N. Y.), 1971.

3.12.28.Billington, Ray Allen "Why some historians rarely write history: a case study of Frederick Jackson Turner". Mississippi Valley Historical Review L (June, 1963) 3—27 p.

3.12.29. Billington, Ray Allen The genesis of the frontier thesis. A study in historical creativity. San Marino (Calif.), 1971.

3.12.30. Billington, Ray Allen Frederick Jackson Turner. Historian, scholar, teacher. N. Y., Oxford, 1973. 599 p.

3.12.31. Billington, Ray Allen "Tempest in Clio's teapot: the American Historical Association rebellion of 1915". AHR 78 (1973)2/348—369p.

3.12.32. Billington, Ray Allen (compiled and introduced by) Allan Nevins on history. N. Y., 1975. 420 p.

3.12.33. Binkley, William C. "Two world wars and American historical scholarship". Mississippi Valley Historical Review 33 (June, 1946) 3—26 p.

3.12.34.Blinkoff, Maurice The influence of Charles A. Beard upon American historiography. Buffalo, 1936.

3.12.35. Borning, Bernard C. The political and social thought of Charles A. Beard. Seattle, 1962.

3.12.36. Bosch Garcia, Carlos — Gili de Perenga, Mercedes — Muro Luis Felipe Romero, Carmen Guia de personas que cultivan la historia de America. Mexico, 1951. 508 p.

3.12.37.Brown, Robert E. Charles Beard and the constitution. Princeton, 1956.

3.12.38. Brown, Robert E. Carl Becker on history and the American Revolution. East Larsing (Mich.), 1970.

3. 12. 39. Callcott, G. H. History in the United States. 1800—1860. Its practice and purpose. L., 1970. 239 p.

3. 12. 40. Cantor, Norman Frank Perspectives on the European past. Conversations with historians. N. Y., 1971.
    1. From prehistory to the scientific revolution. 359 p.
    2. From the Ancien Régime to the present day. 362 p.

3. 12. 41. Cartosio, Bruno Die labor history in den USA. 1999. Zeitschrift für die Sozialgeschichte des 20. und 21 Jahrhunderts. 3(1988)4/75-91 p.

3. 12. 42. Cartwright, William Holman—Watson, Richard L. (eds.) The reinterpretation of American history and culture. Washington, [1973]. 554 p.

3. 12. 43. Caughey, J. W. Hubert Houve Bancroft. Historian of the West. Berkeley, 1946.

3. 12. 44. Caughey, J. W. — Frantz, Joe B. — Jacobs, Wilbur Turner, Bolton and Webb. Three historians of the American frontier. Seattle, 1967.

3. 12. 45. Cohen, Morris R. American thought. A critical sketch. Edited by Felix S. Cohen. Glencoe (Ill.), 1954. Chapter 2: "American ideas on history".

3. 12. 46. Cohen, Warren I. The American revisionist. The lessons of intervention in World War I. Chicago, 1967.

3. 12. 47. Coleman, Peter J. "Beard, Mc Donald and economic determinism in American historiography. A review article". Business Historical Review XXXIV (Spring, 1960) 113—121 p.

3. 12. 48. Commager, Henry S. The search for a usable past and other essays in historiography. N. Y., 1967.

3. 12. 49. Cooke, Jacob E. Frederick Bancroft: historian. Norman, 1957.

3. 12. 50. Coser, Lewis Refugee scholars in America. New Haven, 1984. (Separate chapter on the historians).

3. 12. 51. Crowe, Charles "The emergence of progressive history". Journal of the History of Ideas XXVII (January-March, 1966)109—124p.

3. 12. 52. Cruden, Robert James Ford Rhodes. The man, the historian, and his work. Cleveland, 1961.

3. 12. 53. Cunliffe, Marcus — Winks, Robin W. (eds.) Pastmasters. Some essays on American historians. N. Y., 1969.

3. 12. 54. Curti, Merle "The democratic theme in American historical literature". Mississippi Valley Historical Review XXXIX (June, 1952) 3—28 p.

3. 12. 55. Curti, Merle Probing our past. New York, 1955. (A collection of studies on the problem of democracy in American historiography: F. J. Turner etc.)

3.12.56.Darnell, Donald G. William Hickling Prescott. Boston, 1975.140p.

3. 12. 57. Davenport, F. Garvin The myth of southern history. Historical consciousness in twentieth century southern literature. Nashville, 1970.

3.12.58.Deininger, Whitetaker T. "The skepticism and historical faith of Charles A. Beard". Journal of the History of Ideas XV (1954)573—589p.

3.12.59.Dementev, I.P. "Osnovnye napravleniâ i školi v amerikanskoj istoriografii poslevoennogo vremeni". VI 1976/11/67—90 p.

3. 12. 60. Dewolfe-Howe, M. A. The life and letters of George Bancroft. 1—2. N. Y., 1908.

3. 12. 61. Donovan, Timothy Paul Historical thought in America. Postwar patterns. Norman, 1973. 182 p.

3. 12. 62. Donovan, Timothy Paul Henry Adams and Brooks Adams: The education of two American historians. Norman, 1961.

3. 12. 63. Doughty, Howard Francis Parkman. N. Y., 1962.

3. 12. 64. Dusinberre, William Henry Adams: the myth of failure. Charlottesville, 1980. 250 p.

3. 12. 65. Eisenstadt, A. S. Charles Mclean Andrews: A study in American historical writing. N. Y., 1955. 273 p.

3. 12. 66. Eisenstadt, A. S. (ed.) The craft of American history. 1—2. N. Y., 1966.

3. 12. 67. Elkins, Stanley — McKritick, Eric "A meaning for Turner's frontier". Political Science Quarterly LXXX (1954) 321—353p., 565—602p.

3. 12. 68. Farnham, Charles H. A life of Francis Parkman. Boston, 1900.

3. 12. 69. Feis, Herbert et al. The historians and the diplomat. The role of history and historians in American foreign policy. Ed. by Francis L. Loewenheim, N. Y., 1967.

3. 12. 70. Fischer, Fritz "Objektivität und Subjektivität — ein Prinzipienstreit in der amerikanischen Geschichtswissenschaft". *In:* Aus Geschichte und Politik. Festschrift zum 70. Geburtstag von Ludwig Bergsträsser. Düsseldorf, 1954.

3. 12. 71. Flower, Milton E. James Parton. The father of modern biography. Durham (N. C.), 1951.

3.12.72. Freidel, Frank "American historians: a bicentennial appraisal". Journal of American History 63 (1976) 1/5—20 p.

3.12.73. Gale, Robert Lee Francis Parkman. N. Y., 1973. 204 p.

3.12.74. Gardniner, L. Harvey William Hickling Prescott. University of Texas Press, 1969.

3.12.75. Gatel, Frank Otto — Weinstein, Allen (eds.) American themes, essays in historiography. Oxford University Press, 1968. 493p.

3.12.76. Gay, Peter A loss of mastery. Puritan historians in colonial America. N. Y., 1968.

3.12.77. Genovese, Eugene D. "William Appleman Williams on Marx and America". Studies on the Left 6 (January-February 1966) 70—86 p. (On radical history, a review of Williams' "The Great Evasion").

3.12.78. Gernet, Jacques "L'histoire en Extreme-Orient". Revue Historique 228 (1962) 1. Criticism on works of Bearley, Pulleybank and Hall.

3.12.79. Gershay, Leo "Carl Becker on progress and power". AHR LV (1949) 22—35 p.

3.12.80. Gettleman, Marvin E. (ed.) The Johns Hopkins university seminary of history and politics, 1877—1912. N. Y., 1987.

3.12.81. Gillespre, Neal C. The collapse of orthodoxy. The intellectual ordeal of George Frederick Holmes. Charlottesville, 1972. 273p.

3.12.82. Goldman, Eric F. "Origins of Beard's »Economic Origins of the Constitution«". Journal of History of Ideas XIII (April, 1952)234—249p.

3. 12. 83. Gressley, Gene M. "The Turner thesis: a problem in historiography". Agricultural History **XXXII** (October, 1958) 227—249p.

3. 12. 84. Guberman, J. The life of John Lothrap Motley. The Hague, 1973. 155 p.

3.12.85. Guggisberg, Hans Rudolf Das europäische Mittelalter im amerikanischen Geschichtsdenken des 19. und des frühen 20. Jahrhunderts. Basel und Stuttgart, 1964. 182 p.

3. 12. 86. Guggisberg, Hans Rudolf Alte und neue Welt in historischer Perspektive: sieben Studien zum amerikanischen Geschichts- und Selbtverständnis. Berlin-Frankfurt am Main, 1973. 154p.

3.12.87. Guggisberg, Hans Rudolf "The uses of the European past in American historiography". Journal of American Studies 4 (1970) 1—18 p.

3. 12. 88. Handlin, Oscar "History: A discipline in crisis?" *In:* The American Scholar 40 (1971) 447—465 p.

3.12.89. Handlin, Oscar "A twenty year retrospect of American Jewish historiography". American Jewish Historical Quartely 65 (1976)4/295—309p.

3. 12. 90. Heilbroner, Robert L. The future as History. The historic currents of our time and the direction in which they are taking America. N. Y., 1959.

3.12.91. Herbst, Jurgen The German historical school in American scholarship: a study in the transfer of culture. Ithaca, 1965.

3.12.92. Higby, Chester P. Present status of modern European history in the United States. Chapel Hill, 1926.

3. 12. 93. Higham, John (ed.) The reconstruction of American history. Harper Paperback, 1962.

3. 12. 94. Higham, John — Krieger Leonard — Gilbert, Felix History. The development of historical studies in the United States. Englewood Cliffs, 1965. Including Gilbert's long essay on historical writing in nineteenth and twentieth century Europe.

3. 12. 95. Higham, John Writing American history; essays on modern scholarship. Bloomington, 1970.

3. 12. 96. Higham, John History. Professional scholarship in America. N. Y., 1973. 241 p.

3. 12. 97. Hoffer, Peter Charles Liberty or order: two views of American history from the revolutionary crisis to the early works of George Bancroft and Wendel Phillips. N.Y. 1988. 309 p.

3. 12. 98. Hofstadter, Richard The progressive historians: Turner, Beard, Parrington. N. Y., 1968. 498 p.

3. 12. 99. Hofstadter, Richard — Lipset, Seymour Martin (eds.) Turner and the sociology of the frontier. N. Y., 1970. 232 p.

3. 12. 100. Holt, W. Stull (ed.) Historical scholarship in the United States, 1876—1901: as revealed in the correspondence of Herbert B. Adams. Baltimore, 1938.

3. 12. 101. Holt, W. Stull "The idea of scientific history in America". Journal of the History of Ideas 1 (1940) 352—362 p.

3. 12. 102. Holt, W. Stull "Historical scholarship". *In*: American scholarship in the twentieth century *(ed. Merle Curti)*, Cambridge, Harvard University Press, 1953.

3. 12. 103. Holt, W. Stull Historical scholarship in the U. S. A. Seattle, 1967. (20th century)

3. 12. 104. Hoover, Dwight W. (ed.) Understanding Negro history. Chicago, 1968. 432 p.

3. 12. 105. Horovitz, David Joel Isaac Deutscher: the man and his work L., 1971. 254 p.

3. 12. 106. Howe, Mark Antony De Wolfe The life and letters of George Bancroft. 1—2. 1908. Republished (Da Capo Press) 1970. 294,364p.

3. 12. 107. Howe, M. A. De Wolfe James Ford Rhodes: American historian. N.Y., 1929.

3. 12. 108. Hunt, E. N. "The New economic history". History LIII., (February, 1968.) On R. W. Fogel's econometric methods.

3. 12. 109. Hutchinson, W. T. Marcus W. Jernegan essays in American historiography. Chicago, 1937. 417p. Discussion of leading American historians from George Bancroft to Vernon L. Parrington.

3.12.110. Igrickij, Urij Ivanovic Myfi buržuaznoj istoriografii i real'nost' istorii. Sovremenaâ amerikanskaâ i anglijskaâ istoriografiâ Velikoj Oktoberskoj socialisticeskoj revolûcii. M., 1974. 279 p.

3. 12. 111. Jacobs, Wilbur R. (ed.) The historical world of Frederick Jackson Turner. New Haven, 1968.

3. 12. 112. Jacobs, Wilbur (ed.) Frederick Jackson Turner's Legacy. San Marino (Calif.), 1965.

3. 12. 113. Jameson, J. Franklin The history of historical writing in America. N. Y., 1891. Reprint, N. Y., 1961., 1969.

3. 12. 114. Jameson, J. F. — Channing, Ed. The present state of historical writing in America. Worcester (Mass.), 1910.

3.12.115. An historian's world. Selections from the correspondence of *John Franklin Jameson. Edited by* Elizabeth Donnon, Leo F. Stock. Philadelphia, 1956.

3.12.116.Jordy, William H. Henry Adams: Scientific historian. New Haven, 1952. 327 p.

3.12.117.Kammen, Michael The past before us. Contemporary historical writing in the United States. Ithaca, Cornell Univ. Press, 1980. 524 p. Contemporary US historiography on the history of Europe and Africa.

3.12.118. Kammen, Michael "Moses Coit Tyler, the first professor of American history in the United States". The History Teacher 17 (November 1983) 61—85 p.

3. 12. 119. Kennedy, Thomas C. "Charles A. Beard and the »Court Historians«". Historian XXXV (August, 1963) 439—450 p.

3.12.120.Kezirian, Richard American history: major controversies reviewed. Dubuque (Iowa), 1987.

3. 12. 121. Kraditer, Aileen S. "American radical historians on their heritage". Past and Present No.56 (August, 1972) 136—153 p.

3.12.122.Kraus, M. History of American history. N.Y., 1937.

3.12.123.Kraus, M. The writing of American history. Norman, University of Oklahoma Press, 1953. Revised edition 1985. 445 p.

3. 12. 124. Kroeby, Clifton B. — Wyman, Walker D. (eds.) The frontier in perspective. Madison, 1957.

3.12.125.Landberg, L.C. "La New Economic History negli Stati Uniti. Rassegna dei resultati". Quaderni storici 1976/382—401 p.

3. 12. 126. Leopold, Richard W. "The historian and the federal government". Journal of American History 64 (1977)15—23. p.

3. 12. 127. Lerner, Robert E. "Turner and the revolt against E. A. Freeman". Arizona and the West V (Summer 1963) 101—108. p.

3. 12. 128. Levenson, J. C. The mind and art of Henry Adams. Boston, 1957.

3. 12. 129. Levin, David History as romantic art. Bancroft, Prescott, Motley and Parkman. Stanford (Cal.), 1959

3. 12. 130. Lewis. H. R. — McGann, Th. F. The new world looks at its history. Austin, 1963.

3. 12. 131. Link, Arthur S. — Rembert, Patrick W.(eds.) Writing southern history. Essays in historiography in honour of Fletcher M. Green. Baton Rouge (Louisiana), 1965.

3. 12. 132. Loesdau, A. "Präsentismus in der bürgerlichen Historiographie der USA". ZfG 1966/7/ 1069—1091 p.

3.12.133.Loesdau,Alfred Globalstrategie und Geschichtsideologie. Zur Analyse der bürgerlichen Historiographie der USA in der Klassenauseinandersetzung zwischen Sozialismus und Imperialismus. Berlin, 1974. 200 p.

3.12.134.Loesdau,Alfred "Die Reflexion des Nationalismus in der gegenwärtigen Geschichtsschreibung der USA". Jahrbuch für Geschichte 14 (1976) 373—396 p.

3.12.135.Loewenberg, Bert James American history in American thought. Christopher Columbus to Henry Adams. N. Y., 1972. 731 p. A remarkable review with numerous bibliographical references to American historiography by *Eigham, John* H T 1974/1/78—83p.

3. 12. 136. Loewenheim, Francis L. (ed.) The historian and the diplomat. The role of history and historians in American foreign policy. N. Y., 1967.

3. 12. 137. Lyon, Melvin Ernest Symbol and idea in Henry Adams. Lincoln, 1970. 326 p.

3.12.138. Mane, Robert Henry Adams on the road to Chartres. Cambridge, 1971. 288 p.

3. 12. 139. Marks, Harry J. "Ground under our feet. Beard's relativism". Journal of the History of Ideas XIV (1953) 628—633 p

3.12.140. Maruskin, Boris Iljic Istoriâ i politika. Amerikanskaâ buržoaznaâ istoriografiâ sovetskogo obšestvo. M., 1969. 393 p.

3.12.141. Meier, August — Rudwik Elliot Black History and the historical profession: 1915—1980. Urbana-Chicago, University of Illinois Press, 1986. 380 p.

3. 12. 142. Morton, M. J. The terrors of ideological politics. Liberal historians in a conservative mood. Cleveland, 1972. (An interesting case against the writings of the »consensus« historians; examines the works of A. Schlesinger Jr., Richard Hofstadter, Daniel Boorstin and others).

3. 12. 143. Mowrey, George E. "The uses of history by recent presidents". Journal of American History LIII. (June 1966) 6—18 p.

3.12.144. Murray, James G. Henry Adams. N. Y., 1974. 174 p.

3. 12. 145. Nettels, Curtis "Frederick Jackson Turner and the New Deal". Wisconsin Magazine of History 57 (March, 1934) 257—265p.

3.12.146. Nichols, Roy F. "Postwar reorientation of historical thinking". AHR LIV (Oct., 1948) 79—80 p.

3.12.147. Nichols, Roy F. A historian's progress. N. Y., 1968.

3. 12. 148. Noble, David W. Historians against history. The frontier thesis and the national covenant in American historical writing since 1930. Minneapolis, 1965. 197 p. An examination of the role of ten historians in defending the »national covenant«, the belief in the divine sanction of the USA.

3. 12. 149. Noble, David W. The end of American history: democracy, capitalism and the metaphor of two words in Anglo-American historical writing, 1880—1980. Minneapolis, 1985. 166 p.

3. 12. 150. Novick, Peter That noble dream: the »objectivity question« and the American historical profession. Cambridge, 1988.648p.

3.12.151. Nye, R. B. George Bancroft: Brahmin rebel. N. Y., 1954.

3.12.152. Parish, Peter J. Slavery: history and historians. N.Y., 1989.195p.

3. 12. 153. Pease, Otis A. Parkman's history. The historian as literary artist. New Haven, 1953.

3. 12. 154. Perkins, Dexter — Shell, John The education of historians in the United States. N. Y., 1962. 243 p.

3. 12. 155. Poinsatte, Charles Robert Understanding history through the American experience. L., 1976. 214 p.

3.12.156. Pressley, Th. J. Americans interpret their civil war. N.Y.,1965.

3. 12. 157. Rabb, T. — Rotberg, R. (eds.) The new history: the 1980s and beyond. Studies in interdisciplinary history. Princeton, 1982. Published also in Journal of Interdisciplinary History 12 (1981—82)1—2.

3. 12. 158. Riegel, Robert "American frontier theory". Journal of World History III (1956) 356—380 p.

3.12.159. Robinson, F.E. Scholarship and cataclysm. Teaching and research in American history. 1939—1945. Stanford, 1947.

3. 12. 160. Robinson, James Harwey The new history. Essays illustrating the modern historical outlook. N. Y., 1916., Springfield, (Mass.), 1958. N. Y., (Free Press), 1965. With introduction by *Wish, Harvey.*

3. 12. 161. Rockwood, Raymond O. Carl Becker's »Heavenly City« revisited. Ithaca - N. Y., 1956.

3. 12. 162. Ross, D. "Historical consciousness in nineteenth century America". AHR (October, 1984) 909—928 p.

3.12.163. Rule, John — Handen, Ralph (eds.) "Bibliography of works on Carl Lotus Becker and Charles Austin Beard". HT 5 (1966).

3.12.164. Rystad, Göran "In quest of usable past: foreign policy and the politics of American historiography in the 1960s". Scandia 48(1982)217—230p.

3. 12. 165. Samuels, Ernest The young Henry Adams. Cambridge (Mass.), 1948. 378 p.

3. 12. 166. Samuels, Ernest Henry Adams. The middle years. Cambridge (Mass.), 1958.

3. 12. 167. Samuels, Ernest Henry Adams. The major phase. Cambridge (Mass.), 1964.

3. 12. 168. Sanders, Jennings B. Historical interpretations and American scholarship. Yellow Springs, 1966. 138 p.

3. 12. 169. Saveth, Edward N. American historians and European immigrants, 1875—1925. N. Y., 1948. 244 p.

3. 12. 170. Saveth, Edward N. "A science of American history". Diogenes No. 26 (1959) 107—222 p.

3. 12. 171. Saveth, E. N. American history and the social sciences. N. Y., 1965.

3. 12. 172. Schlesinger, A. M. New viewpoints in American history. N. Y., 1922.

3. 12. 173. Schlesinger A. M. "American history and American literary history". *In: Foerster, Norman (ed.)* The reinterpretation of American literature. N. Y., 1928. 160—180 p.

3. 12. 174. Schlesinger, A. M. and Committee on the Planning of Research (ed.) Historical scholarship in America. Needs and opportunities. N. Y., 1932.

3. 12. 175. Schnool, Rainer Die New Left history in den USA. Studien zur historisch-politischen Konzeption und zum konkret-historischen Geschichtsbild. Potsdam, Pädagogische Hochschule, 1984. 284 p. (Diss. B.)

3. 12. 176. Sevost'ânov, G. N. (ed.) Osnovnye problemy istorii SŠA v amerikanskoj istoriografii, 1861—1918 gg. M., 1974. 357 p.

3. 12. 177. Shaw, Peter "Blood is thicker than irony... Henry Adams' History". New England Quarterly 40 (June 1967) 163—187 p. (On Adams' political views.)

3. 12. 178. Sheehan, Donald — Syrett, C. Harold (ed.) Essays in American historiography. Papers presented in honor of Allan Nevins. N. Y., 1960. 320 p.

3. 12. 179. Shyrock, R. H. "American historiography. A critical analys and a program". American Philosophical Society Proceedings CXXXVII (1943) 35—46 p.

3. 12. 180. Simenson, Harold P. "Frederick Jackson Turner. Frontier history as art". Antioch Review XXIV (Summer, 1964) 201—211p.

3.12.181.Siracusa,JosephM. New left diplomatic histories and historians. The American Revisionists. Port Washington, 1973. 138 p.

3. 12. 182. Skotheim, R. A. American intellectual histories and historians. Princeton — N. Y., 1966. (Recurrent problems and characteristic themes in the history of American ideas.)

3.12.183.Smith, Charlotte Watkins Carl Becker: on history and the climate of opinion. Ithaca-N. Y., 1956.

3.12.184.Smith, William R. History as argument. Three patriot historians of the American revolution. The Hague, 1966. (On David Ramsay, Merci Otis Warren, John Marshall.)

3.12.185. Social Science Research Council. The social sciences in historical study. A report of the Committee on Historiography. Bulletin 64. N. Y., 1954.

3. 12. 186. Sogrin, Vladimir Viktorovic Kritičeskie napravleniâ nemarksistkoj istoriografii SŠA XX veka. M., 1987. 268 p.

3.12.187.Sorenson, Lloyd, R. "Historical currents in America". American Quarterly VII (1955) 234—46. p.

3. 12. 188. Sorenson, Lloyd "Charles A. Beard and German historiographical thought". Mississippi Valley Historical Review XLLII (1955) 274—97 p.

3. 12. 189. Starokin, Robert "The negro: A central theme in American history". Journal of Contemporary History 3, No.2 (April 1968) 37—53 p.

3. 12. 190. Stephenson, Wendell H. Southern history in the making. Pioneer historians of the South. Baton Rouge (Lousiana), 1964.

3.12.191. Sternher, Bernard Consensus, conflict and American Historians. Indiana University Press, 1975. 432 p.

3. 12. 192. Strout, Cushing The pragmatic revolt in American history. Carl Becker and Charles Beard. New Haven, 1958.

3. 12. 193. Susman, Warren I. "The useless past: American intellectuals and the frontier thesis: 1910—1930". Bucknell Review 11 (March, 1963) 1—20 p.

3.12.194.Swierenga,RobertP.(ed.) Quantification in American history: theory and research. N. Y., 1970. 417 p.

3.12.195. Turner, Frederick J. The west as a field for historical study. *In:* Annual report of the American Historical Association for the year 1896. Washington, 1897.

3. 12. 196. Dear Lady The letters of *Frederick Jackson Turner* and Alice Forbes Hooper Perkins, 1910—1932. Edited by Ray Allen Billington with the collaboration of Walter Muir Whitehill. San Marina (California), 1970. 437 p.

3. 12. 197. Tyrrell, Ian R. The absent Marx: class analysis and liberal history in twentieth–century America. Westport (Conn.), 1986.270p.

3.12.198.Unger,I. The "New Left and American history. Some recent trends in United States historiography". AHR 72 (July, 1967) 1237—1263 p. A criticism of radical historians.

3. 12. 199. Van Tussel, David Recording America's past. An interpretation of the development of historical studies in America, 1607—1884.Chicago,1960.

3. 12. 200. Van Tussel, David "From learned society to professional organisation: the American Historical Association". **AHR** 89 (October, 1984) 929—956 p.

3. 12. 201. Wado, Mason Francis Parkman: heroic historian. N.Y., 1942.

3.12.202. Webb, Walter F. The great frontier. Boston, 1952.

3. 12. 203. Webb, Walter F. "The historical seminar: its outer shell and its inner spirit". Mississippi Valley Historical Review 42 (1955)

3. 12. 204. Welch, William American images of Soviet foreign policy: an inquiry into recent appraisals from the academic community. New Haven — N. Y., 1970. 316 p.

3.12.205. Wilkins, Burleigh Taylor Carl Becker. A biographical study in American intellectual history. Cambridge (Mass.), **MIT** Press and Harvard University Press, 1961.

3. 12. 206. Wilson, Clyde N. (ed.) Dictionary of literary biography. Vol. 30. American historians, 1607—1865. Detroit, 1984. 382p.

3.12.207. Wise, Gene American historical explanations. Homewood (Ill.), 1973.

3.12.208. Wish, Harvey The American historian. A social-intellectual history of the writing of the American past. N.Y., 1960. 366 p.

3.12.209. Wish, Harvey (ed.) American historians: a selection. N. Y.,—Oxford University Press, 1960.

3.12.210.Wish, Harvey "The American historian and the new conservatism". South Atlantic Quarterly 65 (Spring 1966) 178—191 p.

3. 12. 211. Woodward, C. Vann American attitudes toward history. N. Y.-Oxford, 1955.

3. 12. 212. Woodward, C. Vann "Clio with soul". Journal of American History 56 (June, 1969) 5—20 p. (On negro history)

3. 12. 213. Woodward, C. Vann Thinking back: the perils of writing history. Baton Rouge (La.), 1986. 158 p. (Historiography of the southern states)

3.12.214. Zagorin, Perez "Carl Becker on History. Professor Becker's two histories: A sceptical fallacy". AHR LXII (1956) 1—11 p. A response: *Gershay, Leo* "Zagorin's interpretation of Becker. Some observations". ibid. 12—17 p.

3. 12. 215. Zieger, Robert H. "Workers and scholars. Recent trends in American labor historiography". Labor History 13 (Spring 1972) 245—266 p.

3.13.Venezuela

3. 13. 1. Brito Figuerod, Federico Temas y ensayos de historia social venezolana. Caracas, 1985.

3. 13. 2. Damas, German Carrera Historiografia marxista venezolana y otros temas. Caracas, 1967.

3. 13. 3. Damas, G. C. Historia del historiografia venezolana (Textos para su estudio). Caracas, 1961. 650 p.

3. 13. 4. Damas, G. C. Cuestiones de historiografia venezolana. Caracas, 1964.

3. 13. 5. Diaz Sanches, Ramón Evolucion de la historiografia en Venezuela. Caracas, 1956. 19 p.

3. 13. 6. Gabaldas, Márquez Joaquin Muestrario de historiadores coloniales de Venezuela. Caracas, 1948. 368 p.

3. 13. 7. Mieres, Antonio La concepcion historiografica en Eloy G. Gonzalez. Caracas, 1974.

4

Africa and the Middle East

4. 1. Africa in general

4. 1. 1. Afiglo, Adiela Eberechukwu The poverty of African historiography. Lagos, 1977. 25 p.

4. 1. 2. Davidson, Appolon Borisovic (ed.) Istoričeskaâ nauka v stranah Afriki. M., 1979. 299 p.

4. 1. 3. Gordon, David C. Self-determination and history in the Third World. Princeton University Press, 1971. Development of critical history in newly independent countries.

4. 1. 4. Jewsiewicki, Bogumil—Newbury, David S. (ed.) African historiographies: what history for which Africa? Beverly Hills, Sage Publications, 1986. 320 p.

4. 1. 5. Markov, W. "Afrikanische Geschichtsschreibung heute". ZfG 12 / 1964 / 1 / 28-45p.

4. 1. 6. Neale, Caroline Writing independent history: African historiography 1960-1980. Westport (Conn.), 1985. 208 p.

4. 1. 7. Rowe, John A. "»Progress and a sense of identity« African historiography in East Africa". Kenya Historical Review 5 (1977) 1/23—34p.

4. 1. 8. Smolin, G. A. (ed.) Istoriografiâ istočnikovedenie istorii stran Afriki i Azii. Leningrad, 1983. 129 p.

4. 1. 9. Ursu, Dmitrij Pavlovic "Stanovlenie nacional'noj istoriografii v stranah Tropičeskoj Afriki". VI 1979/8/ 70-84 p.

4. 1. 10. Ursu, Dmitrij Pavlovic Sovremennaâ istoriografiâ stran Tropiceskoj Afriki, 1960-1980. M., 1983. 261 p. With an English summary. Bibliography 227-253 p.

4. 2. Arab countries

4. 2. 1. Crabbs, Jack A. The writing of history in nineteenth–century Egypt: a study in national transformation. Detroit—Cairo, 1984. 227 p.

4. 2. 2. Holt, P. M. — Lewis, Bernard Historians of the Middle East. Oxford University Press, 1962. 520 p.

4. 2. 3. Maryliouth, David S. Lectures on Arabic historians. Calcutta, 1930.

4. 2. 4. Rosenthal, Franz A history of Muslim historiography. Leiden, 1952. 558 p. Second, revised edition 1968. 653 p.

4. 2. 5. Sauvaget, J. Historiens arabes. Pages choisies, traduites et présentees par – . Paris, 1946. 192 p.

4. 2. 6. Tarabyn, Ahmed Arab historiography and historians in modern times. Damascus, 1970. 248 p.

4.3. Israel

4. 3. 1. Kachan, Lionel The Jew and his history. L., 1977. 164 p.

4. 3. 2. Mahler, Raphael "Darke hahistoriografi-gah hay-yisre elit bam-mé' à há^{c}èsrim". Had-dåbår 5710(1949-50) 422-430 p. A general introduction to the methods of 20th century Israeli historiography.

4. 3. 3. Taubler, Eugen Aufsätze zur Problematik jüdischer Geschichtsschreibung 1908-1950. Hrg. und eingeleitet von Selma Stern-Taubler. Tübingen, 1966. 63 p.

4.4. Madagascar

4. 4. 1. Valette, Jean L'Historiographie malgache, son passé, son devenir. Tananarive, 1959. 3 p. Extract from the Bulletin de Madagascar, n^{0}157/June1959/.

4.5. Nigeria

4. 5. 1. Hess, Robert Auker Perspectives of Nigerian historiography 1875-1971. The historians of modern Nigeria. Harvard University, Phil. Diss. 1972. (Available on microfilm)

4. 6. South Africa

4. 6. 1. Jaarsveld, F. A. van Die Afrikaner se geskiedsbeeld. Pretoria 1958. 33 p. South-African historiography.

4. 6. 2. Jaarsveld, F. A. van Ou en nuwe in die Suid-Afrikaanse geskiedskrywing. Pretoria, 1961. 60 p. Summary in English: Old and new trends in South-African historiography.

4. 6. 3. Wright, Harrison M. The burden of the present: liberal-radical controversy over southern African history. Cape Town, 1977. 137 p.

4.7.Tunisia

4. 7. 1. Abd al–Salam, Ahmad Les historiens tunisiens des XVIIe, XVIIIe et XIXe siècles. Essai d' histoire culturelle. Paris, 1973.590p.Bibliography523-540p.

5
Asia

5. 1. Asia in general

5. 1. 1. Beasley, W. G. — Pulleyblank, E. G. (eds.) Historical writing on the peoples of Asia. Historians of China and Japan. N. Y.—Oxford, 1962. 351 p.

5. 1. 2. Fairbank, John K. "East Asian views of modern European history". AHR LXII (1957) 527-536 p.

5. 1. 3. Gordon, David C. Self-determination and history in the Third World. Princeton University Press, 1971. Development of critical history in newly independent countries.

5. 1. 4. Philips, C. H. (ed.) Historians of India, Pakistan and Ceylon. L., 1961.

5.2. South–East Asia in general

5. 2. 1. Hall D. G. E. (ed.) Historians of South-East Asia. N. Y. — Oxford University Press, 1961.

5. 2. 2. Uzânov, A. N. (ed.) Nacional'naâ istoriografiâ stran ûgo-vostocnoj Azii. M., 1974. 245 p.

5.3.China

5.3.1.Charbonnier, Jean L'interprétation de l'histoire en Chine contemporaine, 1-2. Paris, 1978. 960 p. Univ. VII. Diss.

5.3.2.Dirlik,Arif Revolution and history: the origins of Marxist historiography in China, 1919-1937. Berkeley at Los Angeles, 1978.299p.

5. 3. 3. Dubs, Hamer H. "The reliability of Chinese histories". Far Eastern Quarterly VI (1946) 23-43 p.

5.3.4.Feuerwerker,Albert(ed.) Approaches to modern Chinese history. University of California Press, 1967.

5. 3. 5. Feuerwerker, Albert (ed.) History in Communist China. Cambridge (Mass.), 1968.

5. 3. 6. Feuerwerker, Albert — Cheng, S. Chinese communist studies of modern Chinese history. Cambridge (Mass.), 1961.

5. 3. 7. Gardner, Charles S. Chinese traditional historiography. Cambridge (Mass.), 1961. 124 p.

5. 3. 8. Hall, John W. — Wright, Arthur F. "Historians of China and Japan". AHR (1962) 78-85 p.

5. 3. 9. Hall, John W. "Historiography in Japan". *In:* Teachers of history. Essays in honor of Lawrence Bradford Backard. Edited by H. S. Hughes. Ithaca — N. Y., 1954.

5. 3. 10. Han, Yu-Shon Elements of Chinese historiography. Hollywood (Calif.), 1955. 246 p.

5. 3. 11. Hsien, Winston Chinese historiography on the revolution of 1911. A critical survey and a selected bibliography. Stanford, 1975. 165p.

5.3.12. Leutner, Mechthild Geschichtsschreibung zwischen Politik und Wissenschaft. Zur Herausbildung der chinesischen marxistischen Geschichtswissenschaft in den 30-er und 40er Jahren. Wiesbaden, 1982. 379 p.

5. 3. 13. Pilz, Erich (ed.) Maoistische Geschichtsschreibung. Bochum, 1984. 278 p.

5.3.14. Prusek, Jaroslav "History and epics in China and in the West". Diogenes No. 42. (Summer 1963) 20-43 p.

5.3.15. Pusey, James R. Wu Han: attacking the present through the past. Cambridge (Mass.), 1969.

5. 3. 16. Schneider, Laurence A. Ku Chieh-Kang and China's new history: Nationalism and the quest for alternative traditions. Berkeley — L., 1971. 337 p.

5.3.17. Schütte, Hans-Wilm Marxistische Geschichtsheorie und neue chinesische Geschichswissenschaft. Aspekte der Periodisierungsdebatte der fünfziger Jahre: eine Untersuchung der Ausgangspositionen im Hinblicke auf die Gesellschaft der frühen Zhou-Zeit. Hamburg, 1980. 344 p.

5. 3. 18. Simons, Stefan Das Bild Qin Shihuang's in der Geschichte des ersten Kaisers von China. 1949-1979. Hamburg, 1984. 240p.

5. 3. 19. Staiger, Brunhild Das Konfuzius-Bild im kommunistischen China. Die Neuberwertung von Konfuzius in der chinesisch-marxistischen Geschichtsschreibung. Wiesbaden, 1969. 143 p.

5. 3. 20. Vâtkin, Rudolf Vsevolodovic — Tihvinskij, S. L. "O nekotoryh voprosah istoričeskoj nauki v KNR". VI 1963/10/ 13-20 Published Also in German: "Über einige Fragen der Geschichtswissenschaft in der Volksrepublik China". ZfG 1964/3/403-422 p.

5. 3. 21. *Vâtkin, R. V. — Ivistunova, N. P.* (ed.) Istoričeskaâ nauka v KNR. M., 1971. 303 p. Bibliography: 298-301 p.

5. 3. 22. *Vâtkin, R. V.* "Istoričeskaâ nauka KNR na sovremennom étape". VI 1979/2/ 76-83 p.

5. 3. 23. *Watson, Burton* Sso-ma Chi'on, grand historian of China. N. Y., 1958.

5. 3. 24. *Wei Jing-Pang* "Les historiens chinois sous la dynatie Ts'ing 1644-1911".Sinologica (Basel) 1948/4/291-321 p.

5. 3. 25.*Weigelin — Schwiednik, Susanne* Parteigeschichtsschreibung in der VR China. Typen, Methoden und Funktionen. Wiesbaden, 1984. 248 p.

5.4. India

5. 4. 1. *Banerjee, Tarasankar (ed.)* Indian historical research since independence. Calcutta, 1987. 119 p.

5. 4. 2. *Devahuti, D. (ed.)* Problems of Indian historiography. Delhi, 1979. 190 p.

5. 4. 3. *Devahuti, D.* Bias in Indian historiography. Calcutta, 1980. 407 p.

5. 4. 4. *Ghoshal, U. N.* The beginnings of Indian historiography and other essays. Calcutta, 1944.

5. 4. 5. *Guha, Ranajit* An Indian historiography of India: a nineteenth-century agenda and its implications. Calcutta, 1988.

5. 4. 6. *Sen, S. P.* (ed.) Historians and historiography in modern India. Calcutta, 1963. 464 p.

5. 4. 7. Webster, John C. B. (ed.) History and contemporary India. London, 1971.

5.5. Indonesia

5. 5. 1. Berg, Cornelis Christian De evolutie dev Javoanse geschiedschrijving. Amsterdam, 1951. 146 p. Bibl. 143—173 p.

5. 5. 2. Kahin, G. McT.—Resnik, G. J.— Soedjatmoko, M. A. An introduction to Indonesian historiography. Ithaca—N.Y., 1965. 427 p.

5. 5. 3. Nichterlein, Sue "Historicism and historiography in Indonesia".HT13/1974/3/253—272p.

5.6. Japan

5. 6. 1. Chang, Richard T. Historians and Meiji statesmen. Gainesville, 1970. 105 p.

5. 6. 2. Comité Jaapanais des sciences historiques (ed.) L'état actuel et les tendances des etudes historiques au Japan. Tokyo, 1960.

5. 6. 3. Hall, John W. "Historiography in Japan". *In:* Teachers of history. Essays in honor of Lawrence Bradford Backard. Edited by H.S. Hughes. Ithaca—N.Y., 1954.

5.6.4. Japanese National Committee of Historical Sciences (ed.) Recent trends in Japanese historiography. *In:* Japan at the 13th International Congress of Historical Sciences in Moscow. Tokyo, 1970.328p.

5. 6. 5. Nohara, Shiro et al. Kindai Nihon niokern rekishigaku no hattatau. 1–2. Tokyo, 1976. 220, 202 p. A comprehensive work on the development of historical science in Japan.

5. 6. 6. Paskov, S. S. Sovremennaâ âponskaâ burzoaznaâ istoriografiaâ. M., 1982. 168 p.

5. 6. 7. Zahl, Karl F. Der Wandel des japanischen Geschichtsbildes nach dem Zweiten Weltkrieg. Hamburg, 1983. 89 p.

5.7.Mongolia

5. 7. 1. Bira, Š. Voprosy istorii, kultury i istoriografii MNR. (Sbornik trudov) Ulan-Bator, 1977. 450 p. It can serve as an introduction to Mongolian historiography.

6
Australia

6.1. Crawford, R.M. Making history. N.Y., 1985. 120 p.

6.2. Inglis, K. S. C. E. W. Bean, Australian historian. Queensland, Australia, 1970.

Index of authors

Index of persons discussed

Index of subjects

Agrarian history 2.10.69.
American civil war 3.12.156.
American revolution 2.11.41., 3.12.38., 3.12.184.
Ancient history 1.100., 1.425., 1.428., 1.429., 2.22.66., 2.23.2.
"Annales" school 2.9.1., 2.9.2., 2.9.6., 2.9.15., 2.9.16., 2.9.18., 2.9.21., 2.9.26., 2.9.38., 2.9.39., 2.9.43., 2.9.69., 2.9.76., 2.9.80., 2.9.109., 2.9.117., 2.9.122.
Archeology 1.174., 2.21.19., 2.21.20.
Art and history 1.289., 1.478., 1.507., 1.511., 1.634., 3.12.128., 2.12.129., 3.12.153.

Bias in history 1.116., 1.159., 5.4.4.
Bielefeld school 2.10.109.
Black history 3.12.104., 3.12.141., 3.12.189., 3.12.212.
Bolshevism 2.10.306.
"Bourgeois" historians
- in general 1.144., 1.145., 1.304., 1.344., 1.345., 1.350., 1.383., 1.413., 1.420., 1.450., 1.522., 1.567., 1.599., 1.603., 1.604., 1.605., 1.606., 1.607.
- Eastern Europe 2.10.468.
- Bohemia 2.6.35., 2.6.36., 2.6.37.
- France 2.9.1., 2.9.52., 2.9.82.
- Germany 2.10.38., 2.10.96., 2.10.106., 2.10.123., 2.10.127., 2.10.213., 2.10.249., 2.10.254., 2.10.334., 2.10.337., 2.10.341., 2.10.364., 2.10.376., 2.10.393., 2.10.398., 2.10.399., 2.10.402., 2.10.403., 2.10.405.
- Great Britain 2.11.52., 2.11.90.
- Hungary 2.13.23.
- Italy 2.15.2.
- Soviet Union 2.22.83., 2.22.89., 2.22.90., 2.22.118.
- USA 3.12.7., 3.12.110., 3.12.132., 3.12.133.

Catholic historians
- Hungary 2.13.44.
Cambridge Modern History 2.11.37.
Church history 1.95., 1.414., 1.508., 2.10.382., 3.7.3
Civil war in Russia (1919—1921) 2.22.105.
Class struggle 1.244., 1.442., 2.22.119., 2.22.121., 3.12.197.
Colonial historiography 3.7.1., 3.13.6.
Conservatism
- Germany 2.10.198.
- USA 3.12.210.
Constitutional history 1.71.